FUNNY
OLD GAME

The

Report

Love great sportswriting? So do we.

Every month, Pitch Publishing brings together the best of our world through our monthly newsletter — a space for readers, writers and fans to connect over the books, people and moments that make sport so captivating.

You'll find previews of new releases, extracts from our latest titles, behind-the-scenes interviews with authors and the occasional giveaway or competition thrown in for good measure.

We also dip into our back catalogue to unearth forgotten gems and celebrate timeless tales that shaped sporting culture.

Scan the **QR code** and join the growing Pitch Publishing reader community today.

FUNNY OLD GAME

THE MOST BIZARRE AND AMUSING TALES FROM THE WORLD OF FOOTBALL

ALAN FERGUSON

First published by Pitch Publishing, 2026

1

Pitch Publishing
9 Donnington Park, 85 Birdham Road
Chichester, West Sussex, PO20 7AJ
www.pitchpublishing.co.uk
info@pitchpublishing.co.uk

Set in Sina 9.8/12,5pt

Typeset by Pitch Publishing

Cover design by Olner Design

Printed and bound in India by Replika Press Pvt. Ltd.

The authorised representative in the EEA is
Easy Access System Europe OÜ, Mustamäe tee 50, 10621 Tallinn, Estonia gpsr.requests@easproject.com

A CIP catalogue record for this book is available from the British Library

ISBN 978-1-83680-261-7

Papers used by Pitch Publishing are from well-managed forests and other responsible sources

For Giorgia

INTRODUCTION

EVERYONE KNOWS that the modern game of football was invented in Britain, Real Madrid always win everything and Jimmy Hill was a bit of a fool, but do you know which team of ex-public school toffs won the very first FA Cup Final back in 1872 – or which big club has been cursed and will never win another European trophy?

No? What about this? Which English club wanted to install electric fencing at their ground? Or which football match started a war? You didn't know that either? In that case, this is the book for you.

Funny Old Game is a thrilling collection of over 200 stories from Britain and around the world recounting some of the weirder stuff to happen on a football pitch.

The stories are random and so is the order in which they appear. It just seemed more exciting that way!

There's a lot of fun stuff, tons of trivia and bizarre records; a little bit of history, reports about the most famous (and infamous) matches, and plenty of the more obscure and much sillier 'funny ha-ha' and 'funny peculiar' moments featuring maverick players, bad referees, unruly mascots and mischievous ball boys to keep you amused.

As Winston Churchill once said, 'Writing a book is an adventure. To begin with it is a toy then an amusement. Then it becomes a mistress, and then it becomes a master, and then it becomes a tyrant and, in the last stage, just as you are about to be reconciled to your servitude, you kill the monster and fling him to the public.'

So here it is. Enjoy!

A GREAT NOISE IN THE CITY

THE EARLIEST known reference to a game of football was written by the cleric William FitzStephen in his 12th-century work *Descriptio Nobilissimae Civitatis Londoniae*.

FitzStephen wrote, 'After lunch all the youth of the city go out into the fields to take part in a ball game. The students of each school have their own ball; the workers from each city craft are also carrying their balls. Older citizens, fathers, and wealthy citizens come on horseback to watch their juniors competing, and to relive their own youth vicariously: you can see their inner passions aroused as they watch the action and get caught up in the fun being had by the carefree adolescents.'

It was during the high Middle Ages (1000-1300) when the informal kickabouts such as those described by FitzStephen evolved into organised games of mob football – a violent, unruly game which usually involved two rival village teams kicking an inflated pigskin ball back and forth through the streets. The winner was the first to drag the ball by any means possible towards their opponent's marker – or goal – located at the opposite end of the village. The games could last all day and were often drunken, rowdy affairs with many injuries and even the odd fatality.

The Royal Shrovetide Football match held at Ashbourne in Derbyshire has been described as the oldest, largest and the most chaotic of all the mob football games still played today. The annual event is contested on Shrove Tuesday and Ash Wednesday between the Up'ards and Down'ards (those born north or south of the River Henmore which flows through the centre of the town) with no limit on the number of participants and a field of play roughly three miles long between the goals.

Various monarchs throughout the late Middle Ages (1300-1500) then took it in turn to ban people from playing football.

First off the mark, on 13 April 1314, was the Lord Mayor of London, Nicholas de Farndone, who issued a proclamation on behalf of Edward II banning football from being played on the streets because of all the disruption and social unrest it caused, 'For as much as there is great noise in the city, caused by hustling over large balls from which many evils may arise which God forbid, we command and forbid, on behalf of the king, on pain of imprisonment, such game to be used in the city in the future.'

Edward III outlawed football, believing that it distracted the youth from practising their archery skills. The year was 1349 and the need for skilled archers was most acute at this time because of the Black Death and the Hundred Years' War, with the young men of England either dying of the plague or being slaughtered on the battlefields of France faster than they could be replaced. Edward IV then re-imposed the ban in 1477 after declaring, 'No person shall practice ... football and such games, but every strong and able bodied person shall practice with the bow for the reason that the national defence depends upon such bowmen.'

Henry VIII banned football in 1540. He ruled over England for 36 years from 1509 until his death in 1547 and is best remembered for his extraordinary marital merry-go-round, his wild lifestyle and for initiating the English Reformation. He has also been credited with owning the earliest known pair of football boots. Henry wasn't always a gout-ridden old fatty; in his younger days he was quite a keen sportsman and enjoyed riding, jousting, tennis and presumably playing football since his footwear collection for 1526 was recorded as '45 velvet pairs and one leather pair for football'. By 1540, however, poor Henry was the size of a small house and had to be carried, pushed and hauled around his palaces by an army of servants and obviously felt that if he couldn't play football any more, then nobody else should either!

Then the Puritans, a religious reform movement within the Church of England which emerged in the mid-16th century, banned football. They were dissatisfied with the limited extent of the English Reformation and advocated for much stricter religious reforms, a rigorous enforcement of public morality and the creation of a more disciplined and God-fearing society. They eventually seized power in England after the English Civil War and established the Commonwealth of England in 1649 under the leadership of Oliver Cromwell. These guys were such a cheerless bunch of oddballs that they banned everything: theatre, gambling, dancing, popular songs, drinking, the wearing of makeup or colourful clothing and working on the Sabbath. They even banned Christmas! And, of course, they banned most sports, including football, which they described as 'a friendly kind of fight ... a bloody and murdering practice' and a distraction from proper religious observance.

It wasn't until the Restoration in 1660 that Joe Public was finally allowed to kick a football again.

The modern game of football evolved from the sports played at the English public schools in the 19th century. Prior to the Factory Act of 1850, most working-class people were expected to work their arses off 12 hours a day, six days a week, and so they neither had the time nor the energy to kick a ball about. Unsurprisingly, it was the posh kids from the posh schools who invented organised ball games and set the rules. The Eton Field Game is the earliest known form of football resembling the modern game with the rules being codified at Eton College possibly as early as 1815. However, the Cambridge Rules of 1848 became the first widely accepted set of rules and regulations for the sport. The set of 11 laws was first devised by a group of football enthusiasts at the University of Cambridge in an attempt to standardise the different codes and conventions of play practiced at various public schools. Tripping, pushing and holding opponents was outlawed, catching the ball was not allowed although stopping it with your hands was permissible, and an early attempt at the offside rule was also observed.

The Foot-Ball Club, founded in 1824 in Edinburgh by the lawyer John Hope, was the first documented club dedicated to playing football and the first to describe itself as a 'football club'. It was quite a posh affair with membership seemingly limited to doctors, accountants, lawyers and other professional types living in the upmarket New Town area of the city. The style of football they played resembled mob football, with surviving club records describing games involving up to 39 players with the 'kicking of shins and such tumbling' allowed. The club played its games in the Dalry area of Edinburgh, sticks were used for goalposts and someone called a 'chairman' was employed as a referee.

Sheffield FC has been recognised by FIFA as the oldest club in the world still playing football. During the winter of 1855/56, the players at Sheffield Cricket Club organised a few kickabouts among themselves as a way of keeping fit until the start of the new season. However, it wasn't until two years later that an actual football club was formally established by two of their members, William Prest and Nathaniel Creswick, at a meeting on 24 October 1857.

Those two gentlemen also devised the Sheffield Rules at a meeting of club officials on 28 October 1858. These were the first set of detailed laws of the game published by any football club. The original set of rules and the many revisions that followed had a major influence on the development of the game: pioneering the use of crossbars, introducing free kicks, corner kicks, overhead throw-ins and a half-time change of ends, and outlawing kicking, tripping or holding. A regulation requiring teams to play in separate colours was also included, 'Each player must provide himself with a red and dark blue flannel cap, one colour to be worn by each side.' In 1862, the Sheffield Rules were updated to include the possibility of counting rogue goals – when the ball was touched down after being kicked between two flags placed four yards either side of the goalposts – as a means of deciding a winner in the event of a drawn game.

The Sheffield Rules were later adopted by other clubs from the Midlands and the north of England as they were formed, making them one of the most popular sets of footballing laws during the late 19th century.

Britain's second-oldest football club, Hallam FC, played Sheffield FC in what is now known as the 'Rules derby' for the first time on 26 December 1860. This match has been recognised by FIFA as the oldest fixture in world football. The world's very first competitive game was played at Hallam's ground, Sandygate Road in Sheffield, using Sheffield Rules and resulted in a 2-0 victory for the visitors. The 16-a-side match kicked off at 1pm with the Sheffield FC founder and captain Nathaniel Creswick credited with scoring the first goal. A match report appeared in the *Sheffield Daily Telegraph* three days later and mentioned how the occasion was greatly appreciated by the large number of spectators, many of whom were 'extremely liberal with their plaudits' when the tackles went in and 'equally unsparing' with their criticism when the players slipped and fell in the snowy conditions. It was apparently an entertaining game, played in a good spirit with the white blanket of snow covering the pitch and the contrasting red and blue strips of the Sheffield and Hallam players giving the match 'a very picturesque appearance'. This was the earliest known newspaper report of any football match ever published.

The early game in England usually involved one player charging, head down, up the field trying to dribble the ball past his opponents and being followed by his team-mates ready to seize any loose balls. Team formations usually consisted of just a couple of defenders and seven or eight attackers or 'dribblers' tasked with making their way up the field towards their opponent's goal. If the player with the ball was tackled, hacked down or bundled off the ball, the players following along behind him would take over and have a go themselves. It was never going to be a style of play that would conquer the world with its beauty! It was only when the first Scottish club, Queen's Park, was formed in 1867 that things began to change after their players started passing the ball around the field. It was the first major tactical innovation in the game's short history and changed football for ever. It may have been the English who invented and codified the sport but it was the Scots, principally the players at Queen's Park, who first embraced the 'combination game' style of play which was exported all around the world.

The world's earliest known football tournament was the Youdan Cup, named after the Sheffield theatre proprietor and football enthusiast Thomas Youdan who sponsored the tournament and provided the trophy. The Sheffield Rules competition began with two knockout rounds involving 12 local teams. The first competitive matches ever played in England were the six Youdan Cup first-round ties, which all kicked off at 3pm on 16 February 1867. The final was played on 5 March 1867 between Hallam and Norfolk FC and attracted around 3,000 spectators. They didn't have much to cheer about, however, as the match ended goalless with Hallam only being awarded the trophy on account of the two rogue goals they'd scored. The trophy was to be presented by Thomas Youdan himself during a special celebratory dinner at the Adelphi Hotel in Sheffield on 11 March 1867 but he was too ill to attend – and the trophy wasn't ready in time either! According to the *Sheffield Daily Telegraph,* this was due to 'the protracted time which would have been required in its manufacture' and so Hallam were presented with a fancy claret jug instead. It's to be assumed that the cup was eventually made and awarded to Hallam as it appears to have gone missing shortly afterwards, and didn't resurface again until 1997 when a Scottish antiques collector contacted the club and sold it back to them.

Although the Sheffield Rules had been widely adopted by clubs in the Midlands and the north, that wasn't the case in London and the south of the country, where everyone was still doing their own thing.

The London solicitor Ebenezer Cobb Morley founded Barnes FC in 1862 and served as the team captain until 1867. Their first recorded match was a 2-0 win over Richmond FC on 29 November 1862. A month later, on 20 December 1862, they met another local team, Blackheath FC, who preferred playing a rugby-style game that allowed running with the ball and 'hacking' (kicking shins), and both teams were forced to agree the rules to be followed beforehand. Realising that different clubs were still playing by different rules, he wrote a letter to the *Bell's Life* newspaper, proposing a governing body for the sport 'with the object of establishing a definite code of rules for the regulation of the game' similar to how the Marylebone Cricket Club (MCC) had regulated the rules of cricket. That letter eventually led to the historic meeting at the Freemasons' Tavern in Camden on 26 October 1863 when representatives from 11 London and suburban football clubs got together to form the Football Association.

The Association Rules drafted by Morley were the modern game's first set of laws, drafted over a series of six meetings between the FA's founding member clubs and finally agreed upon on 8 December 1863. The first match played under Association Rules was a hastily arranged little kickabout between Barnes and their local rivals Richmond

FC (who weren't even an FA member club). The 15-a-side, 90-minute exhibition match played on 19 December ended in a rather disappointing 0-0 draw, with the *Sporting Gazette* later reporting that 'very little difficulty was experienced on either side in playing the new rules – their simplicity preventing disputes arising'. However, it's probably fair to say that the Richmond lot weren't all that excited about playing football under these new rules. They never joined the FA and eventually became founding members of the Rugby Football Union (RFU) instead.

The first official match played using Association Rules took place on 9 January 1864 with an FA President's XIV beating an FA Secretary's XIV 2-0 at Battersea Park in London. The two teams were captained by Arthur Pember and Ebenezer Cobb Morley, and included the best players of the day, including Charles W. Alcock who scored both goals. The first match played using Association Rules by two actual FA member clubs took place on 30 January 1864 when N.N. Kilburn hosted Barnes and beat them 3-0. Although the home side were convincing winners, *Bell's Life* did at least single out that man Ebenezer Cobb Morley for his 'very pretty play'.

Time passed and before long most clubs were playing matches using the Association Rules. Now all they needed was a competition.

In 1871, Charles W. Alcock, in his new role as FA secretary, proposed that 'a challenge cup should be established … for which all clubs belonging to the Association should be invited to compete'. Of the 50 FA member clubs at that time, 15 accepted the invitation to take part in the first Football Association Challenge Cup, although by the time things eventually got under way on 11 November 1871, this number had been reduced to 13. The FA Cup is now the world's oldest existing national football tournament and the oldest domestic cup competition.

The Scots established their own competition two years later. Although the Scottish Football Association Challenge Cup is the second-oldest competition in the world, the actual trophy is the oldest and was first presented to Queen's Park as winners of the inaugural 1873/74 tournament.

The games of football and rugby played at the English public schools in the mid-19th century existed as different variations of the same sport. However, when the FA drew up the Association Rules in 1863, the two games became quite separate and were soon referred to as rugby football and association football. It's often assumed that the word 'soccer' is an Americanism but it's actually thoroughly British in origin and was invented by students at the University of Oxford when they used the names 'rugg-er' and 'assocc-er' to distinguish between the two sports. There was a fad among the students at the Oxbridge universities at the time to add an 'er' on to the end of words to form jocular nouns such as fresher (freshman) or brekker (breakfast). At some point the 'a' and an 's' were dropped and 'assocc-er' became 'soccer' and started to be used by people outside of the university colleges too. However, 'soccer' never really became more than just a nickname in Britain and by the early 20th century the two sports were already more commonly known as just rugby and football.

Football was initially a game played by gentlemen, with any disputes being settled by the two team captains. It wasn't ideal as decisions were often reached only after a lengthy delay. As the game got faster and more competitive, and the number of disputes during play inevitably increased, two umpires were introduced, one representing each team, who ran around their own half of the pitch waving a big stick or a handkerchief in the air to signal any infringement of the rules. An actual referee was only employed to stand on the touchline as a timekeeper and act as an arbitrator between the two umpires should a dispute arise between them. It wasn't until 1891 in a major restructuring of the laws that the referees were promoted to the role they have today and the umpires were demoted to running the line.

International football began when Scotland first played England on 30 November 1872 at the Hamilton Cricket Ground in Glasgow.

The English Football League was formed in 1888 and is the oldest football league competition in the world. The clubs had been arranging their own fixtures up until this point, an ad hoc mixture of FA Cup games, friendlies and inter-county games, but it was all a little chaotic and had proven to be an unreliable way of earning money. It was the Aston Villa director William McGregor who first proposed the idea of forming a league 'where ten or 12 of the most prominent clubs in England' could 'combine to arrange home and away fixtures each season'. His proposal was accepted by the FA on 17 April 1888 and the first league games were played on 8 September 1888.

Preston North End were the world's first league winners. They'd moved into the top spot after a 4-0 victory over Wolverhampton Wanderers in only their second game of the season, on 15 September 1888, and stayed there until being crowned champions as early as 5 January 1889 with three games remaining. At the end of the 22-match season they remained unbeaten, earning themselves the nickname of the 'Invincibles'. Preston were also the first team in the world to do the double after beating Wolves 3-0 in the FA Cup Final on 30 March 1889. They finished the inaugural 1888/89 season unbeaten in all competitions.

The Scottish League began in 1890 and a year later the first overseas league was established in Argentina. More countries soon developed their own leagues and cup competitions, and then everything else followed ...

EPIC OPENING CEREMONY FAIL
1994

The opening ceremony of the 1994 World Cup in the USA was staged on a stifling hot day at Soldier Field in Chicago on 17 June 1994 before the game between Germany and Bolivia. The show commenced with the popular TV celebrity Oprah Winfrey standing on a giant football-shaped podium and welcoming an estimated global television audience of around 750 million people.

She then introduced the pop star Diana Ross before tumbling off the podium and twisting her ankle!

Ms Ross duly emerged from the far end of the stadium singing and dancing with a group of excitable children before running down the length of the pitch where she was supposed to kick a football into an oversized net. The plan was simple enough: the ball had been lined up on the penalty spot for her, the fake goalkeeper had been instructed not to save her shot, the goal had been moved forward to the edge of the six-yard box, and the crossbar had been rigged to split in two and fall apart as soon as the ball hit the back of the net. The idea being that she'd kicked the ball with such power and fury that it had broken the goal.

All she had to do was kick the ball straight down the middle, but she tried to place it in the left-hand corner of the net with disastrous results. Her run-up was confident enough and she gave the ball a good whack but her aim was way off.

It went well wide of its target but, instead of retaking the kick or wandering back to the centre circle to be consoled by all those excitable kids, Ms Ross decided to celebrate her embarrassing miss as if everything had gone to plan. The goal had still fallen apart as expected, and so she just ran through the middle of the broken posts and headed off towards the stage to sing another song much to the amusement of around 750 million people!

A JOKE TOO FAR
1977

The Italian midfielder Luciano Re Cecconi was an irreplaceable part of the 1973/74 Serie A-winning Lazio team. *L'Angelo Biondo* (The Blond Angel) was well known for his speed, strength and athleticism on the pitch – and his mischievous sense of humour off it.

And it was that mischievous sense of humour and, more particularly, his love of a good practical joke that ultimately led to his premature death at the age of 28 years old.

He'd gone out with a couple of his mates on the evening of 18 January 1977. At some point, they'd all thought what jolly good fun it would be to raid a jewellery store and stage a fake robbery. They masked their faces and then burst into the nearest jewellers waving their guns and yelling, 'Hands in the air! This is a robbery!' Apparently, at that time, the Lazio players were well known for holding extreme right-wing political views and it wasn't all that unusual for some of them to wander around town with a handgun tucked into their belts!

Unfortunately for them, this particular store had been robbed for real just a few weeks earlier and, in the meantime, the owner had bought himself a shotgun for protection. Without hesitation, he grabbed his shiny new gun and fired off a round, hitting Luciano in the chest.

His last words were purportedly, 'It's a joke! It's just a joke!'

A MIND-BOGGLING SHOW OF SHAME
2013

Possibly the least subtle bit of match fixing ever seen!

Two Nigerian non-league teams, Plateau United Feeders and Police Machine, were level on points going into the final game of the 2013 season with promotion to the lowest level of the Nigerian Professional Football League still to be decided. Plateau played Akurba, and Police Machine played Bubayaro, with the games kicking off at the same time. Both teams were winning comfortably at half-time so goal difference would likely determine who clinched that coveted promotion spot.

At full time Plateau had won 79-0 and Police Machine had won 67-0, meaning Plateau were crowned champions – but not for very long.

The Nigerian Football Federation (NFF) had smelt a very obvious rat and immediately launched an investigation.

Both teams had clearly been informed of the first-half score in the other match and then everyone had kept in contact with everyone else on their mobile phones as the two teams tried to outscore each other in the second half. It was only 7-0 and 6-0 at half-time with Plateau adding 72 more goals and Police Machine another 61 after the break. Surely, the greatest second-half performances ever seen on a football pitch! Apparently, both matches were full of dubious refereeing decisions, lots of own goals, outrageous goalkeeping errors and inexplicably long periods of extra time. Club officials were even seen acting as ball boys to avoid any unnecessary time-wasting.

Winning promotion had been important for both teams and it didn't seem to matter if they achieved it by fair means or foul.

An NFF spokesperson called the events 'a mind-boggling show of shame', adding, 'It was embarrassing that in one of the games, a player scored 11 times while in the other, four goals were scored within a minute and a player scored three own goals!'

The NFF eventually suspended all four clubs from the league for ten years and banned their players and staff and all the match officials for life.

ANFIELD'S GREATEST NIGHT
2019

The night when Liverpool staged one of the most remarkable European comebacks ever seen to beat the Spanish champions Barcelona and reach the final of the Champions League.

They'd lost the first leg of their semi-final 3-0 at the Camp Nou on 1 May 2019; their star strikers Mohamed Salah and Roberto Firmino were injured and couldn't play in the return match six days later, and they were up against a rampant Barcelona team full of world-class players led by the classiest of them all, the five-times Ballon d'Or winner Lionel Messi. Manager Jürgen Klopp was forced to start with regular substitute Divock Origi up front with Sadio Mané playing alongside him on the left and Xherdan Shaqiri, who hadn't started a game for over four months, on the right.

Even their most optimistic fans gave them little chance of turning things around.

But after a frantic start, Liverpool were soon rewarded with a goal from Origi to give them some hope. Barcelona's social media manager didn't seem all that concerned, however, after posting on X (Twitter), 'We score, Liverpool need FIVE – and we're going to get at least one …agreed?' And at half-time, with the scoreline stalled at 1-0, he probably thought his team were still on course for an easy victory.

At the break there was more bad news for Liverpool when it was discovered that the injury picked up by their versatile full-back Andy Robertson after his first-half collision with

Luis Suárez was more serious than first thought and would force him out of the game. Klopp then brought on the Dutch midfielder Georginio Wijnaldum in his place.

Liverpool started the second half as they had done the first, piling on the pressure and attacking the Barcelona goal, and they were finally rewarded for their persistence in the 54th minute when supersub Wijnaldum doubled their lead – then he made it 3-0 just two minutes later. Two goals in 122 seconds that had suddenly and very unexpectedly swung the tie in Liverpool's favour.

The score was now 3-3 on aggregate but Liverpool weren't settling for extra time. They continued attacking and with only 11 minutes left on the clock they won a corner. What followed was perhaps one of the most memorable few seconds of football ever seen at Anfield.

Trent Alexander-Arnold had run down the right wing and then deliberately seemed to hit the ball against Sergi Roberto to win a corner rather than try and cross it into the middle. He took his time placing the ball in the correct spot, and then strolled away, as if he was leaving the kick to somebody else, before quickly running back and sweeping the ball into the box where an unmarked Origi was waiting. The ball bobbled along the ground straight to the striker who half-volleyed his shot into the back of the unguarded goal. The Barcelona keeper and his defenders had still been standing around organising themselves for the corner and weren't even looking at Alexander-Arnold as they thought he'd walked away from the ball. By the time they realised what was happening, Origi was running away to celebrate what would turn out to be the match-winning goal.

The tie ended in a truly remarkable 4-3 aggregate win for Liverpool and a place in the Champions League Final against Tottenham Hotspur on 1 June. Barcelona had been completely outmanoeuvred, outfought and outplayed.

They'd been way too relaxed about making it through the tie and then had their arses handed to them by an under-strength Liverpool side. They deserved nothing more than a humiliating defeat, especially that cocky little social media manager.

And what of their superstar Lionel Messi and his striking partner Luis Suárez that night? Well, Messi was fairly anonymous (which was surprising considering his electrifying performance in the first leg a week earlier) and Suárez seemed content just to play the role of the pantomime villain by revelling in the jeers from the home fans every time he touched the ball. The former Liverpool player wasn't particularly popular among the Anfield faithful after over-celebrating a goal in the first leg, but in a strange way he actually redeemed himself that night after forcing Robertson out of the game. If it hadn't been for him, Wijnaldum might not have come on, which meant he definitely wouldn't have scored those two goals to draw Liverpool level.

It wasn't just the goalscorers who'd won the match for Liverpool. Their Brazilian goalkeeper Alisson Becker had made five big saves on the night to keep the game alive, four of them when the score was still 1-0. The first was from Messi, then Philippe Coutinho and Jordi Alba and then Suárez just before Liverpool doubled their lead. Messi was then denied another goalscoring opportunity much later in the match when Liverpool were 3-0 up.

At the final whistle, the Barça players slinked off the pitch with their heads bowed. The Liverpool players had tears in their eyes; everyone was hugging everyone else, and the fans were cheering and waving their little scarves in the air as they belted out 'You'll Never Walk Alone'.

In a post-match interview with BT Sport, Jürgen Klopp stated, 'I've watched so many football games in my life and I cannot remember a lot like this, playing against maybe the best team in the world. Winning is already difficult but winning with a clean sheet ... I don't know how the boys did it. These boys are fucking mentality giants. It's unbelievable!'

No doubt BT Sport then had to apologise to their viewers for Klopp's outdoor language!

Liverpool went on to claim their sixth European Cup/ Champions League victory after beating Tottenham 2-0 in the final in Madrid.

THROWING IN THE TOWEL
1906

The 1906 Intercalated Games was a multi-sport event held in Athens, which was promoted at the time as the 'Second International Olympic Games in Athens' by the International Olympic Committee. The idea was to begin staging the Olympics in Greece every four years, since the 1900 and 1904 Games in Paris and St Louis had been largely overshadowed by a World's Fair being held in the two cities at the same time. It was a chance for the IOC to re-launch the Olympic Games as a standalone event but the initiative failed miserably. As it turned out, the 1906 Intercalated Games was the first and last event of its kind and in the intervening years even the IOC has disowned it by deciding not to recognise any of the medal winners.

The football tournament was held between 23 and 25 April 1906 and featured only four teams – one national team and three city teams from the Kingdom of Greece/Ottoman Empire – Denmark, Athens, Smyrna (with players from some kind of artists' commune called Friends of the Arts more adept at waving paintbrushes around a canvas than kicking a football around a field) and Thessaloniki (made up of mainly traders and merchants from England, France and Armenia who were based in the city).

The stars of the tournament were undoubtedly Denmark. They breezed through their semi-final against the artists 5-1 to meet Athens in the final, which took place on 24 April.

The Athenians were probably feeling fairly upbeat about their chances before the final having thrashed the merchants 5-0 in their semi-final, but on the day they were a goal down after only one minute – and trailed 9-0 at the break.

And so they decided not to bother playing the second half. There was no real point. They were being well and truly stuffed by the Danes, there was no chance of them scoring a goal, let alone mounting a comeback, and so to save themselves any further embarrassment, they just threw in the towel.

The final was therefore decided after only 45 minutes when the Athenians refused to come out of their dressing room to play the second half.

You'd think the organisers might have cut their losses but for reasons best known only to themselves they decided to continue with the tournament by hastily arranging what they thought would be another series of matches to determine the silver and bronze medal winners. But the Athenians were still sulking and refused to take part in those matches too, so it was only the artists and the merchants left to battle it out. They met each other the following day but it wasn't much of a battle with the merchants winning 12-0.

PIONEERS OF THE GAME
1867

The first football club in the world outside of England and Wales, Queen's Park, was formed on 9 July 1867.

However, being the first club in Scotland also meant being the only club in Scotland and the players were forced to organise matches among themselves, just as the Sheffield FC players had done in England, with 'Married v Singles', 'Smokers v Non-Smokers' and other such games being staged to keep themselves amused until another club could be formed. It wasn't until over a year later when they played their first competitive match against another team, beating the newly formed Thistle FC 2-0 at the Queen's Park Recreation Ground in Glasgow on 1 August 1868.

Queen's Park regularly experimented with different playing styles and have been credited with being the first to abandon the old-fashioned 'dribbling and backing up' style of play based around kick-and-rush manoeuvres, hacking and rough play to practice the modern 'combination game' which favoured individual skill, teamwork and possession football. They also ran the game in Scotland, effectively fulfilling the role of the sport's governing body until the Scottish Football Association was formed in 1873, by promoting the Association Rules north of the border, championing local and regional cup competitions and arranging friendly matches and international fixtures.

In 1875 they introduced the matchday programme. The first programme was printed for a friendly against Wanderers FC at Hampden Park on 9 October 1875. It was just a single piece of card listing the date, venue and the line-ups. Although both teams played with different-coloured shirts, they weren't numbered and the players were only recognisable to the crowd from the caps and stockings they were wearing, the details of which were also printed in the programme.

A year later, Queen's Park became the first club world champions.

The Football World Championship was a series of ad-hoc matches held between 1876 and 1904 featuring the two best teams in England and Scotland. In effect, it was the world's first international club world cup tournament – even though 'the world' never actually extended any further than the British Isles! The irregular matches attracted various degrees of public interest and press attention and usually resulted in the winners proclaiming themselves to be the new world champions. The first game in the unofficial series was held on 4 November 1876 with Queen's Park playing their old Sassenach rivals Wanderers at the Kennington Oval. *The Sportsman* reported that the Scots 'were undoubtedly superior to their opponents at every point of the game' and this was certainly reflected in the scoreline with Queen's Park running out 6-0 winners.

Queen's Park also regularly competed in the FA Cup between 1871 and 1887.

In 1884, they became the first and only club to reach the finals of both the Scottish FA Cup and the FA Cup in the same season.

The first final was the SFA Cup Final and resulted in an easy victory – but only because the other team didn't bother turning up. They'd been due to play the West Dunbartonshire club Vale of Leven at Cathkin Park in Glasgow on 23 February 1884 but due to illness, injury and a shortage of replacement players, Vale were unable to field a full-strength team. They'd appealed to the SFA to have the match postponed but their request fell on deaf ears and in protest they decided not to bother playing. The SFA committee then voted by a narrow majority just to award the cup to Queen's Park rather than reschedule the match.

The second final was the FA Cup Final and that proved a little more difficult for them. In fact, they actually had to play in that one and ended up losing 2-1. On 29 March 1884, they met Blackburn Rovers at the Kennington Oval to become the first non-English side to play in a FA Cup Final. Although it clashed with a Scotland-Wales match being played in Glasgow on the same day, many of the Scottish players chose to play for club rather than country and Queen's Park were still able to field a strong team. They started as favourites and dominated for most of the 90 minutes but ultimately failed to convert their chances. Following the match, the referee Francis Marindin admitted that Queen's Park probably should have had a second goal. At one point during the game, he thought the ball had passed over the Blackburn goal line but as the Scottish players had failed to claim a goal, he didn't bother awarding one!

THE TAGGED PLAYER
2000

Englishman Gary Croft became the first professional footballer to play a match wearing an electronic tag!

The Ipswich Town defender had served one month of a four-month sentence behind bars for driving while disqualified and perverting the course of justice when he returned to the football field for the first time since his conviction as a 71st-minute substitute in the First Division match against Swindon Town at Portman Road on 15 January 2000.

To the astonishment of everyone in the crowd, he was wearing an electronic ankle tag. Apparently, it was a condition of his early release.

However, Croft still wouldn't be available to play in any evening fixtures because he had to obey a 7pm to 7am curfew!

THE DENIS LAW GOAL THAT RELEGATED UNITED
1974

This is one of the greatest myths in football.

It's been widely reported over the years that Manchester United were relegated to Division Two at the end of the 1973/74 season because of a goal scored by their ex-player Denis Law, with his last kick of a ball as a professional footballer, while playing for Manchester City.

But it's just not true.

To avoid relegation, United had to beat City in their penultimate game of the season on 27 April 1974 and hope fellow strugglers Birmingham and West Ham dropped points in their last remaining matches. Then they had to go and win a rescheduled match against Stoke two days later.

It was do-or-die stuff, but ultimately United fell at the first hurdle due to that infamous goal from Law.

The 'Lawman' later claimed that he didn't want to win the game but didn't want to lose it either. A 0-0 draw was the perfect result for him. But in the 81st minute, he back-heeled the ball across the bobbly pitch and past the United keeper into the net. It was an audacious goal but after realising that it might condemn his beloved Red Devils to Division Two, he didn't celebrate. He even hoped that the referee might disallow it for a foul or an offside but it wasn't to be and the goal became the match winner for City. A few minutes later, Law was substituted and he walked off the pitch with his head bowed.

Then the United fans invaded the pitch and the referee was forced to abandon the game after 85 minutes.

The newspapers would report that Law had won the game for City on the same day that saw United go down and everyone just assumed that he'd been responsible. But that wasn't the case. Birmingham had beaten Norwich and West Ham had picked up a point at Liverpool, meaning that even if Law hadn't scored that goal, United would still have been relegated. They couldn't have caught those two teams, even if they'd won their last two fixtures. As it happened, they then lost to Stoke and finished the season in 21st place, second from bottom in the table.

Denis Law had simply confirmed their fate but he wasn't responsible for it.

It wasn't even the last kick of his career either. Although he retired from the game at the beginning of the following season, he did play one more professional match for City, against Oldham Athletic on 10 August 1974.

Over time the facts have never been allowed to get in the way of a good story and many people still believe it was Law who sent United down with his final kick of a football. The one thing that is true, however, is that his back-heel remains the most famous strike in the history of the Manchester derby.

MORE OWN GOALS THAN GOALS
2013

Long-serving Liverpool centre-back Jamie Carragher scored 12 goals in his 16-year, 737-match club career. Unfortunately, most of them were in his own net – only four went in at the right end and twice as many at the wrong end!

Seven of those own goals came in Premier League matches; two of them in front of the Kop end against rivals Manchester United in the north-west derby on 11 September 1999, making him the first Premier League player to score two own goals in a single match. With only three minutes on the clock, he got on the end of a Ryan Giggs cross and headed the ball past his own keeper, and then with half-time fast approaching, a loose ball in the penalty box ricocheted off his body and into the net for what proved to be the winning goal. It was certainly one of the most memorable games of his career but for all the wrong reasons.

His most favoured team seemed to be Tottenham, having scored three Premier League goals for them – exactly the same number as he scored for Liverpool.

It should also be noted that he scored the same amount of league goals against Liverpool as some of the greatest strikers – Wayne Rooney, Sergio Agüero, Olivier Giroud and even Alan Shearer. His only non-Premier League own goal didn't go unnoticed either because that came in the 2006 FA Cup Final when he opened the scoring for West Ham United after only 21 minutes.

FLIPPING THE BIRD
2024

Cagliari only unveiled their mascot in 2023 but it has already become one of the most loved in Italy and around the world.

Pully is a 9ft-tall pink flamingo who dresses in the *rossoblù* colours of the club.

He suddenly became famous after the Serie A game against Napoli on 15 September 2024 when he appeared on the pitch alongside the Cagliari players to stand in front of their supporters. There's a strange tradition in Italy that if a team doesn't play well, the players sometimes feel obliged to appear in front of their own fans to apologise and accept the abuse being hurled at them.

When the Cagliari players strolled towards the Curva Nord, Pully tagged along too. The photos of him bowing his head and looking shamefaced by his team's poor performance in a 4-0 defeat went viral – and even the angriest fans must have had a little smile on their face when they saw that bloody big bird skulking around in front of them.

THE SHORTEST CAREER
1997

English striker Joe Sheerin was signed to Chelsea between 1996 and 2000. He made his Premier League debut as a last-minute substitute for Gianfranco Zola against Wimbledon on 22 April 1997 but he never actually touched the ball before the referee blew his whistle for full time. Sheerin never played for Chelsea or any other top-level team again, with his 60-second appearance in this game now recognised as the shortest-ever playing career in the Premier League.

THE FIRST FA CUP COMPETITION
1871

The FA Cup is the world's oldest domestic cup competition and the world's oldest existing national football tournament.

The competition is open to all FA-registered league and non-league teams in all ten levels of the English Football League System with the winning team qualifying to play in the following season's FA Community Shield and the UEFA Europa League.

Although the Football Association was formed in 1863, it wasn't until 1871 when the FA secretary Charles Charles W. Alcock proposed the new competition. Of the 50 FA member clubs at that time, 15 accepted the invitation to take part in the first tournament, including Scottish club Queen's Park, although by the time the first-round ties were due to be played, this number had dropped to 13 – Barnes, Civil Service, Clapham Rovers, Crystal Palace, Donnington School, Hampstead Heathens, Hitchin, Maidenhead, Marlow, Queen's Park, Royal Engineers, Upton Park and Wanderers.

The rules of the competition stipulated that each team should have 11 players and a game should last 90 minutes. At the time, the existing Laws of the Game didn't even make reference to these two fairly basic points. However, there was no provision for extra time. When a match finished in a draw, either a replay would be arranged or both teams would just be allowed to proceed to the next round.

Although there were seven first-round matches scheduled to be played on 11 November 1871, only four of them actually took place. Royal Engineers and Wanderers both won their matches by a walkover after their opponents Reigate Priory and Harrow Chequers suddenly withdrew from the tournament. Queen's Park and Donnington School couldn't agree on a venue, so they were both allowed to progress to the next round. Likewise, Hampstead Heathens received a bye because there was an odd number of teams and they had nobody to play. Hitchin and Crystal Palace did play each other, with the game finishing in a 0-0 draw, but no replay was ever organised and so both teams were placed in the second round. The remaining three ties resulted in wins for Barnes, Maidenhead and Clapham.

Queen's Park and Donnington School were drawn against each other again in the second round. This time the school club withdrew from the tournament rather than pay the cost of the train fares to Glasgow, and Queen's Park were afforded a bye to the next round. There were also wins for Crystal Palace, Hampstead Heathens, Royal Engineers (against Hitchin who only fielded eight players) and Wanderers.

The quarter-finals were played in January 1872; by now there were only five teams left. The match between Wanderers and Crystal Palace finished 0-0 but both teams were allowed through to the next round. Queen's Park didn't have anyone to play so they received a bye – somehow, they'd reached the semi-finals without actually kicking a ball. In the remaining match, Royal Engineers beat Hampstead Heathens 3-0. After that defeat, the Heathens never played another competitive match and the club folded later that same year. It's probably fair to say they didn't accept defeat lightly.

Both semi-finals were played at the Kennington Oval and both finished in 0-0 draws. Royal Engineers then went on to beat Crystal Palace 3-0 in the replay. However, things weren't quite so simple for Queen's Park. After their first game against Wanderers, they withdrew from the tournament because they couldn't afford the train fares back to London again for the replay.

The first FA Cup Final was contested between Wanderers and Royal Engineers at the Kennington Oval on 16 March 1872. It kicked off at 3.05pm in front of around 2,000 spectators and was refereed by Alfred Stair. Both teams had attacking line-ups, with Wanderers fielding eight forwards and Royal Engineers seven. The British Army Sappers were the pre-match favourites but Wanderers won the coin toss and chose to defend the Harleyford Road end, leaving their opponents with the sun and the wind in their faces.

After only ten minutes, Royal Engineers' Edmund Creswell suffered a serious injury after breaking his collarbone during a charge on goal. With no substitutes available, he refused to leave the pitch and played on in great pain until the end of the match. *The Sportsman* reported, 'Too much praise cannot be accorded to him for the pluck he showed in maintaining his post, although completely disabled and in severe pain, until the finish.'

Wanderers took the lead after only 15 minutes with a goal from Morton Betts who was playing under the pseudonym of A.H. Chequer.

Back then, it wasn't at all unusual for a player to turn out for more than one team during the season. Sometimes clubs would even loan each other players if one of them arrived short-handed for a match. Morton actually played his football for Harrow Chequers (Old Harrovians) but they'd failed to show for their first-round match and had been disqualified. However, it seems that Morton wasn't to be denied his chance of FA Cup glory and that's why he'd turned out for Wanderers, as A.H. Chequer (A Harrow Chequer). It's unclear if the guy was trying to avoid being cup-tied or if he was just trying to be funny.

The goal itself was a relatively simple tap-in coming after a successful dribble through the opposition's defence by his team-mate Walpole Vidal. The rules at that time demanded a change of ends after every goal but the Engineers were unable to take advantage of the more favourable conditions and Wanderers continued to dominate.

After 20 minutes, Wanderers captain Charles W. Alcock slotted the ball past the opposition keeper William Merriman but the goal was disallowed as his team-mate Charles Wollaston was adjudged to have handled the ball. Wanderers remained on top and it was only due to some outstanding goalkeeping from Merriman that the score remained at 1-0.

Despite a late rally from the Engineers, Wanderers held on to their slender lead to win the first FA Cup Final. *The Field* claimed that it was 'the fastest and hardest match that has ever been seen at The Oval' with Wanderers showing 'some of the best play, individually and collectively, that has ever been shown in an Association game'.

Wanderers didn't receive the trophy at the end of the match; that tradition didn't begin until 1882. Instead, they had to wait a month until the FA president Ebenezer Cobb Morley presented them with it at a specially arranged dinner in some fancy London restaurant.

The following season, whereas all the other teams competing in the 1872/73 FA Cup had to fight their way through the rounds, Wanderers were automatically awarded a spot in the final. This was the first and only occasion when the holders were given a bye straight through to the following year's final.

That match took place on 29 March 1873 against Oxford University at Lillie Bridge in Fulham, London. Unusually, the match kicked off at 11.30am to allow people to watch the University Boat Race taking place that afternoon along the River Thames. The Oxford side dominated the early stages of the match but it was Wanderers who scored first against the run of play after 27 minutes when their charismatic captain Arthur Kinnaird outpaced the Oxford defence and slotted the ball home. Later in the game, Oxford moved their goalkeeper Andrew Leach up the field to play with the strikers in a desperate attempt to get an equalising goal. It must have seemed like a good idea – right up until the point when the Wanderers forward Charles Wollaston broke through their defence and hit the ball into an empty net. *The Field* reported that the shot would have been easily saved if the goalkeeper had still been standing in his goal. Wanderers won 2-0 and became the first back-to-back winners of the FA Cup.

* * *

Wanderers, the London-based amateur club of former public schoolboys, had originally been founded as Forest FC in 1859 but it wasn't until 15 March 1862 that they actually played a game of football after meeting Crystal Palace in a 15-a-side Cambridge Rules fixture.

In 1863, the club became founding members of the FA and began playing by Association Rules. A year later they changed their name to Wanderers FC, reflecting their desire to play football at various different locations in and around London and avoid the expense of owning their own ground. Among the players who represented the club was the so-called 'father of football' Charles W. Alcock, along with Arthur Kinnaird – regarded as the greatest player of his day – and perhaps the most famous and celebrated Victorian sportsman of them all, W.G. Grace. Although Grace is better known as a cricketer, having captained the England, Gloucestershire, Gentlemen and MCC teams, he also had a great enthusiasm for athletics, golf, bowls and curling, and still found the time to turn out for Wanderers every now and again too.

Wanderers were by far the most popular and successful team of the era and won the FA Cup five times between 1872 and 1878.

They continued to dominate the game right up until the late 1870s when their fortunes started to decline after more and more public schools decided to establish their own football teams and many of their old-boy players chose to play for those sides instead.

By the mid-1880s, the amateur public school teams were being outplayed by the professional teams from the north of England. By then, the golden age of amateur football in England had come to an end and Wanderers FC was dissolved in 1887.

WHEN THE CHAIRMAN DIDN'T KNOW BEST
1997

In 1992, Michael Knighton bought Carlisle United, promising to invest in the club and take them out of the lower divisions.

At the end of the 1996/97 season they won promotion to the Second Division and on 20 April 1997 they beat Colchester United on penalties to win the Football League Trophy. However, after a poor start to the following season, Knighton sacked the team's manager Mervyn Day but then couldn't find a suitable replacement, so he just appointed himself to the role instead! He'd only played a bit of youth-team football and was understandably better known as a businessman and entrepreneur than a sportsman but that didn't stop him from believing he could do better than any of the jobless professionals out there.

Alas, things didn't go quite as he'd hoped because Carlisle were relegated back to the Third Division in 1997/98 and then spent the early part of the following season bouncing around the relegation zone. Knighton's vanity was costing them dearly. Finally, after winning only 19 of his 68 games in charge, he had the good sense to sack himself. He no longer had the financial resources to run the club and had understandably become unpopular with the fans.

Nigel Pearson was eventually brought in as the new manager to try and avoid the drop into the Conference. But it was touch and go whether he'd succeed right up until the last kick of the last game.

On 8 May 1999, Carlisle needed to beat Plymouth to avoid relegation. With the score at 1-1 and only ten seconds left on the clock, they won a corner and their emergency on-loan goalkeeper Jimmy Glass ran up to the opposition penalty area. Then, with the very last kick of the game, he volleyed the ball into the Plymouth net for a shock injury-time goal to record a 2-1 win and guarantee Carlisle's future in the Football League. Their journeyman keeper had saved their arses with perhaps the greatest last-gasp goal ever seen in the history of the English Football League.

It wasn't until 2002 that Michael Knighton finally had the good sense to sell up and move on.

BIG LOSERS
2013

Antigua Barracuda played a whole season without a single win ... or even a draw!

Based in St John's, Antigua, they were the island's first full-time professional team, although they actually played their football in the US-based USL Pro league. Unfortunately, they only played for three seasons before being wound up in 2014. Things started to go wrong for them in 2012 during their second season when the other teams in the league suddenly refused to travel thousands of miles to a remote Caribbean island just to play a game of football, and so the United States League (USL) ordered them to relocate to the US mainland and play all of the following season's games away from home.

As a result, they finished the 2013 season with no points and a goal difference of -80 (scoring 11 times and conceding 91) after losing all 26 games.

When former West Ham, Swindon and Portsmouth defender Adrian Whitbread took over as their manager halfway through that fateful season, the team were broke and living in a modest hotel in Tampa, Florida, which acted as their base. He had to rely on his own contacts or the generosity of their next opponents to arrange training facilities for them. And when all else failed, they just had to be content with a kickabout in the hotel car park! For his first game in charge, he was shocked to discover that they wouldn't be flying to face Richmond Kickers but driving instead, with the club's entire personnel of 18 players and four backroom staff squeezing into a fleet of minivans for the ten-hour journey to Virginia. Sometimes, they couldn't even afford to hire cars. They once had to walk from their hotel to the stadium for a game played in Los Angeles.

Although Whitbread helped out where he could by dipping into his own pocket to cover some of the day-today costs, the players and staff weren't getting paid and a few of them, including the team's physio, just walked out mid-season and returned home to Antigua.

By the end of the 2013 season, the players who remained were all exhausted. The long road trips, bad results, sleepless nights in strange hotels, the club's financial difficulties, and the worry of failing to provide for their families back in Antigua had all taken a toll on their welfare. But they still had a good sense of togetherness and the margins of defeat had actually decreased as the season progressed. Their good spirits and the problems they'd endured earned them a great deal of respect and admiration from their opponents. On one occasion, after a game against Phoenix FC, some of the home fans even invited them all out for a beer.

However, Antigua Barracuda were still homeless and penniless at the end of the 2013 season which meant there was no 2014 season with the club withdrawing from the USL Pro league on 6 January 2014.

BIGGER LOSERS
2016

The amateur team Longford AFC were even bigger losers.

They were playing in Division Two of the Gloucestershire Northern Senior League back in 2015/16 and ended their 30-game season with no wins, no draws, 30 losses and a goal difference of -216 after scoring ten times and conceding 226 - an average of 7½ goals every game! No wonder the press had dubbed them the 'worst team in Britain'.

For the game against Wotton Rovers on 12 March 2016, the 53-year-old former Nottingham Forest and England defender Stuart Pearce was asked to play for them – 14 years after his last appearance as a player – in an effort to try and stop the rot. It was all part of a publicity stunt arranged by the insurance company Direct Line to promote its #directfix marketing campaign.

Pearce's appearance had seen the usual crowd of one man and his dog grow to around 450 people. Such was the interest in the game that the local branch of the British Cactus and Succulent Society had very generously agreed to hold its usual Saturday afternoon meeting away from the village hall which overlooks the pitch, so the football club could use it.

Having recently racked up losses of 15-0, 16-0 and 17-0, Pearce's presence obviously had an effect, even though he only appeared for the second half, because they only lost 1-0 that day. And that one goal they conceded came from a penalty.

It was a direct fix of sorts but Direct Line were probably hoping for a win.

THE BASTARD IN BLACK
1878

Segar Bastard was a solicitor, amateur sportsman and the first football referee who really was a bastard! He played cricket for Essex and the MCC and football for Upton Park between 1873 and 1887. As a referee, he took charge of the 1878 FA Cup Final and the first-ever international match between England and Wales in 1879.

Unfortunately, there doesn't seem to be any record of whether he was true to his name or not.

THE SCANDAL OF STAMFORD BRIDGE
2009

Chelsea hosted Spanish giants Barcelona in the second leg of their Champions League semi-final on 6 May 2009, after drawing 0-0 at the Camp Nou a week earlier. After only nine minutes, Chelsea midfielder Michael Essien hit a spectacular volley to give the home team the lead. But this match was played back in the days when away goals counted for double in the event of a draw, so Chelsea really needed a second to ease their jitters.

That second goal never came thanks mainly to the match official Tom Henning Øvrebø turning down FIVE penalty appeals.

The first came in the 23rd minute after the Barcelona full-back Dani Alves fouled Florent Malouda inside the box – and Mr Øvrebø awarded a free kick just outside the box instead. Just three minutes later, Eric Abidal appeared to hold back Didier Drogba after pulling on his shirt but the Norwegian official failed to spot any infringement, his whistle remained silent and play continued, much to the disgust of the Ivorian striker.

Probably the most controversial incident occurred ten minutes from time. After Gerard Piqué handled the ball under pressure from Nicolas Anelka, Mr Øvrebø again failed to spot anything untoward and waved play on. It was the clearest penalty of the night to everyone in the stadium and certainly everyone watching on TV with the advantage of seeing the slow-motion replay of the incident. Everyone except Mr Øvrebø, who seemed to think it was perfectly acceptable for the Spanish defender to suddenly start using his hands to control the ball.

Then Yaya Touré appeared to pull down Anelka as they chased for the ball. This was by far Chelsea's weakest penalty appeal of the five, so there was no chance of getting anything for that one.

And in the last few seconds of the game, after Barcelona had equalised with a stoppage-time goal from Andrés Iniesta, Samuel Eto'o appeared to block a last-gasp shot from Michael Ballack with his arm inside the box – but Mr Øvrebø yet again refused to point to the spot. The Chelsea midfielder ran after him like a man possessed and yelled in his face demanding a penalty. But the more Chelsea appealed and the more melodramatic those appeals became, the more belligerent Mr Øvrebø became in refusing them.

At the final whistle, the Chelsea players surrounded Mr Øvrebø. Drogba had been substituted but that didn't stop him from sprinting back on to the pitch and telling the referee exactly what he thought of him before bellowing down the lens of a TV camera, 'It's a disgrace! It's a fucking disgrace!'

Chelsea defender José Bosingwa said during a post-match interview with the Portuguese TV station RTP, 'I don't know if he's a referee or a thief. I don't have any words to describe that man that was on the pitch. We have nothing against Barcelona's goal but the penalties that he didn't give us and his way of managing the game weren't right at all. This referee should never referee a game again. What happened was a disgrace. It was a well-contested game but the referee came to spoil the game.'

Such was the level of anger among the home crowd that Mr Øvrebø was assigned police protection getting out of the ground after the game and was forced to change hotels. Some Chelsea fans were convinced that Barcelona had been playing with 12 men that night because the UEFA president Michel Platini was desperate to break the English dominance of the tournament after five Premier League clubs had reached the final in the previous four years. A little fanciful perhaps considering that Mr Øvrebø had also red-carded the Barcelona defender Eric Abidal in the 66th minute, which would have almost certainly benefited the home team.

Many years later in an interview with *FourFourTwo* magazine, Guus Hiddink, Chelsea's manager at the time, commented on the game and the referee's perceived lack of integrity: 'Some people argued it was fixed. While deep down I don't believe that, perhaps it was the only time I started to doubt it.'

Tom Henning Øvrebø has also had time to reflect on his performance that night and now accepts that some of his decisions were a bit controversial, but still remains unconvinced that Chelsea would have made it through to the final if he'd rewarded some or even all of their appeals with a spot kick.

But he would say that, wouldn't he?

THE CLUMSY CAPTAIN
1993

Arsenal were the first team to win both the FA Cup and the League Cup in the same season. It was also the first time in history that both finals were contested by the same two teams. On 18 April 1993 they beat Sheffield Wednesday 2-1 in the League Cup Final, and on 20 May they beat them again by the same scoreline in a replay of the FA Cup Final.

Steve Morrow played in the League Cup Final, scoring his first goal for Arsenal and winning the game for them. In the post-match revelries, his captain Tony Adams attempted to lift him up on to his shoulders but he slipped and fell – and so did Morrow, who landed awkwardly and broke his arm. He was then rushed to hospital and never got the chance to collect his medal. The injury also ended his season, forcing him to miss the upcoming FA Cup Final. However, at least he was invited back to Wembley on that occasion to receive his League Cup medal before the kick off.

Ironically, this time he was the only player to leave the stadium with a medal, because the match went to a replay after a 1-1 draw.

SENDING THE WRONG MESSAGE
1995

Birmingham City's 1-0 Football League Trophy Final victory over Carlisle United on 23 April 1995 was the first British match settled by a golden goal.

It was still goalless when Paul Tait scored the winner after 103 minutes. He then whipped off his shirt to reveal a T-shirt underneath bearing the slogan 'Birmingham City – Shit on the Villa' before running about the field celebrating his team's win.

He was later reprimanded by the Professional Footballers' Association, charged by the FA for bringing the game into disrepute, and fined two weeks' wages by his club!

THE BOGOTÁ BRACELET INCIDENT 1970

As part of their preparations for the 1970 World Cup in Mexico, England had planned a couple of friendly matches against Colombia and Ecuador to help them acclimatise to the heat and get used to playing at a high altitude.

The squad left their base in Mexico City and arrived in the Colombian capital, Bogotá, checking into the Hotel Tequendama on 18 May 1970.

They had been warned not to wander around the city. It was unsafe and everyone had been confined to the hotel. As there wasn't much to keep them amused, they all spent a bit of time hanging around the shop in the hotel lobby browsing for gifts to take back home.

That evening, captain Bobby Moore had accompanied his team-mate Bobby Charlton into the shop to have a little look around. They left shortly afterwards, without buying anything, and were standing around in the lobby when the shop's assistant Clara Padilla suddenly ran out and accused them of stealing a valuable 18-carat diamond and emerald bracelet from a display case. The players protested their innocence and allowed themselves to be searched. Team manager Alf Ramsey quickly arrived on the scene and took charge of the situation, negotiating with the hotel staff and then the police when they turned up later. Both players later made an official statement after being questioned and the matter seemed to have been resolved after they received an apology from the hotel staff for the misunderstanding.

The match against Colombia went ahead as planned on 20 May with England winning 4-0. The team then flew to Quito in Ecuador for another game, on 24 May, this time against Ecuador, which they won 2-0, before returning to the Hotel Tequendama to await a flight back to Mexico City. It had been proposed beforehand that the team should travel via Panama instead to avoid any further problems in Colombia but the idea was strongly rejected by Ramsey and Moore in case it gave the impression of some wrongdoing on their part.

As the players stepped off the plane on 25 May, a British Embassy official informed Moore that he was required to answer a few more questions about the theft. As the rest of the squad travelled back to the hotel, he was taken into custody by machine gun-toting cops and whisked away to a downtown courtroom to appear in front of a judge. Apparently, a new witness, 26-year-old street vendor Álvaro Suárez, had come forward, claiming to have seen Moore take the bracelet. The judge was apparently unconvinced of the England skipper's innocence because he ordered him to be detained in prison while the case was investigated further.

'He might be the best footballer in the world, the most attractive, distinguished and most highly regarded of anyone, a friend of Her British Majesty even. But that doesn't mean he's not a kleptomaniac,' added the shop owner Danilo Rojas, on learning of Moore's detention.

Luckily, the director of the Federación Colombiana de Fútbol, Alfonso Senior Quevedo, realised it wasn't a great look if the England captain was banged up in one of the city's notorious jails and pleaded with the judge to let Moore stay with him under house arrest. His request was granted and two policemen were assigned to watch over him day and night.

Meanwhile, the rest of the squad set off for Mexico without their captain. One of the other players, Jeff Astle, was a notoriously bad flyer and he'd had a few drinks to calm his nerves during the flight. But by the time they'd landed in Mexico City, he was a little worse for wear and had to be carried off the plane by his team-mates, leading one Mexican newspaper to brand them all as 'a team of drunks and thieves'.

Moore showed remarkable fortitude during his detention; he was always the perfect English gentleman. However, on one occasion, the temptation to get one over on his dopey guards proved too much even for him. He got them drunk one night and was able to sneak out early the following morning for a run and then enjoy a big plate of ham and eggs before they'd crawled out of their beds. He could have made his escape and been halfway back to England by the time those two goons knew what was going on.

He was generally perceived as being innocent of the crime, with Ramsey remarking, 'I should have thought that the integrity of this man would be enough to answer these charges. It is too ridiculous for words.' Even the Colombian press were on his side, with *El Tiempo* writing, 'We should have more faith in his [Moore's] statements than those of the witnesses who contradict themselves and lack seriousness.' João Saldanha, the former Brazil coach, called the allegations 'disgraceful' and went on to describe a similar experience he had endured at the same hotel when he was staying there with his club team Botafogo.

But Clara Padilla was sticking to her story, 'Nobody, and I repeat nobody, other than him [Bobby Moore] could have been the author of the jewel's disappearance. I'm sure of that.'

On the second day of his detention, Moore was hauled in front of the judge again, but after several hours of questioning he was still none the wiser and ordered a re-enactment of the crime to take place at the hotel with all the protagonists present. Padilla repeated her well-rehearsed and oft-told story that she'd seen Moore slip the bracelet into his blazer's left-hand pocket. Presumably he was still wearing the same blazer because he then challenged the judge to find that infamous left-hand pocket. It was the mic drop moment – because the blazer didn't have a left-hand pocket. Poor Clara Padilla then changed her story a few more times but eventually even she didn't believe what she was saying any more and just burst into tears before running from the hotel.

The judge was also a little curious to know why the mysterious eyewitness Álvaro Suárez waited for four days to come forward and why the value of the bracelet had also increased from £500 to £6,000 during the course of the investigation. It was later revealed that Danilo Rojas had bribed Suárez for his testimony and was just plucking figures out of the air whenever he was asked about the bracelet's value.

Rather wisely, the judge decided that there was insufficient evidence to justify Moore's continued detainment, all the charges against him were dropped and he was finally released from custody on 28 May. The hotel gift shop was closed soon afterwards and Clara Padilla fled to the USA, never to be seen or heard from publicly ever again.

It is generally assumed that the incident was either a poorly executed attempt to extort money from the English FA or an equally poorly executed plan to have Moore ruled out of the World Cup, weakening England's chances of winning the tournament.

SEVEN GOALS UNLUCKY
1922

Following a 1-1 draw at Clarence Park, St. Albans on 18 November 1922, Dulwich Hamlet and St Albans City met again in south London to decide their FA Cup fourth-round qualifying tie.

This was the match where neither side fielded their regular goalkeeper, which undoubtedly contributed to the exaggerated 8-7 scoreline; the match that ended farcically in near darkness, and the match in which the St Albans striker Wilfred Minter famously scored all seven of his team's goals – and still ended up on the losing side!

Thirty minutes in, St Albans were leading 3-1 after Minter – known to friends and family as Billy – had scored his first hat-trick. By the 60th minute, however, Dulwich were ahead 5-3, but then Minter rose to the occasion again and notched up another treble in ten minutes to nudge his team into a 6-5 lead. With only five minutes remaining, however, Dulwich scored again to level the score at 6-6 and send the match into extra time.

Dulwich struck first in extra time and then, as the light began to fade, Minter nodded in his seventh goal of the day to equalise five minutes from time. The two teams appeared to be heading towards yet another replay until the referee stopped play a few moments from full time to award the home team a free kick after his linesman had signalled a foul. The ball was then lobbed into the box and headed into the net by W.J. Davis to the delight of the few home fans who could still make out what was happening on the pitch.

The *Daily News* reported, 'It is right and proper to congratulate Dulwich Hamlet, but one would have preferred to have seen the tie all square at the end, for St Albans played a wonderful forward game and it is a tragedy for Wilfred Minter that although scoring each of the seven goals for the Herts club, the gifted centre-forward found himself at last on the losing side.'

St Albans may have been defeated but at least they got their name in the record books as the losing team in an FA Cup tie to score the most goals. The fact that Minter had scored all of them just makes this match all the more remarkable.

EVERTON TWO
2009

Britain's largest open-air shopping centre, Liverpool ONE, was officially opened on 1 October 2008.

A year later, when Everton opened a second club store in the new centre, they rebranded their original stadium store as Everton One and named the new store Everton Two as a subtle way of trolling their rivals Liverpool. Because whenever anyone had to write the new store's address – Everton Two Liverpool ONE, 11 South John Street, Liverpool L1 8BU – the first line would always read like a match scoreline in Everton's favour.

It was either very clever or very petty!

THE GENTLEMEN PLAYERS
1882

Corinthian FC was formed in 1882 by the former Finchley player Nicholas Lane Jackson to challenge the dominance of Scottish football.

England had just suffered a series of six losses to Scotland and he believed this was because most of the Scots' players all came from the same club and were used to playing together whereas the England players were drawn from many different clubs and only met up for the first time on the day of the match. To address this problem, he invited the best university and ex-public school amateur players to join his new team. They'd continue to play for their regular club sides at the weekends but would also play midweek fixtures for Corinthian against the best sides in England in order to provide the national team with a good pool of footballers who regularly played together.

The original name for the team was the Wednesday Club but following a suggestion by one of their first players, Harry Swepstone, it was changed to Corinthian FC. As the club rules stated that they shouldn't compete in the FA Cup (or any other competition), they only ever played friendlies, exhibition games and charity fundraising matches, many of which took place overseas.

During the late 19th century, the majority of players selected to play for England were also Corinthian players, and for two matches against Wales, in 1894 and 1895, the entire team was chosen to represent their country – the only times this has ever happened for an England fixture.

Corinthian were able to challenge many of the top professional sides. In 1889 they were the only team to beat the Preston North End 'Invincibles' team, and in 1904 they beat Manchester United 11-3, which to this day remains their heaviest defeat. If the club had competed in the FA Cup, there's a fair chance they would have won it many times. Shortly after Blackburn Rovers beat Queen's Park in the 1884 final, Corinthian beat Blackburn 8-1 and, after Bury defeated Derby County in the 1903 final, Corinthian beat them 10-3.

By the early 20th century Corinthian were considered to be the best team in the world.

The club has been credited with popularising football around the world, promoting sportsmanship and fair play, and championing amateurism. The players were all gentlemen and prided themselves on never knowingly committing a foul against an opponent or acting in an improper manner on the field. So when William McCrum of Irish club Milford FC first proposed the idea of introducing the penalty kick to penalise any tripping, holding or handling of the ball within 12 yards of the goal line and the International Football Association Board then approved the idea in 1890, it was greeted with much derision by the Corinthian players, especially by their popular captain C.B. Fry who said it was 'a standing insult to sportsmen to have to play under a rule which assumes that players intend to trip, hack and push opponents and to behave like cads'. They had no option but to accept a referee's ruling if they were awarded a penalty but if it was a Corinthian man adjudged to have committed a foul in the area, their keeper was instructed just to stand aside, lean against the goalpost and watch along with everyone else as the penalty taker struck the ball into an empty net.

Their tour of South Africa in 1897 was the first time that the Corinthian gentlemen embarked on an overseas trip. It was also the first tour by any British club outside of Europe. They played a total of 23 matches against club sides and the South African national team, winning 21 of them and drawing two. The tour began with a 4-0 win against Cape Town Civilians on 17 July 1897 and ended with a 2-1 win in the last of their three matches against a South African XI on 13 September. Corinthian scored 113 goals and conceded only 15 with their biggest victory being a 10-1 thrashing of Griqualand FC on 28 August 1897. Considering the long journeys, the hard grounds and the ridiculously packed schedule, the 14 players who undertook the tour did a remarkable job.

Corinthian became the most travelled club in the world after undertaking over 20 foreign tours between 1897 and 1939 to promote the game and show Johnny Foreigner that it should always be played with style, honour and a sense of decency.

Corinthian's influence would spread around the world; Arthur Johnson was an expat player for Real Madrid who later went on to manage the club between 1910 and 1920, during which time he decided to adopt the same all-white strip for his players in honour of Corinthian, who were his favourite side.

As part of their six-match Brazilian tour of 1910, Corinthian played AA Palmeiras on 31 August. In the crowd that day were five local railway workers who were so impressed by the elegant play of the English team that they immediately decided to form a football team of their own, Sport Club Corinthians Paulista, now one of the biggest and most successful clubs in South America.

NOT WINNING ANYTHING WITH KIDS
1995

On the opening day of the 1995/96 Premier League season, Manchester United lost 3-1 away to Aston Villa. The home team had taken a commanding 3-0 lead into half-time with United only managing a late consolation goal. Their manager Alex Ferguson had overhauled his team during the summer break and had fielded a team of youngsters against Villa with disastrous results.

On *Match of the Day* that evening, when asked by the show's host Des Lynam for his appraisal of United's performance, the ex-Liverpool player and resident pundit Alan Hansen pointed out the lack of star names in the team and scathingly remarked, 'You can't win anything with kids.'

United would not lose again until November. They only lost twice in the new year and eventually surpassed rivals Newcastle in the race to win the Premier League title. They also enjoyed an impressive FA Cup run, reaching the final and then beating Liverpool 1-0 to complete a domestic double. Ferguson was also named Premier League Manager of the Season. So much for not winning anything with kids!

It has since transpired that Hansen's derogatory comment was constantly mentioned throughout that season to inspire the Manchester United players to greater things. The club shop later began selling T-shirts printed with his infamous words, such was everyone's delight at him getting it so spectacularly wrong.

FIFTEEN SECONDS OF MADNESS
1992

The backpass rule was introduced by the International Football Association Board in 1992 to discourage time-wasting and reduce defensive play. The incident often cited as prompting the rule change occurred in a 1990 World Cup match between the Republic of Ireland and Egypt on 17 June when the Irish goalkeeper Pat Bonner spent a combined total of SIX minutes of game time pissing about with the ball, picking it up, putting it down again, dribbling it around his area or just passing it back and forth to his defenders.

The 1992/93 season was the first to incorporate the new rule and the early games were full of slapstick comedy moments played out by terrified goalkeepers and nervous defenders. And nobody made a bigger fool of himself than the Sheffield United keeper Simon Tracey as he struggled to gain possession of the ball without picking it up during the Premier League match against Tottenham on 2 September 1992.

It just wasn't his day. He'd already been booked as early as the fourth minute and had let in two goals – and then in the 84th minute he seemed determined to demonstrate just how totally hopeless he was at adapting to the new law.

It all started with an innocent backpass and was followed by 15 seconds of total madness. Rather than booting the ball out of the stadium like a lot of keepers might have done, Tracey made the foolish decision to try and dribble his way out of trouble and inadvertently became the star of his own little comedy show. It was a decent enough first touch but then he got a bit cocky and tried to dummy and outrun an oncoming Tottenham player before being forced to run with the ball towards the touchline and kick it out of play. Then, instead of sprinting back to the safety of his own box, he tried to retrieve the ball before anyone else could by indulging in a rather undignified and ultimately unsuccessful wrestling match with a ball boy. The ball ended up rolling back on to the pitch, a Tottenham player picked it up and attempted to take a quick throw-in but was then rugby-tackled to the ground by Tracey. The referee had no option but to show him a second yellow card and then a red one.

***

Over the years many players have tried to get around the law with a bit of fancy play. By coincidence, two of the most famous incidents occurred in 2017.

In the 30th minute of the Ligue 1 game between Nantes and Paris Saint-Germain on 21 January 2017 at the Stade de la Beaujoire, the PSG midfielder Marco Verratti received the ball from his goalkeeper Kevin Trapp but instead of playing it upfield, he decided just to play it back to his keeper by getting down on his hands and knees and heading the ball along the ground so he could pick it up and restart play. The referee was not impressed, deeming his actions as unsportsmanlike, so he booked Verratti for ungentlemanly conduct and awarded Nantes an indirect free kick.

Ivan Perišić was another player who fell foul of the law when he was playing for Inter Milan against Roma at the Stadio Olimpico in a Serie A game the following month. In the sixth minute, when he had possession of the ball in his own penalty area, he nonchalantly flicked it up into the air and headed it back to his goalkeeper Samir Handanović. As soon as the pass was completed, the referee stopped play and ran halfway across the pitch to show him a yellow card.

It seems that Verratti and Perišić hadn't been quite as clever at beating the backpass rule as they initially thought because FIFA had already made provisions for some smart-arse player trying their luck. Football's official laws clearly stated that players were not allowed to use trickery in order to get around the rule: 'A player may pass the ball to his own goalkeeper using his head, chest, knee etc. However, if, in the opinion of the referee, the player uses a deliberate trick – such as flicking the ball to his head with his foot and heading it to the goalkeeper or kneeling and deliberately pushing the ball to the goalkeeper with his head or knee – he must be cautioned for ungentlemanly conduct.'

THE FIRST WORLD CUP
1930

The FIFA World Cup is the most prestigious international football competition and the most widely followed sporting event in the world.

FIFA had been arranging the football competitions at the Olympic Games, beginning in Paris in 1924, and it was the success of these mini tournaments which prompted them to start organising something similar themselves. Plans were finalised in 1928 to hold the first World Cup in Uruguay, in 1930. Uruguay were the footballing superpower at that time and the gold medal winners at the Olympics Games in Paris, then Amsterdam in 1928, so the South American nation seemed like the perfect choice to host the first competition.

Every FIFA-affiliated country was sent an invitation and asked to confirm their participation. But only 13 North and South American countries RSVP'd their willingness to take part. Uruguay was a long way from home for the European nations with the lengthy boat trip and the cost of the journey overshadowing any enthusiasm they may have had for the new tournament. It was only after the personal intervention of the FIFA president Jules Rimet that Belgium, France, Romania and Yugoslavia all agreed to take part.

This was the only World Cup where the participating teams didn't have to play any qualifying games first.

All the matches were played between 13 and 30 July 1930 at just three stadiums in Montevideo. The 13 nations were organised into four groups with only the first-placed teams progressing to the knockout stage. The opening France-Mexico and USA-Belgium games kicked off simultaneously at 3pm on 13 July and were the first World Cup matches ever played.

Argentina and Uruguay were the tournament favourites with Argentina quickly establishing themselves as the bad boys of international football with some pretty rough play right from the off against France on 15 July. There was a hostile atmosphere inside the ground and the referee did nothing to relieve the tension by inexplicably blowing the final whistle six minutes early, just as the French winger Marcel Langiller was through on goal and looked certain to score. Argentina's second game, against Mexico, ended in an easy 6-3 win. Their first-choice striker and captain, Manuel Ferreira, had returned home to sit a law exam so Guillermo Stábile had taken his place in the team, scoring three goals and eventually becoming the tournament's top scorer – and then never playing for his country again! Argentina's last group game was a 3-1 win over Chile and featured a big fight between the players, which had to be broken up by the police.

Argentina (Group 1), Yugoslavia (Group 2), Uruguay (Group 3) and USA (Group 4) all progressed to the knockout stage where, rather bizarrely, both of the semi-finals ended 6-1.

During the Argentina-USA game on 26 July, the South Americans bullied their way to victory: one US player had his leg broken, another had four teeth knocked out and a third ended up in hospital with stomach injuries. At one stage, the US medic rushed on to the field to complain about the rough treatment his players were receiving; he threw down his medical bag full of glass bottles containing various lotions and potions, and started remonstrating with the referee. Unfortunately, the bag burst open, a few bottles were smashed, including one full of chloroform, the fumes overpowered him and he had to be carried off the field again by his own players.

Things weren't much calmer in the other semi-final the following day, between Uruguay and Yugoslavia. Brazilian referee Gilberto de Almeida Rêgo controversially disallowed a perfectly good Yugoslavia goal for a very dubious offside before allowing a goal from Uruguay's Peregrino Anselmo to stand despite the ball going out of play during the build-up and being kicked back on to the field by a helpful policeman!

Argentina and Uruguay then met each other in the final at the Estadio Centenario in Montevideo on 30 July.

The gates were opened at eight o'clock in the morning, six hours before kick off, and by noon the stadium was already full, with 93,000 excited fans. The atmosphere surrounding the game was tense with a ring of armed troops being deployed around the field; fans were searched for weapons on their way into the ground, and the referee, John Langenus, only agreed to officiate a few hours before kick off after receiving assurances that a boat would be on standby in the harbour to whisk him away to safety should things turn nasty after the game. The Belgian had already had to break up a few scuffles and deal with a chaotic pitch invasion during his two previous tournament matches, so he wasn't about to take any chances with this one.

Just to make things worse, Argentina and Uruguay couldn't agree on which ball to use. They'd both brought one to the match and each insisted on using their own ball. It's uncertain how the stand-off was resolved as two versions of the story have emerged, one a little more far-fetched than the other. Either the referee walked out on to the pitch carrying both balls and it was only decided which would be used just before kick off with the toss of a coin (which Argentina won and meant playing the whole match with their Scottish-made Tiento ball), or it was agreed that both balls should be used, Argentina's during the first half and Uruguay's slightly larger and heavier T-Model ball for the second half.

Uruguay took the lead after only 12 minutes with a goal from Pablo Dorado but Argentina equalised eight minutes later through Carlos Peucelle and then went into the break leading 2-1 after a 37th-minute Guillermo Stábile strike. In the second half Uruguay came out fighting and equalised soon afterwards with a 57th-minute goal from Pedro Cea. Santos Iriarte made it 3-2 in the 68th minute and then their one-armed attacker Héctor Castro put the result beyond any doubt by netting Uruguay's fourth goal after 89 minutes.

Uruguay had beaten the bully boys of Argentina 4-2 to become the first champions of the world.

The 'Victory' trophy was presented to the president of the Asociación Uruguaya de Fútbol after the game by Jules Rimet, and the Uruguayan government declared a national holiday for the following day to celebrate their country's glorious win.

Uruguay hadn't been at all happy about the lack of enthusiasm shown by the European nations for the tournament being staged in South America, so they decided to show their displeasure by boycotting the qualification competition for the 1934 World Cup in Italy, making them the first and only team not to defend their title. And they were still sulking about it four years after that when they refused to play any qualification games for the 1938 World Cup in France too.

The four British teams didn't bother to turn up for the inaugural World Cup and also refused to participate in the second one despite FIFA offering England and Scotland direct entry into the finals without playing any qualifying games. FA committee member Charles Sutcliffe called the competition a 'joke', claiming that 'the national associations … have quite enough to do in their own international championship, which seems to me a far better World Championship than the one to be staged in Rome'.

As a point of interest, Uruguay have only won that first World Cup and then the 1950 tournament in Brazil, but have four stars above the badge on their shirts. This is because FIFA recognises their two wins at the Olympic Games in 1924 and 1928 as world championships and therefore equivalent to World Cup victories.

THE HAMPDEN ROAR
1929

Alec Cheyne has been credited with instigating the famous 'Hampden Roar' in his debut for Scotland in their British Home Championship win over England on 13 April 1929.

The match was described by *The Times* as 'distinctly disappointing' with the hard ground and a strong, blustery wind combining to prevent both teams from playing good football.

Then, with the game seemingly heading towards an inevitable 0-0 draw, Scotland were awarded a corner in the 89th minute. Cheyne stepped up and whipped the ball into the penalty box – and straight into the goal to win the game.

The ball had flown into the far corner of the net assisted by 'the very element that had nearly spoiled the great game of the season'. His Olympic goal lifted the roof off Hampden with the 110,000 elated Scottish fans continuing to cheer their team well beyond the final whistle.

Scotland had lost their outside-right Alex Jackson through injury after 40 minutes and had been forced to play the remainder of the game with just ten men. Jackson had been taken to hospital about a mile away from the ground to receive treatment for his injury but later claimed that the roar of the fans had been so loud that he could hear it and knew that Scotland had scored.

THE SERIAL STREAKER
1994

At one time, Mark Roberts was the world's most famous naked man. His first streak at a football ground in Britain was during an Everton-Liverpool match on 21 November 1994. Mark whipped off his clothes, squeezed past a steward and then ran down the steps and on to the pitch at Goodison Park. As the game continued around him, he decided to sprint the full length of the pitch and shake hands with the Everton goalkeeper Neville Southall. As some fans gawked at his dangly bits bouncing around, others read the message written on his back and his butt cheeks – 'BRIAN CLOUGH IS AN→ ↓ ←' (with all the arrows pointing to his arsehole) – making reference to the loudmouth manager's derogatory comments in his recently published autobiography about what he said was the bad behaviour of the Liverpool fans during the Hillsborough disaster in 1989. Mark was eventually apprehended by the police and led off the field to great applause from the crowd.

Mark was a compulsive streaker who stripped off more than 500 times in over 20 countries. He first ran nude at a Rugby Sevens game in 1993 in Hong Kong and has since appeared naked or semi-naked all around the world at football matches, racecourses, snooker tournaments, a Miss World contest, the summer and winter Olympics, Wimbledon, the Running of the Bulls, Super Bowl XXXVIII and even the Crufts dog show and a Turner Prize awards ceremony.

There was, however, one time when he kept his clothes on and everyone else around him was naked! In 2002, he filmed a Spanish TV advert for Athletic Club in Bilbao where he was seen streaking across the pitch fully clothed during a nude football match. The players, the referee, the crowd and even the policemen chasing him were all naked but Mark was wearing the club's new range of sportswear.

* * *

Britain's first streaker was actually an Australian. Michael O'Brien ran stark-bollock naked across the pitch at Twickenham during an England v France rugby union international on 20 April 1974. He was apprehended by

PC Bruce Perry who famously placed his helmet over the man's junk to save all our blushes. When being interviewed about the event afterwards, PC Perry commented, 'It was an extremely cold day and Michael had nothing to be proud of.'

ONE TEAM IN TALLINN
1996

The FIFA delegate for the World Cup qualifier between Estonia and Scotland on 9 October 1996, Jean-Marie Gantenbein, had originally expressed doubts about the standard of the temporary floodlighting installed at the Kadriorg Stadium in Tallinn and then, after a Scotland training session on the evening before the game, the Scotland manager Craig Brown seemed equally as unimpressed by their low level of brightness and questioned their suitability for use in such an important match. Although Brown sent a late-night fax to FIFA highlighting the problem, he still made it clear that Scotland would nevertheless fulfil their obligations and play the match.

The FIFA Executive Committee called an emergency meeting early the following morning and upheld Scotland's protest. They ruled that the proposed kick off time of 6.45pm should be brought forward to 3pm and informed both the Scottish and Estonian football associations of their decision.

Now it was the turn of the Estonians to throw their toys out of the pram. They claimed the team wouldn't be ready in time; their training ground was over 60 miles away from the stadium, and the new earlier kick off time would prove a logistical nightmare for both their part-time players and the fans. More importantly, however, they were upset that the change would result in a loss of valuable TV revenue. The BBC had agreed to pay them £50,000 to show the match live in Scotland but the new kick off time meant the game clashing with coverage of a memorial service for the Dunblane massacre. There was no way a football match would take precedence over that and no chance the BBC would still pay them the same kind of money just to show highlights of the game, so the Estonians decided not to accept the FIFA ruling. They would play at 6.45pm – or not at all.

Although FIFA and Scotland were informed of their decision, everyone just assumed they were bluffing but at 2.30pm, when the Scotland players were busy warming up on the pitch and the Estonian team were still enjoying lunch at their hotel, it soon became evident that their threat to boycott the game was very much real.

At 2.57pm, the referee led the Scotland team out on to the pitch to the chants of 'One team in Tallinn, there's only one team in Tallinn' from the Tartan Army. Although the national anthems weren't played, all the other pre-match formalities were observed; the linesmen even checked the goal nets for any holes! Handshakes were exchanged and a coin tossed, and then Billy Dodds kicked off and passed the ball to his captain John Collins before the referee blew his whistle to end one of the most farcical games in World Cup history.

The Estonian team eventually arrived at the stadium later in the afternoon just as the Scotland squad were on their way to the airport.

Jean-Marie Gantenbein said at the time that Scotland would most probably be awarded the game with a default win of 3-0, but at another emergency FIFA Executive Committee meeting held on 7 November 1996, it soon became apparent that he'd been talking out of his arse because it was decided to play the match again, this time at a neutral venue. For whatever reason, FIFA had capitulated to the Estonian FA's appeals and completely ignored their own strict rules by announcing that the game should be replayed.

That match took place some four months later on 11 February 1997 at the Stade Louis II in Monaco and ended in a boring 0-0 scoreline.

THAT KUNG-FU KICK
1995

Eric Cantona (known as 'King Eric' to the Stretford End faithful) played for Manchester United between 1992 and 1997, scoring over 80 goals in 185 matches and winning four Premier League titles and two FA Cups. He brought skill, flair and leadership to the team; he was instrumental in ending the club's horrendous 26-year wait for a league title, and inspired a whole new generation of young, creative footballers which would eventually lead to United dominating English football for over two decades. Eric was revered by his team-mates, worshipped by the fans, and adored by his manager Alex Ferguson.

Having said all that, the great man had a bit of an off-day when United travelled to south London for the match against Crystal Palace on 25 January 1995.

Cantona and Palace's Richard Shaw had been involved in a series of ugly clashes during the first half and the Frenchman was pissed off with the referee for not showing his opponent a yellow card. Three minutes after the restart, he foolishly decided to take matters into his own hands by kicking out at Shaw and was rightly shown a direct red.

As Cantona was walking towards the tunnel, a gobby Palace fan called Matthew Simmons left his seat and ran down the terracing towards the touchline to yell abuse at him. Although he later claimed to have merely shouted something innocuous like, 'Off! Off! Off! It's an early bath for you, Mr Cantona!' others around Simmons have asserted that what he actually shouted was, 'Fuck off back to France, you French bastard!' Whatever it was, Cantona didn't take kindly to it. He ran across to where the loudmouth fan was standing, jumped in the air and kicked out at him like he was suddenly Bruce Lee. He then fell backwards over the advertising board but sprung to his feet and threw a few well-aimed punches before being restrained by a steward and accompanied off the pitch by the United goalkeeper Peter Schmeichel. Meanwhile, other United players arrived to confront the idiot fan and other Palace supporters arrived to confront the players with everyone tussling with everyone else before the police finally arrived on the scene to calm the situation.

Cantona was later fined by his club and the FA, and received a nine-month ban. He was also prosecuted by the police and found guilty of assault, although his two-week prison sentence was later overturned on appeal to 120 hours of community service which he served coaching kids at Manchester United's training ground. At a press conference called by the player after the Appeals Court decision, he famously told the assembled reporters, 'When the seagulls follow the trawler, it's because they think sardines will be thrown into the sea. Thank you very much,' and then stood up and walked out of the room.

The United players had expected Alex Ferguson to give them a good bollocking after that game at Selhurst Park. They hadn't played well; they'd dropped two points against a poor Palace side and, most shockingly, their star striker had just been red-carded after attacking a member of the public.

And sure enough, they weren't disappointed.

Sir Alex almost ripped the door off its hinges as he stormed into the dressing room; his jacket was off and his sleeves were rolled up; steam was coming out of his ears and he was frothing at the mouth. The plates of sandwiches and the pots of tea and coffee which had been laid out on the benches in the middle of the room were violently sent flying into the air as he launched into his X-rated rant.

The former United forward Lee Sharpe, who also played in that infamous match, recounted the tense dressing-room showdown while speaking on the after-dinner circuit in 2007. Like everyone else, he'd just assumed that King Eric would cop the worst of it but Sir Alex surprised everyone when he started having a go at him and Gary Pallister and Paul Ince.

Sharpe reported Ferguson's words, 'F****** Pallister, you can't head anything, you can't tackle. Incey, where the f*** have you been? Sharpey, my grandmother runs f****** faster than you! You're all a f****** disgrace. Nine o'clock, tomorrow morning, I'm going to run your f****** balls off in training. F****** shocking!'

With all that off his chest, only then did Ferguson finally turn his attention to the fiery Frenchman, 'And Eric. You cannae go around doing things like that, son.'

And that was all Ferguson said on the matter.

DOWN TO THE WIRE
2012

Manchester City sealed their first championship victory since 1968 and their first Premier League title on the last day of the 2011/12 season with surely the competition's most exciting ending.

Manchester United had travelled away to mid-table Sunderland and City were at home to relegation-threatened Queens Park Rangers; a win for City would have guaranteed them the trophy while United needed three points and their rivals to slip up. Wayne Rooney gave United the lead after 23 minutes and they were top of the table, but then Pablo Zabaleta scored for City 16 minutes later to move them back to the top. At half-time, City still had the advantage.

However, three minutes after the restart, Djibril Cissé equalised for QPR; United were now only 42 minutes away from picking up their 13th Premier League title.

City were then thrown a lifeline when QPR's Joey Barton was sent off for violent conduct after 55 minutes following a clash with Carlos Tévez. All their fans just assumed that it would only be a matter of time now before there was a goal and, sure enough, 12 minutes later, the ball hit the back of the net again. But it was QPR who'd taken the lead after Jamie Mackie was left unmarked in the box and headed the ball past Joe Hart in the City goal. Yet again, the crowd at the Etihad were stunned into silence and the United fans at the Stadium of Light were rejoicing as they looked set to be crowned Premier League champions.

City needed two goals now with just over 20 minutes of normal time remaining. It seemed like an improbable task.

Manager Roberto Mancini threw on two strikers, Edin Džeko and Mario Balotelli, in search of a breakthrough. City then spent those last 20 minutes camped out in the QPR half, firing shot after shot at their goal and then watching them being cleared away. QPR still needed all three points to be certain of avoiding the drop and they were defending their lead as if their lives depended on it.

As the clock ticked towards full time, the fourth official signalled for five minutes of stoppage time. QPR were still winning 2-1 and some of the disconsolate City fans were in tears as they started to make their way out of the stadium.

Then, after two of the additional minutes, Džeko rose to head in a corner to level the score. But now they only had three minutes left to try and get the winner.

Meanwhile, the United match had ended. They'd finished their campaign with a 1-0 win and the players and staff all stood around on the pitch waiting to know if they were going home to Manchester as champions or runners-up.

Then the impossible happened.

Sergio Agüero received the ball on the edge of the QPR box, played a one-two with Balotelli, dodged a tackle from Taye Taiwo and then fired his shot past Paddy Kenny into the net. As the United players shook their heads in disbelief and wandered off the pitch in Sunderland, the City players and their fans celebrated their first Premier League title win.

The winning goal was timed at 93 minutes 20 seconds. It has since been recognised as one of the greatest moments in the history of the Premier League. The exaggerated reaction of Sky Sports commentator Martin Tyler screaming 'AGÜEROOOOOO!!', sustained for several seconds, as he watched the ball go in captured the public's imagination and is probably more famous than the actual goal itself now.

City and United had both ended the season with 89 points but it was City who had secured the title with a superior goal difference of just +8, +64 to +56, making them the fifth different club to win it and, to date, the only ones to do so on goal difference.

QPR avoided relegation after fellow strugglers Bolton dropped points against Stoke. But nobody really cared about that.

* * *

Six years later Manchester City were also involved in the LEAST exciting title win.

'The Centurions' are considered the greatest team ever to win the Premier League. They finished the 2017/18 season 19 points clear of second-placed Manchester United and recorded the biggest winning margin in the history of the Premier League, but their complete dominance over the other teams also made for the dullest end to any campaign. They hold the record for most points (100), most goals (106), best goal difference (+79), most wins (32) and the most consecutive victories (18) and equalled the record for the earliest title win when they clinched it on 15 April 2018 with five games still left to play.

REPAINTING THE SPOT
1977

With only minutes remaining in a Division One encounter at the Baseball Ground on 30 April 1977, Derby County were 3-0 up against ten-man Manchester City and were then awarded a penalty.

But this was the 70s, long before decent undersoil heating and artificial pitches, when the 18-yard box resembled a muddy, churned-up field rather than the green baize of a snooker table like they do today, so it wasn't all that surprising when Gerry Daly picked up the ball and stepped up to the spot – only to discover that the spot had disappeared!

After the City keeper Joe Corrigan had attempted to help the referee by pacing out 12 yards himself but was then booked for his cheek, a call was put out for the only man who could save the day.

Moments later a groundsman emerged from the stands carrying a bucket of paint, a brush and a tape measure. He held one end of the tape on the goal line and the referee walked away with the other end to measure out the 12 yards. Once the correct distance had been agreed upon, the groundsman ran forward and splashed a big blob of white paint on the mud to mark the spot.

Everything was as it should be again; Daly scored from the newly painted spot.

THOSE FAMOUS RED AND WHITE SHIRTS
1933

Arsenal ran out on to the field wearing their iconic red shirts with the white collar and the white sleeves for the first time in their home match against Liverpool on 4 March 1933.

They had played in all-red shirts until their manager Herbert Chapman decided to shake things up a bit. It has often been suggested that he was inspired by a fan in the crowd wearing a similar jersey but the idea actually originated with the renowned *Daily Mail* cartoonist Tom Webster.

Webster had played a round of golf with the Chelsea chairman Claude Kirby and had turned up wearing a sleeveless blue pullover with a white polo shirt underneath. It was a look that inspired Kirby to suggest a change of kit to his manager David Calderhead, but he thought it was a daft idea and so it was soon forgotten about. However, Webster later met up with Herbert Chapman and recounted the story. He was a lot more receptive to the idea of his team wearing a dual-coloured shirt and immediately sought permission from the Football League to change the Gunners' home kit to red shirts with white sleeves and a white collar.

But when the Arsenal players first appeared in their new shirts, it was actually two shirts they were wearing: a red sleeveless one worn over their long-sleeved white away shirt. Chapman couldn't wait for the fancy new shirts to be manufactured, so the players were asked to make do with the less fancier DIY versions for a while!

NOT FOOLING ANYONE
1976

Kettering Town were the first British club to play with a sponsor's name on their shirts.

The former Wolves player Derek Dougan was appointed player-manager of Kettering in 1975 and one of his first tasks was to broker a shirt sponsorship deal with a local tyre company, Kettering Tyres. The team shirts emblazoned with the company's name were first used in a Southern League match against Bath City on 24 January 1976.

However, the initiative was unsanctioned by the FA and four days later they ordered the club to remove the name from their shirts. Dougan attempted to get around the directive by changing the wording to 'Kettering T' and claiming that it had nothing to do with the sponsors but referred instead to the name of the club. It didn't fool anyone, least of all the FA, who repeated their demand to remove the wording or face a fine of £1,000. Dougan was eventually forced to back down and the sponsorship deal was cancelled.

A year later, Kettering, Derby and Bolton submitted a joint proposal to the FA to allow shirt sponsorship, which was accepted on 3 June 1977. Ironically, Kettering were then unable to find a sponsor for the following season.

UNDER THE FLOODLIGHTS
1878

The first football game ever played under floodlights was a special exhibition match staged between two teams made up of players from the local Sheffield football clubs, representing the Blues and Reds, at Bramall Lane in Sheffield on 14 October 1878.

Kick off was at 7.30pm with a crowd of 30,000 spectators each paying sixpence for entry.

Four lamps were perched on top of four 30ft-high wooden towers erected at each corner of the ground with the power being generated by two portable engines positioned behind each goal. The *Sheffield Telegraph* reported that 'many of the ladies, once within the rays, shot up umbrellas as they would parasols to shield them from the sun at mid-day' and *The Times* commented that 'the brilliance of the light dazzled the players and sometimes caused strange blunders'.

ODD ONE OUT
1885

Jimmy Forrest was the first professional player ever to appear for England.

The Blackburn Rovers half-back played for his country 11 times between 1884 and 1890, making his debut against Wales on 17 March 1884 in the inaugural 1883–1884 British Home Championship.

However, when he was included in a team to play Scotland on 21 March 1885 at the Kennington Oval, the Scottish Football Association objected to his selection as he was known to be a professional player. He was eventually allowed to appear in the match but only after he'd agreed to wear a different-coloured shirt from the rest of his team-mates and Blackburn had agreed not to pay him his £1 wages for the week of the match.

He actually played in his light blue and white club shirt while the rest of his team-mates turned out in their traditional white shirts.

THE FIRST SUPERSTAR OF FOOTBALL
1872–1882

An outstanding sportsman, a pioneer of the game and one of the most visible figures in the history of football, Arthur Kinnaird, 11th Lord Kinnaird was one of the best players of his generation and undoubtedly the first footballing superstar, having played in seven out of the first nine FA Cup finals between 1873 and 1882 and then assuming the role of president of the Football Association for 33 years from 1890 until his death in 1923.

Kinnaird made his FA Cup debut for Wanderers in their 2-0 win over Oxford University in the 1873 final, captaining the side and scoring their first goal, and made his last appearance for Old Etonians in their 1-0 win over Blackburn Rovers in the 1882 final. In total he won the cup three times with Wanderers and twice with his old school team, and in the course of his career he played in every position from goalkeeper to striker.

He also co-founded the FA in 1863, helped arrange the world's first international match in 1872, and later gained his one and only international cap playing for Scotland against England on 8 March 1873.

He had a very distinctive playing style and was known as a fierce competitor and one of the game's toughest tacklers with a fondness for hacking down opponents. Nicholas Lane Jackson, founder of the Corinthian club and editor of the weekly sports magazine *Pastime*, once wrote, 'Lord Kinnaird's energy was expended as much on the shins of his opponents as on the ball.' An anecdotal story about him involved his mother expressing her concern to a friend that her son may arrive home one day with a broken leg, to which the friend had supposedly replied, 'You must not worry, madam, if he does, it won't be his own!'

In his time as a player, and later as the FA president, he was instrumental in transforming football from an obscure pastime played by a bunch of old toffs into Britain's national sport. When a new FA Cup was commissioned in 1910, he was given the old one to keep in gratitude for his unrivalled contribution to the game.

Arthur was only an amateur sportsman, and playing football was no more than just a hobby for him. Off the field he was a businessman and a banker but he was also a philanthropist, devoting a lot of his time and money to good causes, running a school for street urchins and undertaking work for the YMCA and many other charities, as well as promoting evangelical religion through his work with the Church of Scotland.

THE CANCELLED OWN GOAL
1877

Arthur Kinnaird might have been one of those dashing Victorian gentleman in his youth and one of those cuddly, old grandfatherly types with a big bushy beard in later life, and he may have been a thoroughly decent chap who played for the most successful football team of the late 19th century and did all that good work for charity, but that's not to say he wasn't above the odd bit of underhandedness when the occasion suited him.

Wanderers were the reigning FA Cup holders and had won the competition in 1872, 1873 and 1876. Oxford University had also won the cup in 1874. Their meeting on 24 March 1877 was the first time an FA Cup Final had been contested by two previous winners.

It was also the first FA Cup Final to register an own goal.

Both teams were playing a 2-2-6 formation of two full-backs, two half-backs and six forwards, in line with the attacking style of play that was popular at the time. Kinnaird was playing in goal for Wanderers even though he'd appeared as an outfield player in their three earlier cup final appearances. At that time the goalkeeping position wasn't really considered particularly specialised and players often took it in turn to stand between the posts; a bit like school playground games when nobody wants to go in goal!

After only 15 minutes, Oxford were awarded a corner and the ball was kicked high towards the goalmouth. Although Kinnaird caught it easily enough, he then stepped back over his goal line, the Oxford players appealed and the referee Sydney Wright awarded a goal. Kinnaird might have been a little embarrassed by his clumsiness but he was as mad as hell with Mr Wright for allowing the goal to stand. He and his team-mates tried to bully the poor chap into changing his mind but Mr Wright stood his ground and ordered the players back to the centre circle for the restart. The record books would now show the great Arthur Kinnaird as the first player ever to score an own goal in an FA Cup Final.

Later in the game, Charles Wollaston was injured and he swapped places with Kinnaird. Back then, substitutions weren't allowed and so injured players were discouraged from leaving the field. They were just expected to carry on regardless, often in goal, where it was assumed they'd be less of a liability. Wanderers eventually equalised four minutes before the end of normal time with a goal by Jarvis Kenrick and the final went into extra time. Seven minutes later, William Lindsay got the winner and Wanderers managed to hold on to their 2-1 lead until the end to retain the trophy.

However, Kinnaird was still not happy about having that own goal chalked up against his name. He informed his fellow FA Committee members that the ball had definitely not crossed the line and then insisted that the goal should be annulled, even though all the newspaper reports had agreed with the referee's decision to allow it and had printed the final score as 2-1. Nevertheless, the FA members accepted Kinnaird's word as a gentleman and struck the goal from their records, changing the scoreline to 2-0 (despite the fact that if Oxford hadn't scored, there wouldn't have been any need to play extra time, and therefore the second Wanderers goal should also have been annulled). But what the hell, it wouldn't be Kinnaird's name in the record books any more and that was the most important thing!

It wasn't until the 1980s when the FA finally rectified their mistake and officially reinstated the original 2-1 scoreline.

SNACKING ON THE PITCH
2024

Hearts were awarded a penalty just before half-time of their Scottish Premiership clash with rivals Hibernian on 28 April 2024 when their striker Kenneth Vargas went down in the box after trying to outrun defender Will Fish.

Lawrence Shankland then stepped up to the spot and was pelted with objects from the crowd – everything from a lighter and a bottle opener to an old coffee cup and even some Apple AirPods. The Hibs fans were throwing anything they were holding or could find in their pockets, it seemed. It didn't put Shankland off his stride, however, as he smashed the ball high into the left-hand corner of the net to level the score at 1-1. He then stood in front of the away end with his arms aloft celebrating the goal. The supporters were far from amused and started lobbing missiles at him again; one even threw his half-eaten pie. To everyone's surprise, Shankland caught it one-handed, took a big bite out of it and then threw what was left of it back towards the crowd, like it was all part of some elaborate pre-arranged routine.

It was really cool to watch and the perfect 'fuck you' to the opposition fans.

But the strangest part of this story is why anyone should want to waste a perfectly good pie in this way. It's totally incomprehensible. Scottish football might not be the strongest but the pies are to die for.

* * *

As well as coins, flares and bottles, sometimes fans like to throw other things on to the pitch to show their displeasure for a particular player or the club and its officials. A pig's head, Mars bars, tennis balls, toilet rolls, half a dead cat, a severed bull's head, doughnuts, celery, dead fish and even a wheelbarrow have all ended up on the field of play at sometime or another over the years.

Back in 1965, in a Division Three game between Brentford and Millwall at Griffin Park, the visiting Millwall fans lobbed a hand grenade on to the pitch! Brentford keeper Chic Brodie didn't seem all that bothered, though. He just picked it up and threw it into his goalmouth out of the way. Can you imagine modern footballers being so nonchalant? Only later was it discovered to be a dummy grenade.

Of course, sometimes it's an actual person who may end up on the pitch. In 2018, the hot-headed businessman/ owner of PAOK, Ivan Savvidis, marched on to the field accompanied by a couple of burly bodyguards during a Greek Super League 1 match against AEK to confront the referee, who'd just disallowed a goal for his team. Nothing particularly alarming there, except that Savvidis had a handgun strapped to his waist and, for a short while, everyone – especially the match official – was just a little nervous about what might happen next.

Perhaps the most bizarre incident of hooliganism to date involved some of the more intellectually challenged Inter Milan fans when they tried to hurl a moped on to the pitch from the second tier of the Curva Nord at the San Siro stadium during a Serie A game against Atalanta in 2001. The moped belonged to the *capo* of the Atalanta ultras, so the story goes, and it had been captured during a scuffle outside the ground before the game. The moped was vandalised, burned and then dumped over the railings surrounding the seating. Fortunately, the section below was empty so it didn't land on anyone's head but, unfortunately for them, play wasn't interrupted because the moped never made it on to the pitch. The fans just had to watch it crash on to some empty seats – and then stay there.

Makes you wonder what kind of security they had at the stadium. It also makes you wonder which strange supernatural force the Inter fans believed would carry that moped on to the pitch.

WINNING THE GAME AFTER THE FINAL WHISTLE
2020

Manchester United registered their first Premier League victory of the 2020/21 season on 26 September 2020 after narrowly beating Brighton & Hove Albion 3-2 with a match-winning penalty AFTER the referee had blown his whistle for full time.

Brighton had outplayed United for most of the game, enjoying all the possession and firing off 18 shots and hitting the woodwork FIVE times. Leandro Trossard alone had four shots on goal and was responsible for three of the efforts that hit the post or bar. They probably thought they'd snatched a well-deserved point after Solly March headed home an injury-time goal to level at 2-2 and then the referee had blown for full time – but that wasn't the case.

Moments before the final whistle, Harry Maguire had headed the ball towards the Brighton goal; it hit the raised arm of Neal Maupay and was then cleared off the line by March. Although the incident was only brought to the attention of the referee by the VAR officials after the game had ended, he nevertheless decided to award a penalty to the visitors.

Bruno Fernandes then stepped up to the spot to score the winning goal ten minutes into stoppage time with another last kick of the game – and then the referee blew his whistle again for full time.

THE TWO-TEAM WORLD CUP PLAYER
1934

In 1934, Luis Monti became the first player to appear for two different teams at a World Cup.

Monti began his footballing career at Argentina's Club Atlético Huracán in 1921 and then moved to San Lorenzo de Almagro a year later. He was first called up to the national team in 1924. After winning the Campeonato Sudamericano de Fútbol (now the Copa América) in 1927 and a silver medal at the Olympics in 1928, he then turned out for his country in the inaugural World Cup in Uruguay, scoring Argentina's first World Cup goal in their 1-0 win over France on 15 July 1930.

Argentina made it all the way through to the final. It wasn't a great performance from Monti; he seemed a little subdued and might have been suffering from an injury picked up in the semi-final against USA or it might have been the letter he'd received before the game warning him against being a hero and threatening his life and the life of his family if Argentina were victorious. Many of the Argentinian players received death threats before and even during the game and presumably they were all in a bit of a panic going into the half-time break leading 2-1. It was no wonder that they conceded three quick second-half goals and lost 4-2.

Shortly afterwards, Monti received a visit from two mysterious gentlemen with an offer to play football in Italy.

They promised him a huge monthly salary plus bonuses, a new car and a bloody big house as part of the deal, and they seemed to suggest that the man behind it all was none other than the Italian dictator Benito Mussolini. Needless to say, with all that on offer, Monti accepted the job.

In 1930, he joined Juventus and was deployed as a central defender or midfielder. During his nine-year career at the club he made 225 appearances and scored 19 goals, helping them to win four successive Serie A championships between 1932 and 1935.

After becoming an Italian citizen he was quickly called up for the *Azzurri* under manager Vittorio Pozzo. Monti had played 16 times for his native Argentina and eventually went on to play another 18 times for his adopted country between 1932 and 1936, which included five appearances at the 1934 World Cup in his new home country.

Italy began their 1934 campaign with an easy 7-1 victory over the USA and then beat Spain 1-0 in a quarter-final marred by rough play and some very dubious refereeing decisions. They then beat Austria 1-0 in their semi-final with the referee again being criticised for his obvious favouritism towards the host nation. Giuseppe Meazza and Enrique Guaita had both constantly challenged the Austrian keeper Peter Platzer for high balls in the box and after 19 minutes, the two players combined to score Italy's only goal. Platzer had fallen on to the ball near his goal line but Meazza clattered into him and kicked it loose from his grasp. It then rolled against the post and Guaita stabbed it over the line for the goal. According to the Swedish referee Ivan Eklind, it was a perfectly good goal and it was no surprise that the Italian organisers then chose him to officiate the final too.

The 1934 World Cup was marred by the blatant attempts by dictator Benito Mussolini to manipulate the high-profile event for his own political gain and the promotion of fascism. Many historians and journalists have since accused him of widespread corruption in an attempt to influence match results and even the outcome of the tournament itself. It seemed that *Il Duce* also had his own unique way of motivating the *Azzurri* too. On the day before the final against Czechoslovakia, he sent a telegram to the team at their hotel: 'Victory or death gentlemen ... Good luck tomorrow. Win. If not so, crash.' It was a chilling reminder to the lads that they were expected to fulfil their duty and few of them doubted the implications of the word 'crash'.

The final was played on 10 June 1934 at the Stadio Nazionale PNF in Rome, in front of 55,000 mainly Italian fans.

The Czechs were a hard team to beat. They'd already defeated Europe's other fascist superpower, Germany, 3-1 in the semi-final a week earlier and at half-time the score remained goalless. It was time for Mussolini to offer his players a few more words of encouragement, so he fired off another one of his inspirational telegrams and had it delivered to their dressing room: 'You are responsible for the success, but if you fail, may God help you.'

After 71 minutes the unthinkable happened: the Czechs took the lead through a goal from Antonín Puč and then began to dominate the play. In the next ten minutes they could have put the game beyond any doubt but squandered their chances after missing an open goal and hitting the woodwork. Then, much to the relief of everyone, not least the Italian players, Raimundo Orsi equalised in the 81st minute to send the match into extra time. Angelo Schiavio became the hero of Italy just five minutes after the restart when his shot beat the Czech goalkeeper František Plánička to give them a 2-1 lead which they were then able to hold on to until full time.

The fascist anthem 'Giovinezza' rang out around the stadium and the Italians were presented with the Jules Rimet Trophy. They were also given a much larger cup specially commissioned by their greatest fan, Benito Mussolini, because he thought the official trophy was a bit on the small side! He rewarded his players by telling them that they could have anything they wanted – money, jewels, cars, houses and lots of beautiful women.

Luis Monti later recounted the threats he'd received in Uruguay and Italy, 'In Uruguay they would kill me if I won. In Italy they would kill me if I lost.'

At least he had a sense of humour about it all.

THE BATTLE OF BRAMALL LANE
2002

Sheffield United's home match against West Bromwich Albion on 16 March 2002 is the only professional game in the history of English football to be abandoned because one team didn't have enough players left on the pitch.

The Blades had seen three players sent off by the 65th minute – including two substitutes – leaving them with just eight men. By the 82nd minute, another two of their players had to leave the pitch because of injury, leaving only six of them on the pitch and forcing referee Eddie Wolstenholme to abandon the game.

Things hadn't gone too well for the home team right from the off. After only nine minutes, their goalkeeper Simon Tracey was sent off for handling the ball outside the penalty area and denying West Brom an obvious goalscoring opportunity. Their manager Neil Warnock was then forced to send on their substitute keeper Wilko de Vogt and take off an outfield player. The game was fairly quiet and relatively uneventful for the next 56 minutes with the visitors taking advantage of the extra man to secure a 2-0 lead, but then things turned ugly in the 65th minute.

A minute earlier, Michael Tonge had been replaced by George Santos but only seconds after joining the game, Santos was sent off after a poorly timed, two-footed tackle on Andy Johnson. It was a horrific challenge which left the visiting midfielder on the ground writhing in agony. It was obvious to everyone that the tackle had been revenge for the previous season's clash between the two players which had left Santos with a fractured cheekbone. The two sets of players then indulged in a bit of pushing and shoving and, in the scuffle, another Sheffield United substitute, Patrick Suffo, head-butted the West Brom captain Derek McInnes, so he was sent off too.

At this point Sheffield United only had eight players left on the pitch and had used all of their three permitted substitutes. It could so easily have been seven soon afterwards as their captain Keith Curle was lucky to escape a red card after appearing to land a couple of punches on McInnes.

West Brom added a third goal in the 77th minute. Two minutes later, Michael Brown limped off the field with an injury and in the 82nd minute his team-mate Robert Ullathorne followed him, obliging Mr Wolstenholme to abandon the game as IFAB rules state that a match shouldn't continue if there are fewer than seven players on either team.

After the game, West Brom manager Gary Megson screamed, 'There will be no replay! If we are called back to Bramall Lane, we shall kick off and then walk off the pitch. I've been in professional football since [I was] 16 and I'm 42 now. I've never ever witnessed anything as disgraceful as that. There is no place for that in any game of football, let alone professional football.' Neil Warnock simply stated, 'I wouldn't imagine Gary will be having a drink with me tonight.'

West Brom were later awarded a 3-0 win and the three points. Sheffield United were fined £10,000 and the players deemed to have brought the game into disrepute were all fined and handed down lengthy bans. George Santos and Patrick Suffo never played for the Blades again.

THE HALF-TIME KIT CHANGE
1996

It was a familiar story when the two teams met at The Dell on 13 April 1996. Manchester United were challenging for another Premier League title and Southampton were fighting to avoid relegation, so nobody, least of all the home fans, expected Southampton to be winning 3-0 at half-time. They'd gone 1-0 up after only 11 minutes, 2-0 up 12 minutes later and then their star player Matthew Le Tissier had made it 3-0 after 42 minutes. Southampton had taken United apart during an extraordinarily one-sided first half and thoroughly deserved their lead at the break.

But then Manchester United reappeared for the second half literally looking like a different team.

Their manager Alex Ferguson had been convinced that their light grey-coloured away shirts had been the reason for such a poor performance because the players couldn't see each other from a distance in the bright afternoon sunshine, and it has since been reported that the first thing he'd said to them in the dressing room at half-time was, 'Get that kit off, you're getting changed!'

The United players had reappeared wearing their blue and white striped third kit. They did play a lot better in the second half but only managed a late consolation goal from Ryan Giggs in the 89th minute.

Manchester United were later fined £10,000 by the FA for the half-time shirt swap, with Ferguson commenting that it was 'the best £10,000 ever spent'. United went on to win the league that season; the grey shirts were never worn again, and Ferguson is remembered for one of the worst excuses ever made for a team's bad performance.

FROM BAD TO WORSE
1978

Welsh referee Clive Thomas always seemed to interpret the rules of the game in his own very unique way.

For a long time he was most famous for disallowing a perfectly good goal during the FA Cup semi-final between Everton and Liverpool on 23 April 1977. In the dying minutes of the game, Bryan Hamilton deflected a shot into the Liverpool net but Thomas disallowed the goal for handball. However, after the game, he admitted not seeing the handball but was unsure which other part of his body the player could have used to divert the ball into the net if it wasn't his arms or hands, so he denied Everton the goal. In fact, the ball had come off Hamilton's hip. It would probably have sealed a late 3-2 win for Everton and sent them into the final against Manchester United. Instead, the game finished 2-2 and Everton lost the replay 3-0, all because of Thomas's bizarre decision to disallow that goal.

It was one of the daftest calls that any referee had ever made – at least until Thomas made his next daft call a year later in the World Cup match between Brazil and Sweden on 3 June 1978 when his pedantic timekeeping earned him worldwide notoriety.

The game itself was fairly uneventful. Thomas Sjöberg put Sweden ahead in the 37th minute and Reinaldo equalised just before half-time with the score remaining 1-1 as the end of the 90 minutes approached. Brazil had been pushing forward looking for the winning goal and had won a corner, and then another, and then a third in the dying seconds of the game.

Nelinho placed the ball by the corner flag ready to restart the game but then the linesman ordered him to remove it as he hadn't placed it within the confines of the arc. Thomas checked his watch, Nelinho finally took the kick, and then Clive blew his whistle for the end of the game after six seconds of stoppage time with the ball still in the air. He'd then turned his back on the play and began heading towards the tunnel. For him the game was over but behind him Zico had just headed the ball into the Swedish net. The Brazilians celebrated the goal – but not for very long. Their joy was soon curtailed after spotting Thomas shaking his head and pointing at his watch to indicate that the game had already ended and the goal wouldn't count. The Brazilians protested but Thomas dismissed their appeals and continued his purposeful march towards the tunnel. Brazil had apparently scored the winning goal just a fraction of a second too late.

Thomas revelled in the controversy that followed and couldn't wait to start blabbing to the press about the incident: 'I saw the header but I didn't see the ball go into the net. I had turned away. As far as I was concerned, the game was over. The Brazilians have only themselves to blame. They should not have wasted so much time over taking the corner.'

He had been the pre-tournament favourite to referee the final but after his spectacularly bad call in this game, FIFA ordered him to pack his bags and return home. He never refereed another World Cup match again.

THE UNLIKELIEST CHAMPIONS
2016

Leicester City started out as 5000/1 outsiders to win the 2015/16 Premier League title after battling relegation the previous season, and ended up being crowned champions for the first time in their 132-year history. The team, led by their Italian manager Claudio Ranieri, only lost three games in the whole season and their title win has subsequently been described as the most unlikely triumph in the history of team sport.

Seven years before their success they'd been playing third-tier football in League One and their previous best season had been way back in 1928/29 when they'd finished as runners-up in the old Division One. The 5,000/1 odds of them winning the title quoted by the bookies before the season began were actually longer than Elvis Presley being found alive (2000/1) or the Loch Ness Monster being discovered (500/1).

The East Midlands club reached the top of the table with a 3-0 victory over Stoke on 23 January 2016 and stayed there until they were crowned champions on 2 May 2016, two games before the end of the season, after their nearest rivals Tottenham failed to beat Chelsea and gain the necessary three points to continue challenging them for the title. Leicester's most used starting XI had cost only £23m to assemble, far less than Chelsea, Manchester City and Manchester United, who all fielded teams worth more than £150m that season.

Their positive counterattacking football, the manager's relaxed style and even a group of Buddhist monks who'd been drafted in by the club owner Vichai Srivaddhanaprabha to bless the pitch and hand out lucky charms were all credited as contributing to the team's success.

A club spokesman later commented, '[The team] have captured the imaginations of football fans around the world with one of the most brilliant and unlikely sporting triumphs ever seen.' Their achievement attracted global attention for both the club and the city, but, more importantly, the rest of the world finally began to understand that the word 'Leicester' only had two syllables and was actually pronounced 'Less-ter' and not 'Lie-ches-ter'.

THE FIRST OLYMPIC CHAMPIONS
1908

The first Olympic football tournament was held during the 1900 Games in Paris. Three teams took part in the unofficial tournament, only two demonstration matches were played, and no medals were ever awarded. The newly reformed club side Upton Park represented Great Britain, beating Club Français 4-0 at the Vélodrome de Vincennes in Paris on 20 September 1900. The only other match was played three days later with the French team easily beating Belgium's Université de Bruxelles 6-2. Although the International Olympic Committee now credits Great Britain, France and Belgium with the gold, silver and bronze medals as part of its attempt to reconcile past successes in the early Olympic Games with the more familiar modern awards scheme, FIFA has not yet recognised this contest.

A similar ad hoc tournament also took place four years later in St Louis.

The first official FIFA-recognised Olympic Games football tournament took place in London in 1908. Eight teams originally entered – Bohemia, Denmark, France A, France B, Great Britain, Hungary, Netherlands and Sweden; Hungary and Bohemia later withdrew, the former for financial reasons and the latter because they'd subsequently lost their FIFA membership. Their exclusion suddenly allowed the Netherlands and France A to qualify for the semi-finals without playing a game.

The Great Britain team was actually an all-English team. The footballing authorities in the other home nations had refused to nominate any amateur players for inclusion in the squad, so the English just attached a Union Jack to their all-white jerseys and played as Great Britain.

The first match, on 19 October, saw Denmark beat France B 9-0. The former Scotland player John Cameron noted in his 1908 book *Association Football and How to Play It* that this result only served to demonstrate that the French were never likely to excel at playing football. According to him, they were far too polite and way too fond of the fags, 'They puffed away right up to the start of the match, and in the interval had another smoke, finishing up the day by repeating the practice. How different with our ideas!' The way he described the French, it's surprising that they didn't insist on smoke breaks during the match too!

In the only other first-round game, the following day, Great Britain thrashed Sweden 12-1.

In the first semi-final on 22 October 1908, Great Britain beat Netherlands 4-0 with Harry Stapley scoring all four goals. In the second semi-final, Denmark stuffed the France A boys 17-1 with their striker Sophus Nielsen hitting the back of the net ten times. Unsurprisingly, this game still holds the record for the most goals scored in any Olympic match. The French were so dazed and confused by their defeat that they declined to play the third-place play-off on 23 October, so the Netherlands took their place, beating Sweden 2-0 to claim the bronze medal. If only the French hadn't been quite so fond of a smoke.

The final was contested between Great Britain and Denmark on 24 October at White City in London. Goals from Frederick Chapman and captain Vivian Woodward sealed a 2-0 victory for the home team and earned them the gold medal.

Great Britain also won the gold medal in Stockholm four years later.

The final took place on 4 July at the Olympic Stadium in Stockholm and was a repeat of 1908 with Great Britain being led by Woodward and taking on Denmark. The Brits scored all of their four goals in the first half, helped by the fact that one of Denmark's midfield players, Charles Buchwald, limped off injured after only 15 minutes, forcing them to play most of the game with ten men. Denmark mounted a bit of a comeback in the second half but Great Britain held on to win 4-2 and pick up their second Olympic Games gold medal.

Depending on whether you choose to believe the FIFA or the IOC records, Great Britain either became the first back-to-back tournament winners (1908, 1912) or the first three-time winners (1900, 1908, 1912).

A VERY ONE-SIDED MATCH
1973

The Marxist dictator Salvador Allende was elected to power in Chile in September 1970 but was overthrown by the fascist dictator Augusto Pinochet in a *coup d'état* three years later. Many thousands of people were then deemed enemies of the state by the new regime and hauled off to the Estadio Nacional in Santiago to be tortured or killed. Salvador Allende himself refused to be captured and took his own life with a rifle gifted to him by Fidel Castro, the most famous Marxist dictator of them all.

The Soviet Union had been a staunch ally of the overthrown regime; they condemned the military coup, refused to recognise the new government and then broke off all diplomatic relations.

Unfortunately, around about the same time, they were also due to play Chile in a 1974 World Cup qualification play-off.

They'd already met in the first leg in Moscow on 26 September 1973, which ended in a 0-0 draw, but then the Soviets refused to play the return fixture in Santiago because the stadium in which the game was due to take place was being used as an illegal detention centre to intern, torture and kill supporters of Salvador Allende. The Soviets argued that they couldn't travel to Chile but did offer to play the game in a neutral country and sent a letter explaining their position, 'For moral considerations, Soviets cannot at this time play in the stadium of Santiago, splashed with the blood of Chilean patriots.'

Meanwhile, FIFA had established a commission to inspect the stadium where at least 7,000 detainees were being held. Apparently, their representatives walked around the pitch and either saw the prisoners or knew of their presence but still gave the go-ahead for the game to take place. FIFA subsequently rejected the Soviet Union's offer to play in another country and issued them with an ultimatum to accept playing in Chile by 11 November or forfeit the tie.

The Soviets never bothered to travel to Chile; FIFA declared a walkover for the home country and awarded them a 2-0 victory, but then rather bizarrely asked Chile to arrange the match anyway; even more bizarrely, 15,000 people turned up to watch it! The one-sided play-off game on 21 November lasted for just 30 seconds after the Chilean players slowly passed the ball around in mock play before their captain Francisco Valdés walked it into an empty net. The referee then blew his whistle to abandon the game with Chile qualifying for the finals in West Germany.

PLAYER TO SCORE IN EVERY MINUTE OF A MATCH
2014

The two-legged Copa del Rey semi-final game between Atlético Madrid and Real Madrid ended in a 5-0 aggregate win for Real, and it also saw Cristiano Ronaldo completing a quite unique career milestone by becoming the first player ever to score in every minute of a match. Bizarrely, he was only missing a goal in the seventh minute before the start of the second leg on 11 February 2014; the same number as his shirt and the same number as his much publicised CR7 brand. All that changed early in the first half when he was tripped inside the box by Javier Manquillo and Real were awarded a penalty. The Portuguese striker himself then stepped up to the spot and blasted the ball into the bottom-left corner to score that elusive seventh-minute goal and get his name in the record books. Again.

REFUSAL TO WEAR THE SHIRT
2013

In October 2012, the former payday loan company Wonga signed a four-year, £24m sponsorship deal with Newcastle

United and in July 2013 their striker Papiss Cissé suddenly announced that he'd refuse to play in the new Wonga-sponsored kit as the company's trading activities offended his Muslim faith and clashed with his personal beliefs. According to some interpretations of Sharia law, Muslims are not allowed to benefit from money-lending transactions, with the giving and receiving of interest payments being prohibited.

As talks between the player, the club, Islamic law specialists, faith leaders and the PFA on how to resolve the situation broke down, Cissé was left behind in England when the rest of the team flew off to Portugal to attend a pre-season training camp. He had proposed wearing a blank shirt or a shirt emblazoned with the logo of a charity but Wonga and club owner Mike Ashley both rejected this idea. They also pointed out that other Muslim players seemed to have no problem with the new sponsor, breaking a contract was equally frowned upon by the Muslim faith, and he himself had happily worn a shirt featuring the logo of the club's previous sponsor, Virgin Money, who are a banking and financial services company, and whose trading activities should have been equally as offensive to him. Cissé eventually changed his mind and agreed to wear the shirt.

However, his change of heart seemed to coincide with a photograph of him, which emerged on social media, sitting at a blackjack table in a Newcastle casino. As gambling is also prohibited under Sharia law, all of a sudden his heroic stand against promoting Wonga didn't seem quite so heroic any more.

THE UNBEATEN RUN
1989

During the late 80s, Steaua București were one of Europe's top teams, winning five domestic league championships, three Cupa României trophies, the European Cup in 1986 and the European Super Cup the following year.

Steaua didn't suffer a single defeat in any domestic league or cup game for three full seasons between 1986/87 and 1988/89. Their extraordinary unbeaten record of 102 league games (86 wins, 16 draws) and 15 cup ties resulted in winning Divizia A and the Cupa României in three consecutive years. Over this period they scored 322 league goals at an average of just over three per match, and conceded only 63. Their 1988/89 league campaign was the most impressive after winning 31 of their 34 games (a 91.18 per cent win ratio), scoring 121 goals and conceding only 28.

Of course, it helped that the guy who ran the club just happened to be Valentin Ceauşescu, the son of Romania's hard-line communist leader, and their remarkable unbeaten run wasn't without a little controversy along the way.

The 1988 Cupa României Final on 26 June against rivals Dinamo Bucureşti was level at 1-1 until the 90th minute when the Steaua striker Gavril Balint scored what should have been the winning goal, only for the referee to rule it offside. Ceauşescu was so incensed that he ordered his team off the field in protest and the match was never resumed. The government then ordered the media not to report the final score until the following day when the Romanian FA had been told to announce that Gavril Balint's winning goal would stand and Steaua would be awarded the cup. All TV footage of the match was destroyed and the poor referee was informed that he'd never take charge of another match ever again. Bearing in mind the time and the crime, he probably got off lightly!

It wasn't until 1990, after the fall of the communist government, when Steaua finally admitted they'd won the final unfairly.

A DAMN GOOD THRASHING
1885

The biggest margin of victory ever recorded in a professional football match is Arbroath's 36-0 Scottish FA Cup first-round win over Bon Accord on 12 September 1885. Arbroath were already 15-0 up by half-time and then scored another 21 goals in the second half.

It's been claimed that their goalkeeper Jim Milne didn't actually touch the ball in the entire game and spent most of his time sheltering from the rain under an umbrella lent to him by a spectator. The *Scottish Athletic Journal* later reported, 'The leather was landed between the posts 41 times, but five of the times were disallowed. Here and there, enthusiasts would be seen with scoring sheet and pencil in hand, taking note of the goals as one would score runs at a cricket match.'

There were no goal nets back then and many people thought the scoreline could have been even higher if they hadn't wasted so much time retrieving the ball after every goal. The Arbroath striker Jocky Petrie scored 13 goals and unsurprisingly still holds the British record for the most goals scored by any one player in any senior football game.

Coincidentally, on the same day, Dundee Harp were involved in an equally bizarre one-sided SFA Cup game after beating local rivals Aberdeen Rovers 35-0. The referee had actually recorded a score of 37-0 which was disputed by the Dundee Harp club secretary after the game when he claimed that his side had only scored 35 goals. Presumably, he thought he was being awfully sporting about the whole thing but, as it turned out, he should have just kept his big mouth shut because his goody-two-shoes attitude cost his team a place in the record books. The referee acknowledged that it was very difficult for him to keep an accurate score with such a deluge of goals and quickly accepted the lower 35-0 scoreline before wiring the result to the Scottish Football Association's HQ in Glasgow.

GETTING THINGS SO TOTALLY WRONG
1996

Manchester City failed to beat Liverpool on the final day of the 1995/96 season and were relegated from the Premier League after finishing in 18th place.

Bolton and Queens Park Rangers had already been relegated which had left City fighting it out with Southampton and Coventry on the last day to avoid the drop. All three clubs began the day on the same points but City had a worse goal difference than any of their two rivals and needed to better the result of at least one of them to stay up.

However, things didn't start too well for them; Liverpool went 1-0 up after only six minutes when Steve Lomas turned the ball into his own net, and then Ian Rush doubled their lead just before the break. The other two games, Southampton-Wimbledon and Coventry-Leeds, were still 0-0 at half-time and City were now the obvious favourites to go down. But then Uwe Rösler pulled a goal back for them with a 71st-minute penalty and Kit Symons equalised shortly afterwards, leaving City with another ten minutes or so to find a winning goal to complete a remarkable turnaround and be sure of avoiding relegation.

But rather than go for the win, manager Alan Ball instructed his players to kill the game. News had reached their bench that one point would be enough to keep them up, as Wimbledon had taken a 1-0 lead against Southampton, so the players just needed to keep the ball, waste time and play out the remaining few minutes. But the message they'd received had been wrong: the score was still 0-0 at The Dell as it was in the other game and, as things stood, City were still going down. Meanwhile, as the clock ticked down to full time, all the City players were still following their manager's instructions to the letter with Lomas and Rösler dribbling the ball towards the corner flag and keeping it there in an effort to waste as much time as possible.

The fans were confused; they needed another goal but their team were just pissing about with the ball and squandering the few precious minutes they had left to turn things around. Liverpool couldn't have cared less; they weren't moving up or down the table whatever the result and the match was nearly over, so they just let City do their thing without seriously challenging them for the ball.

It was Niall Quinn who first realised their mistake. He'd been taken off injured earlier in the game and had been watching TV in the dressing room as the results from the other games started to come in. Without a moment's hesitation, he sprinted out the door, up the tunnel and along the touchline screaming at his bench that they still needed another goal.

But it was too late; seconds later the referee blew his whistle for full time, and Manchester City were relegated to the second tier on goal difference.

DOING THINGS THE EASY WAY
1998

Giuseppe Bergomi is the first and only player ever to take part in four World Cups without ever playing in a qualifying game.

The Inter Milan defender played for his country in the 1982, 1986, 1990 and 1998 tournaments. As an 18-year-old, he was a surprising late addition to the squad that went to Spain in 1982, becoming the youngest-ever Italian player to be selected for the World Cup finals; Italy automatically qualified as holders for Mexico in 1986 and again as hosts in 1990, and then in 1998, at 34 years-old, Bergomi was again a late call up to the squad for the World Cup in France.

THE ONE-MAN TEAM
1891

On 12 December 1891 it was very cold, a wind was blowing, snow was falling and the Blackburn Rovers players didn't seem all that fussed about playing football – they'd conceded three goals in the first half of their Football League match away to local rivals Burnley and their hearts just weren't in it.

Half-time came and went. The Burnley players were all back on the pitch after the regulation ten-minute interval but the visitors arrived back in dribs and drabs with an obvious lack of enthusiasm for playing another 45 minutes. The referee that day was the ex-player and high-ranking FA official J.C. Clegg, a strict teetotaller and non-smoker with a deep religious conviction, a stickler for the rules and definitely not the type of man to be kept waiting. He warned both teams that he'd start in two minutes; he waited four and then blew his whistle for the kick off when some of the Blackburn players still hadn't reappeared on the pitch.

It had been a fairly tetchy match right from the go with the players seemingly keeping warm by kicking great lumps out of each other. Soon after the restart, Joe Lofthouse of Blackburn and Burnley's Alec Stewart exchanged blows, prompting a massive brawl between everyone else on the pitch. Both players were ordered off the field, and then, in a moment of madness, the officious Mr Clegg dismissed all the other Blackburn players too.

Well, everyone except their goalkeeper, Herbie Arthur. Presumably he'd dutifully remained in his goal as his teammates were slugging it out with their hosts and escaped Mr Clegg's wrath.

Once order had been restored and the Blackburn players had left the field, Mr Clegg waved play on.

Nine Burnley men sprinted towards the lone figure of Arthur at the other end of the field and scored another goal but it was immediately disallowed because they'd all been offside. Then, after a lengthy spell of time-wasting from the goalkeeper, Mr Clegg finally realised just how farcical the situation had become and abandoned the match.

ONE OF EVERYTHING
2021

On 19 September 2021, West Ham had taken the lead after 30 minutes of their Premier League game at home to Manchester United with a goal by Saïd Benrahma; Cristiano Ronaldo equalised for the visitors five minutes later, and then, late in the second half, United went ahead with a goal from Jesse Lingard which looked to have secured them the three points. But six minutes later, deep into stoppage time, United defender Luke Shaw appeared to handle the ball inside the area. After consulting the VAR pitchside monitor, the referee awarded the home side a penalty and the chance to draw level.

West Ham immediately substituted Jarrod Bowen and sent on Mark Noble to take the spot kick. He was a proven penalty taker with one of the best conversion rates in the Premier League and his opponent, David de Gea, had one of the worst records for saving penalties. It looked like West Ham had a good chance of salvaging a point at the death, but Noble squandered the opportunity to be the hero and, instead, De Gea saved easily. It wasn't the best shot; Noble's body movements seemed to give away the direction and height of the ball, and the United goalkeeper made an easy save after palming the ball away to safety.

De Gea and his team-mates celebrated his match-winning heroics, Noble just wandered away with his head in his hands, and a minute later the referee blew his whistle for full time.

However, Noble did at least come away from the match with a new Premier League record – one minute played, one touch, one shot and one missed penalty. Nobody had ever done that before.

ST TOTTERINGHAM'S DAY
2002

It's the day when it becomes mathematically impossible for Tottenham Hotspur to finish above north London rivals Arsenal in the Premier League table.

It was a concept originally created by an Arsenal fan website in 2002; a moveable 'feast day' which usually falls in April or May, and a day for the Gunners fans to gloat about their team's superiority and collect on any outstanding bets made by overly enthusiastic Tottenham supporters at the beginning of the season.

Since 2002 and up to the end of the 2024/25 season, Spurs have only finished above Arsenal six times in the Premier League.

HALF-TIME TEAM TALK ON THE PITCH
2008

Things weren't going too well for Hull City in their Premier League game at Manchester City on 26 December 2008; they were 4-0 down at the break.

Then came the half-time team talk from their manager Phil Brown.

But instead of leading his players down the tunnel and into the dressing room, Brown led them to the far end of the pitch where their supporters were grouped, sat them down and gave them a very public bollocking. Not only was he intent on showing his players how angry he was at their first-half performance, he wanted everyone else in the ground to know too. Some of the players looked close to tears, some stared off into the distance, and others just bowed their heads in shame as Brown laid into them. However, his unorthodox behaviour seemed to have the desired effect because they only conceded one more goal in the second half – and even managed to score one themselves.

Things went a little better for Hull when the two teams met again the following season in the corresponding fixture on 28 November 2009. City may have taken the lead but Hull equalised with a late Jimmy Bullard penalty in the 82nd minute and the match ended in a 1-1 draw. The Hull midfielder almost had his shot saved by Shay Given, possibly because he was already thinking about how he'd celebrate the goal. After the ball sneaked into the bottom-left corner of the net, he called his team-mates together, sat them down and began yelling and wagging his finger at them in a re-enactment of Phil Brown's meltdown of a year earlier.

MATCH OF THE DAY
1964

The BBC's *Match of the Day* is the longest-running football TV show in the world.

Kenneth Wolstenholme introduced the first show, which aired on BBC2 at 6.30pm on 22 August 1964 with highlights from Liverpool's 3-2 home win against Arsenal and match analysis by the former Arsenal defender and Wales international Walley Barnes. As the BBC's newly launched second channel was only available in two cities at that time, London and Birmingham, the Anfield crowd actually outnumbered the TV audience of around 20,000 people by two to one.

THE LISBON LIONS
1967

Celtic were the first British team to win the European Cup, and were also the first of only nine European clubs to date to complete a 'continental treble' by winning their league title, their primary national cup and the European Cup/Champions League in the same season.

After winning the Scottish Division One title and the SFA Cup, Celtic then travelled to Portugal for the final of the European Cup against Inter Milan, which took place on 25 May 1967.

On their way to Lisbon they'd beaten Swiss champions FC Zürich 5-0, Nantes of France 6-2, Yugoslavia's FK Vojvodina 2-1 and Dukla Prague of Czechoslovakia 3-1 (all on aggregate). Then they faced the mighty Inter Milan team who had dominated European football for the last three years, having won the tournament in 1964 and 1965 and then been semi-finalists in 1966. They were the odds-on favourites with most of the pre-match talk focused on them winning a famous *tripletta* of European Cups.

Inter scored in the seventh minute after Jim Craig fouled their striker Renato Cappellini in the penalty box and Sandro Mazzola converted the spot kick. Celtic equalised through Tommy Gemmell after 63 minutes, and Stevie Chalmers scored the winner in the 84th minute.

The game was said to have been a victory for good football with Celtic's stylish attacking play overcoming Inter's more cynical, defensive and less attractive style. Inter didn't win a single corner and forced the Celtic goalkeeper Ronnie Simpson into making only two saves in the whole game. Celtic, on the other hand, had 39 attempts on goal, 13 of which were blocked and/or deflected by the Inter keeper Giuliano Sarti, and two hit the crossbar.

There were no big-name players in the Celtic team, no multimillion-pound superstars; every player was Scottish and every one of their 15-man squad was born within 30 miles of Celtic Park in Glasgow. They were led by their legendary manager Jock Stein, who commented after the game, 'There is not a prouder man on God's Earth than me at this moment. Winning was important, but it was the way that we won that has filled me with satisfaction. We did it by playing football; pure, beautiful, inventive football.'

After flying back to Glasgow the following day, the team were driven to Celtic Park where 50,000 fans had gathered to cheer their heroes. They were later nicknamed the 'Lisbon Lions' and even to this day they are still regarded as Celtic's greatest-ever team.

KICKING THE BALL BOY
2013

Swansea had somehow come away with a 2-0 win from the first leg of their League Cup semi-final against Chelsea at Stamford Bridge, and by the 78th minute of this second leg on 23 January 2013 the score was still 0-0 when the ball went out of play over the Swansea byline. Chelsea winger Eden Hazard was eager to restart the game to avoid any unnecessary time-wasting, so he ran to the touchline to retrieve the ball in order to throw it back to the Swansea keeper for the goal kick.

Unfortunately for him, 17-year-old Charlie Morgan was the ball boy on duty at that particular pitchside spot and he got hold of the ball first. Instead of throwing it back into play, Morgan held on to it, and when Hazard tried to wrestle it off him, the youngster fell to the ground and smothered it with his body. Clearly, he had no intention of giving the ball back, and out of frustration the Belgian tried to kick it free from underneath him.

Morgan played to the crowd, rolling about on the ground like an epileptic show dog, clutching his chest in apparent great pain before suddenly making a miraculous recovery, sitting up and gesturing wildly at his attacker. Eventually, he was helped from the pitch by a couple of the Swansea team medics. Meanwhile, Hazard was claiming that he'd played the ball and not the ball boy but the referee was having none of it and sent him off.

He was still protesting his innocence during the FA investigation of the incident that followed but was nevertheless found guilty of violent conduct and banned for three matches. There were no repercussions for Morgan, however, giving ball boys everywhere the green light to play silly buggers whenever they feel the need and then act like right Charlies about it afterwards.

WALKING IN A GOAL
2019

There's an unwritten rule in football that if a player appears seriously injured and the referee doesn't intervene to stop the game, then the ball should be kicked out of play by the team in possession so that player can receive the necessary medical attention. However, on the penultimate weekend of the 2018/19 Championship season, when Leeds met Aston Villa, that rule was seemingly ignored by the home team and it led to one of the strangest goals ever scored in English football.

In the 71st minute, Villa's Jonathan Kodjia went down with an injury inside the Leeds half and his team-mates expected the home team just to kick the ball out of play so he could receive treatment. Tyler Roberts appeared ready to do just that but instead he passed the ball to Mateusz Klich. Instead of doing the decent thing, however, Klich elected to run with the ball down the left wing, cut inside and curl a low right-footed shot into the goal to put Leeds 1-0 up. The goal sparked pandemonium on the pitch and on the touchline; a big fight broke out in which every player seemed to be involved and, in the immediate aftermath, Anwar El Ghazi was shown a red card for allegedly elbowing Leeds striker Patrick Bamford in the face.

After the referee had restored order and things had settled down, Leeds manager Marcelo Bielsa met with his opposite number Dean Smith and it was agreed that Villa should be allowed to walk in a goal from the kick off to level the score. Seconds later, Bielsa could be seen yelling to his players from the touchline, 'Give the goal! Give the goal!'

From the restart, Albert Adomah was allowed to run towards the opposition goal unchallenged by ten of the Leeds players with only a confused Pontus Jansson – knowingly or unknowingly – disobeying team orders and challenging for the ball. He almost got it, too. Villa didn't celebrate the goal and Jansson got a good bollocking from his team-mates for almost ruining their feelgood moment.

This unprecedented gesture of sportsmanship from Bielsa effectively ended any hopes of automatic promotion for Leeds. They ended the season in third spot and had to be content with a play-off semi-final against Derby County which they lost 4-3 on aggregate. Ironically, Aston Villa, who only finished fifth, went on to win their semi-final against West Bromwich Albion, then beat Derby in the final and were promoted to the Premier League.

THE BAD SUBSTITUTE
2007

Sheffield United winger Keith Gillespie came on in the 53rd minute of his team's 3-1 Premier League defeat at Reading on 20 January 2007 but was sent off immediately after entering the game, even before play had restarted, after jostling for position with Stephen Hunt at a throw-in and elbowing him in the face. It was the quickest red card in Premier League history, timed at just 12 seconds.

* * *

A special mention goes to the Wigan Athletic midfielder Andreas Johansson. He replaced David Thompson after 73 minutes in their Premier League match at Arsenal on 7 May 2006. After running on to the field, he gave away a penalty by fouling Freddie Ljungberg and was sent off: he'd only been on the pitch for 40 seconds and hadn't even touched the ball.

THE PLAYBOY FOOTBALLER
1970s

With his good looks and playboy lifestyle, Manchester United and Northern Ireland icon George Best was the first media celebrity footballer; a sporting superstar who was as much a part of the Swinging Sixties as the pop stars and actors of the day. Commenting on his flamboyant and reckless lifestyle, he once famously remarked, 'I spent a lot of money on booze, birds and fast cars. The rest I just squandered.'

THE MIRACLE MATCH
1950

One of the biggest upsets in World Cup history saw the USA beat England 1-0 on 29 June 1950 in a World Cup group-stage match in Belo Horizonte, Brazil.

England were the 'kings of football' with an impressive postwar record of 23 wins, three draws and only four losses, while the Americans were a hastily assembled team of semi-professionals, seemingly taking part in the tournament just to make up the numbers. Their squad had been selected from all across the US and most of them had never met each other before, let alone played together, prior to this tournament.

Before the match, England were the odds-on favourites with the *Daily Express* claiming, 'It would be fair to give the US three goals of a start,' with even the American coach William Jeffrey comparing his players to sheep being led to the slaughter and telling the press, 'We have no chance!' The opening matches for both countries, on 25 June, seemed to reaffirm these opinions with a comfortable 2-0 win for England against Chile and an emphatic 3-1 defeat for the USA against Spain.

As soon as this game got under way, England laid siege to the American goal. In the first 15 minutes they had six clear shots on goal, forcing several good saves from keeper Frank Borghi and hitting the woodwork twice. It wasn't until the 25th minute that the USA finally managed to get out of their own half and have a shot on goal themselves. England then counterattacked, firing off three further shots in the 30th, 31st and 32nd minutes, but they failed to score.

The Americans had defended well and had weathered the early storm. Then, in the 37th minute, totally against the run of play, they suddenly went 1-0 up. The crowd, who were resolutely supporting the underdogs, watched in amazement as a Walter Bahr shot from 25 yards was deflected off Joe Gaetjens and past the wrong-footed English goalkeeper Bert Williams.

After the break the USA played with a renewed vigour but still spent most of the second half fending off England attacks. They somehow managed to cling on to their 1-0 lead for another 45 minutes and at the final whistle some of their fans ran on to the field to celebrate such an incredible victory. The historic win became known as the 'Miracle Match' and was recounted in the 1996 book *The Game of Their Lives* by the American author/journalist Geoffrey Douglas and later a movie of the same name in 2005.

The match wasn't really covered in any great detail in the British press as it coincided with another historic loss in another sport. Luckily for England, their cricketing counterparts had just suffered their first home defeat in a Test match to the West Indies on the very same day and the newspapers seemed more interested in wallowing in the misery of that occasion rather than reporting on the events in Brazil.

Some of the newspapers didn't even believe the 1-0 scoreline to be true; they'd just assumed there'd been a typing error on the match reports received from the news agencies and decided to print the result as a 10-1 win for England.

A DIFFERENT KIND OF HAT-TRICK 1986

On 21 April 1986, in West Ham's 8-1 Division One win at home to Newcastle, Alvin Martin became the first player to score a hat-trick against three different goalkeepers in the same fixture.

Newcastle goalkeeper Martin Thomas wasn't match fit when he started the game and after conceding four first-half goals, including a fourth-minute close-range shot from Martin, he failed to appear for the second half. His place was taken in goal by centre-half Chris Hedworth but he was unable to prevent Martin from scoring his second goal of the night in the 64th minute.

Shortly afterwards, Hedworth dislocated his shoulder after colliding with the goalpost and was helped off the pitch.

Then it was the turn of Peter Beardsley to stand between the posts and, after the forward conceded two more goals, West Ham were awarded a penalty in the 85th minute. Ray Stewart was their regular penalty taker but Martin wrestled the ball off him. By then the game was won and Martin was being encouraged to take the penalty by the crowd to complete his hat-trick. Despite never having taken one before, and never taking one afterwards, Martin stepped up to the spot and hit the ball into the back of the net.

He might have had the best game of his career and then walked off the field feeling like a hero with the cheers of the home fans ringing in his ears but his manager John Lyall wasn't quite so thrilled about his performance that night and reprimanded him in the dressing room afterwards. His behaviour was deemed unprofessional. West Ham were still in with a shout of winning the title and it could have come down to goal difference on the final day of the season. What if he'd missed that penalty? It could have cost them the trophy.

As it turned out, Liverpool won the First Division that season and West Ham only finished in third place.

THE INTERNATIONAL TEAM OF SHOPLIFTERS
1990

Albania were due to play Iceland in Reykjavík in a European Championship qualifying match on 30 May 1990.

Their party of 37 players and staff had been travelling to Iceland via Rome and London and it was during their three-hour stopover at Heathrow that their otherwise mundane journey turned into something a little more eventful.

As they approached the gate for their connecting flight to Reykjavík, they were stopped by the police on suspicion of shoplifting. They were later found to have stolen watches, perfume, confectionery and other goods to the value of £2,500.

The incident was later blamed on a language problem. Apparently, they'd left the shop without paying after believing that everything was free instead of just duty-free! They'd been confused and it was all just a terrible misunderstanding. But the police weren't convinced and locked them up for 24 hours. Their investigation was only scuppered when they failed to find an interpreter and then it just seemed easier to let them go.

The police then escorted them to the gate and saw them on to the plane just to make sure they didn't get confused again.

Apparently, they already had duty-free goods in their luggage from Rome, so either the security wasn't as tight there or their confusion only began in London.

The Icelandic authorities weren't taking any chances. They met the Albanians on arrival, their luggage was searched and then they were escorted to their hotel and effectively placed under house arrest until the match.

THE HIDDEN TROPHY
1943

The German military had looted banks and plundered treasures from museums and galleries in every country they'd invaded during the Second World War, sending gold, valuable paintings and other precious artefacts back to Germany. After the fall of the Italian dictator Benito

Mussolini in 1943, the Nazis occupied the Italian peninsula and the famous 'Victory' World Cup trophy suddenly became a must-have addition to their collection of stolen treasures.

The trophy had been kept safe in a bank vault in Rome after Italy's victory at the 1938 World Cup but the Federazione Italiana Giuoco Calcio official Ottorino Barassi was fearful that the Nazis would try and snatch it, so he sneaked into the bank vault and grabbed it for himself first. After taking it back to his home in Cremona, he packed it into an old shoebox and hid it under his bed for the remainder of the war.

His house was once searched by Nazi soldiers but unbelievably they forgot to look under the bed!

* * *

The planned 1942 and 1946 World Cups were cancelled due to the Second World War. Germany and Brazil had applied to host in 1942 but inevitably, plans were put on hold with the outbreak of hostilities in Europe and the tournament was cancelled before a host country could be chosen.

FIFA met for the first time after the war on 1 July 1946 and were keen to resurrect their competition as soon as possible but didn't have sufficient time or the financial resources to organise and schedule it for that year. Much of Europe lay in ruins and FIFA failed to find a country willing to devote the time and money needed to stage the competition until Brazil offered to host it on the condition that it took place in 1950 instead of 1949 as FIFA had originally proposed.

Brazil had been favourites to win the 1942 bid, nobody else was interested, so FIFA quickly accepted the offer.

As a result of the 1942 and 1946 tournaments being cancelled, Italy were the reigning world champions for a record-breaking 16 years, one month and six days from 10 June 1934 until Uruguay won the trophy on 16 July 1950.

THE ARAB PRINCE PITCH INVADER
1982

After a credible 1-1 draw against Czechoslovakia in their opening group game on 17 June 1982, Kuwait then met France in their second match four days later. They held out against *Les Bleus* for half an hour before going into the break trailing 2-0 after goals from Bernard Genghini and Michel Platini, and then conceded a third goal from Didier Six soon after the restart. Although Kuwait managed to claw a goal back after 75 minutes, it was clear to everyone that their dream of causing a major World Cup upset was never going to happen.

Things went from bad to worse when Alain Giresse then scored France's fourth goal. The Kuwaitis had stopped playing and had remained rooted to the spot when the midfielder had fired in his shot, after claiming they'd heard the referee blow his whistle to stop the game. Except it wasn't him, it was someone in the crowd.

When the referee Myroslav Stupar ignored their pleas to have the goal disallowed, the Kuwaiti players walked off the pitch in protest and beckoned the president of the Kuwait Football Association, Sheikh Fahad Al-Ahmed Al-Jaber Al-Sabah, down from the stands to try and persuade him otherwise. The Sheikh rushed on to the pitch and told the referee in no uncertain terms that his team would return to their dressing room if the decision to award that goal wasn't overturned. Unbelievably, the referee then succumbed to his threats and cancelled the goal, much to the fury of the French players; the Sheikh retook his seat in the stands, and the match was restarted with a drop ball after a seven-minute delay.

Maxime Bossis scored another fourth goal for France after 89 minutes and the match ended 4-1. The Kuwaitis left the field red-faced and then lost their last game 1-0 to England, bowing out of the tournament in disgrace.

Afterwards, FIFA banned Myroslav Stupar from ever taking charge of another game and Sheikh Fahad was fined £5,000 for his leading role in one of the most farcical incidents in World Cup history.

Sheikh Fahad later invited Michel Platini to play for Kuwait in a friendly against the USSR on 27 November 1988. Platini only appeared for 21 minutes but it was enough for the Kuwaitis to try and frame his guest appearance as some kind of apology for his team's unsporting behaviour six years earlier.

THE PLAYER WHO PREFERRED TO BE ON HOLIDAY RATHER THAN PLAY FOOTBALL
1992

Denmark hadn't qualified for the 1992 European Championship in Sweden but were suddenly awarded a place in the finals just ten days before the start of the competition after war-torn Yugoslavia were disqualified. Most of the Danish players were lying on a beach somewhere but once they got the call, they cut their holidays short, packed their bags and took the first flight to Sweden.

Everyone except Michael Laudrup. The Barcelona striker didn't rate his country's chances, so instead of joining up with the rest of the squad, he just stayed where he was, finished his holiday and watched it all on TV.

Denmark somehow managed to make it through to the final on 26 June 1992 against Germany and then won 2-0. They were suddenly the new champions of Europe, everyone got a nice shiny medal and were hailed as heroes back in Denmark.

Everyone except Michael Laudrup.

THE UNHOLY TRINITY
2021

In Southampton's 9-0 defeat to Manchester United at Old Trafford on 2 February 2021, defender Jan Bednarek became the first Premier League player to score an own goal, concede a penalty and then get sent off in the same match.

The poor man had seemed determined to play a big part in his team's downfall that day. He stuck the ball in his own net after only 34 minutes, conceded a penalty after fouling Anthony Martial late in the second half, and then got himself red-carded for the same offence after the referee reviewed the incident on the VAR's pitchside monitor. At the time, his decision seemed a little harsh, but judging by his team's performance, Bednarek was probably glad to leave the field early.

THE PIE-EATING GOALKEEPER
1894–1908

William 'Fatty' Foulke was the first celebrity footballer.

He is remembered primarily for his long and distinguished career at Sheffield United (1894–1905), although he also spent time with Chelsea (1905–1906) and Bradford City (1906–1908).

Foulke was reportedly 6ft 3in tall and weighed around 26 stone at the height of his 14-year career. He was a temperamental man known for his gamesmanship; he was hugely popular with the fans, and for many years he was also the best goalkeeper in the country. He might have had difficulty in reaching the low shots but there was never any chance of him being barged over the goal line.

He was the subject of much derision and name-calling from the opposition fans due to his enormous bulk and sometimes from his own fans too. It has even been suggested that the chant 'Who ate all the pies?' was originally aimed at him by the Sheffield United supporters. But it was all water off a duck's back for Foulke, who once said, 'I don't mind what they call me as long as they don't call me late for lunch!'

During his time at Sheffield United he won a league championship medal in 1898 and two FA Cups, in 1899 and 1902.

As well as being a big man, he also had a big personality. Opposing players who incurred his wrath were often unceremoniously picked up and dumped into his goalmouth; he'd walk off the pitch if he thought his own players weren't trying hard enough; he liked to swing from the crossbar during matches and on one occasion actually pulled down the goal; and was known to turn up early for pre-match lunches so he could scoff all the food meant for his team-mates.

Most famously, in the 1902 FA Cup Final against Southampton, he fiercely contested the equalising 88th-minute goal scored by Harry Wood, and after the game he ran naked from the Sheffield United dressing room to confront the referee, chasing him into a broom cupboard, where he'd taken refuge in fear of his life. As the poor chap begged for mercy from behind the locked door that Foulke was trying to rip off its hinges, a group of equally scared FA officials approached the big man and eventually persuaded him to return to the dressing room – and put some bloody clothes on!

Although he was a big hit with the fans, the stuffy old codgers at the FA didn't take kindly to his antics, which might explain why the Selection Committee only picked him once to play for England, against Wales in 1897.

In 1905 he was transferred to Chelsea for a fee of £50; he was made captain, and helped the newly formed club to finish the 1905/06 season in third place. Nobody had ever thought of employing kids around the ground to retrieve the ball when it went out of play until Chelsea signed Foulke. To draw even more attention to their larger-than-life goalkeeper,

Chelsea employed two little boys to stand behind his goal in every home game to make him look even bigger and more fearsome than he actually was and to distract the opposition strikers as they charged towards him. Because Foulke wasn't the most agile player in the later stages of his career, the boys were also used to retrieve the ball whenever it went out of play so he didn't have to. In effect, they were the first ball boys.

After playing only 35 games for Chelsea he then moved to Bradford where he finished his career.

Foulke made the headlines again in an FA Cup second-round match against Accrington Stanley on 2 February 1907. Apparently, he turned up wearing the same red jersey as the Accrington players. The referee postponed the kick off and asked everyone to look around for an alternative shirt for him. But finding a different-coloured shirt that would fit a man of his size proved impossible and he was forced to play wrapped in a white bedsheet tied like a Roman toga which had been acquired from a nearby house. Foulke kept a clean sheet that day with Bradford winning 1-0 and also kept his sheet clean too as he wasn't called upon to make a save in the whole game. It has sometimes been suggested that the phrase 'clean sheet' may have originated from his performance that day.

Foulke retired from first-class football at the end of the 1907/08 season and bought himself a pub. He also made a few guest appearances in beat-the-goalie competitions at the amusement arcades along the Blackpool seafront. And when he wasn't pulling pints or making an arse of himself at the seaside, he was to be seen just walking around the streets of Sheffield wearing his cup final medals.

William 'Fatty' Foulke remains in the record books as the heaviest-ever first-class footballer to play anywhere in the world.

FOGGY COMMENTARY
1940

A thrilling and dramatic Edinburgh derby on New Year's Day 1940 was broadcast live on the radio by the BBC.

Unfortunately, the city was shrouded in fog with the players and the estimated 12,000 crowd unable to see anything further than the end of their own noses. Under normal circumstances the match would have been postponed but it was wartime; it was being broadcast to British soldiers fighting overseas, and a cancellation might have alerted the Germans to the weather conditions in Edinburgh. The nearby dockyards at Leith and the Forth Railway Bridge were both major targets for the Luftwaffe and the low clouds would have provided perfect cover for a bombing raid.

The game went ahead with the BBC's match reporter Bob Kingsley being instructed not to mention the fog and provide a commentary as if it was a bright, sunny day. Although he employed runners to go back and forth between the pitch and his commentary position to tell him what was happening, the messages he received were often muddled and only added to the confusion, so for the most part he just made things up as he went along. Luckily, he had a vivid imagination and described a game packed with exciting play, loads of goals, crunching tackles, goalmouth scrambles and near misses.

He didn't know it at the time but his ad-libbing wasn't all that far from the truth.

Hibs went into the break winning 3-2 but then the referee realised that he'd blown his whistle after only 43 minutes and so the teams were led back on to the field again to play out the remaining two minutes – during which time Hearts scored another two goals. In the second half, Hibs went 5-3 down but managed to pull it back to 5-5 before the Hearts striker Tommy Walker scored the winner in the last minute.

Of course, everyone at the stadium had no idea what was happening and the people listening to the match on the radio were following a completely different game. As darkness descended late in the day, many in the crowd drifted away, but there were just as many fans who didn't even know it had finished and remained on the terraces for ten minutes or more after the final whistle. Bob Kingsley even continued his commentary for 15 minutes after the match had ended.

It was reported afterwards that Kingsley was a little disappointed to discover that the real game had turned out to be just as exciting as his imaginary commentary.

THE LEOPARDS OF ZAIRE
1974

Zaire (now the Democratic Republic of the Congo) were the first sub-Saharan African team to qualify for the World Cup. They were also the first team to play all of their group games without scoring a single goal.

The leader of the country, a ruthless dictator by the name of Mobutu Sese Seko, had invested heavily in the national football team, which had led to wins at the Africa Cup of Nations in 1968 and 1974 and, more importantly, a place at the 1974 World Cup in West Germany. He'd showered the players with praise and gifts and, in return, he expected them to do their country proud when they stepped out on to the pitch in the World Cup.

Unfortunately, things didn't go quite to plan.

In their opening Group 2 game, against Scotland on 14 June, they lost 2-0 and then the players threatened to go on strike.

Each team received a huge qualification bonus from FIFA and part of this money was supposed to be passed on to the players. The Zaire team were staying at the same hotel as the Haiti squad and had seen them happily blowing all their bonus money on bags full of clothes, jewellery and other goodies, and were just a little anxious to know when they were going to get the chance to spend some of that FIFA money themselves. On the day before their next game, against Yugoslavia on 18 June, their Minister of Sport finally informed them that their money had been sent straight back to Zaire. The players knew they'd never see a penny of it and threatened not to play their next match, seemingly intent on becoming the first team ever to forfeit a game in the tournament's history. Mobutu got to hear of the threat and phoned the team captain Kidumu Mantantu to make a few threats of his own. He would be watching to see if they turned up or not and Mantantu was left in no doubt that it would be better for them and their families back home if they did.

The players had no choice but to play the game but their hearts weren't in it and they lost 9-0.

Mobutu was back on the phone again and advised the players that if they lost by four or more goals to Brazil in their final group match, on 22 June, there'd be hell to pay. His threat had the desired effect because they only lost 3-0. Coincidentally, Brazil also needed to win by the same margin to guarantee their qualification for the knockout stages so the result suited everyone. At the time, the 'Leopards' had intended to show the world just how well they could really play football and by half-time they were only 1-0 down. However, Kidumu Mantantu has since claimed that a few of the players, including their goalkeeper Kazadi Mwamba, had conspired to fix the result beforehand. Probably a good idea since their lives seemed to depend upon it.

The squad had travelled to Kinshasa airport on their way to West Germany in a luxury coach as national heroes and the newly crowned African champions but had returned in disgrace and were bundled into the back of an old army truck before being whisked away to the presidential palace where Mobutu was waiting for them. Meanwhile, their manager Blagoje Vidinić had wisely decided not to return to Zaire and flew straight back home to Yugoslavia instead. As expected, Mobutu ranted and raged at the players and then kept them all imprisoned in his palace while he decided their fate. Bet it wasn't the swankiest part of the palace either!

Eventually, after four days, they were allowed to leave unharmed. They might have lived to tell the tale but Mobutu had forbidden them from leaving the country, scuppering any thoughts some of them might have had of pursuing a career in Europe.

While in West Germany, Zaire gained worldwide notoriety during their final group game, against Brazil at the Parkstadion in Gelsenkirchen on 22 June.

Late in the match, a free kick was awarded to Brazil just outside the Zaire penalty area but before it could be taken, one of their defenders, Mwepu Ilunga, rushed out of the wall and booted the ball as hard as he could up the field. At the time, some commentators had speculated that perhaps he didn't understand the rules of football but he later claimed that his actions were in protest at the Zairian government withholding that bonus money and threatening their lives, and that he was hoping to be sent off.

Brave man; it's unlikely that Mobutu would have been too pleased by his petulant behaviour.

THE NORTH BANK MURAL
1992

The government inquiry into the 1989 Hillsborough disaster resulted in the Taylor report, which recommended that all Football League grounds should be converted into all-seater stadiums to ensure greater spectator safety. As part of their plans to modernise Highbury, Arsenal decided to knock down their old North Bank stand and replace it with a brand-spanking-new all-seater version. However, vice-chairman David Dein didn't want their home games in the first season of the newly launched Premier League to be played against a backdrop of cranes, cement trucks and scaffolding, so he commissioned a fancy mural to conceal all the building work.

A huge, hand-painted vinyl mural depicting excited little Arsenal fans wearing red and white shirts and waving scarves was eventually erected across the entire width of the pitch at the North Bank end behind the goal.

However, a day before their opening game of the season against Norwich City, the team had been training on the pitch when it was pointed out by one of their players, Kevin Campbell, that there were no black faces in the crowd. The artist was immediately summoned back to Highbury and overnight he added a bit of colour to some of the faces to better represent the team's diverse fanbase. But despite the mural's emergency overnight makeover, the club continued to receive complaints that black people were still underrepresented.

And then things get a bit apocryphal from here.

There were no women and children or disabled people either so they were all painted in too.

But because of all this fiddling around, it was now apparent that some of the children were sitting alone or next to adults who didn't appear to be their parents, prompting criticism from children's charities and adoption agencies. All the kids were subsequently painted the same colour as the nearest adult and another 1,000 portraits were changed into women, including several hundred in saris, burkas and traditional African headgear to cover all their bases. Just for the hell of it, some nuns were painted in too. Fifty Sikhs were also added, some brandishing ceremonial swords, which then brought a complaint from the police. It was rumoured that gay rights groups had complained because there weren't enough homosexuals in the crowd and that a bunch of heterosexuals had then complained that the few homosexuals that were already present in the mural had been painted dangerously near to women and children. The mural wasn't altered but the club were forced to issue a statement saying that homosexuals looked no different from anyone else and posed no threat to women or children at football grounds or anywhere else.

A backdrop of cranes, cement trucks and scaffolding might have been more appealing after all, and much to everyone's relief the mural was taken down a year later.

THE SUBSTITUTE FAN
1994

Lifelong West Ham United fan Steve Davies had travelled with a mate to watch their team play in a pre-season friendly against non-leaguers Oxford City on 28 July 1994. They stood near to where the team's manager Harry Redknapp was sitting in the dugout with Davies passing most of the first half slagging off their underperforming striker Lee Chapman, who was losing tackles and being beaten in the air by smaller players.

West Ham had turned up without a full squad; the players weren't really match fit, and due to substitutions and injuries, Redknapp was soon running out of players to put on the field, so he turned to Davies at half-time and asked him if he'd like to play. Davies had been the loudest voice in the crowd and Redknapp had been listening to him yelling abuse at his players for the whole of the first half and had decided to give him the chance to put up or shut up.

Naturally, Davies jumped at the chance of playing for his beloved West Ham; Redknapp then walked him down the tunnel and into the dressing room. Chapman was told he was off and the new guy was on, and then Davies got changed into his kit. He'd played a bit of Sunday league football but soon realised that Saturday football was a whole different ball game as he struggled to keep up with the pace. But that's not to say he didn't have a good game; playing it safe, making runs, having a few decent touches and making a couple of quality passes, while all the time resisting the urge to wave at his mate in the stand who was looking on in disbelief.

The cherry on top came after 71 minutes. A cross from Matty Holmes found Davies running between two defenders and into the box; he hit the ball as hard as he could and it flew past the outstretched arm of the Oxford keeper into the bottom corner of the net. Davies was living the dream, playing for the Hammers and scoring on his debut – not bad for someone who'd been downing the beers and puffing on the ciggies just half an hour earlier.

At full time Davies walked off the field with the rest of his new team-mates and into the dressing room, jubilant that he'd helped the team to a 4-0 victory. Afterwards, he was asked to return his kit but he somehow managed to sneak away with his shirt as a memento of the occasion.

THE GLOBAL GOALIE
1991–2011

German keeper Lutz Pfannenstiel, known as the 'global goalie', was one of the most eccentric and unpredictable players in football.

In a 20-year career between 1991 and 2011, he signed for 25 clubs in 13 countries and became the first professional footballer to play in leagues governed by all six FIFA confederations – AFC (Asia) , CAF (Africa), CONCACAF (North/Central America & Caribbean), CONMEBOL (South America), OFC (Oceania), and UEFA (Europe).

He began his career in Germany with FC Bad Kötzting (1991–1993) (UEFA) and then, instead of accepting an offer from Bayern Munich, he went to play for Penang FC in Malaysia (1993–1994) (AFC). It was back to Europe after signing for Wimbledon (1994 1995) and Nottingham Forest (1995–1997) before moving to South Africa's Orlando Pirates (1996/97) (CAF). After playing for various Finnish and

German clubs, it was back to Asia again after signing for Geylang United of Singapore (1999–2000). Things didn't go too well for him there. He'd been living the high life, hosting his own TV show and doing a bit of modelling for Armani, but then he was suddenly accused of match fixing and thrown in jail to await trial.

After 101 days inside, Pfannenstiel was released after the charges were unexpectedly dropped, and he hightailed it out of there, moving south in 2001 to New Zealand where he signed for New Zealand's Dunedin Technical (OFC). Pfannenstiel later returned to England and played for Bradford Park Avenue (2001–2002). During a derby game against Harrogate Town on 26 December 2002 he suddenly slumped to the ground after a collision. His lungs had collapsed, he had no pulse and was carted away in an ambulance after being pronounced dead. Seemingly back from the dead, Pfannenstiel then left England again and popped up at various clubs in Norway, New Zealand, Canada, Armenia and Albania, which included spells at Calgary Mustangs (2004) and Vancouver Whitecaps (2007) (CONCACAF) before arriving in South America for the first time and signing for Brazil's Clube Atlético Hermann Aichinger (2008) (CONMEBOL). Then it was back to Norway again and a return to Africa where he ended his playing career in Namibia at Ramblers (2009–2011). He must have been exhausted!

THE VOID MATCH
1999

Arsenal v Sheffield United in the FA Cup fifth round on 13 February 1999 was just another cup tie until Arsenal's Dutch winger Marc Overmars scored one of the most controversial goals in the competition's history.

Sheffield United were the plucky First Division underdogs taking on the Premier League big boys, and early in the second half they were threatening to cause a major upset after a goal from their striker Marcelo cancelled out a first-half header from Patrick Vieira to level the score at 1-1. The visitors were being roared on by their supporters packed into the Clock End and it began to look more and more likely that they could force a replay. Then, in the 76th minute, the game was turned on its head by *that* goal.

The Sheffield United keeper Alan Kelly had kicked the ball out of play so his team-mate Lee Morris could receive treatment for an injury and, as expected, when play was restarted a few minutes later, Arsenal midfielder Ray Parlour then threw the ball back towards him.

Unfortunately, not everyone appeared to understand what was expected of them in this situation.

Arsenal substitute striker Nwankwo Kanu had only been on the field for ten minutes; it was his debut for the club and his first appearance in English football after transferring from Inter Milan, and he probably couldn't believe his luck when he latched on to that loose ball from Parlour, ran down the right wing and swung a cross into the box with none of the Sheffield United players appearing to challenge him.

In fact, the Blades were just standing there rooted to the spot, watching him and wondering what the hell he was doing. Meanwhile, Overmars got on the end of the cross and slotted the ball into an empty net to put Arsenal 2-1 up.

Needless to say, all hell broke loose after that. The Sheffield United players then unconsciously broke off into two groups. One lot ran to confront the referee in the hope that he might be persuaded to disallow the goal, while the other lot went to confront the two villainous Arsenal players who were busy celebrating the goal in front of the North Bank fans. With emotions running high and the away fans chanting 'Shame on Arsenal', it looked for a time that the Blades might walk off the pitch but after an eight-minute delay in which the referee dished out five yellow cards, the goal was allowed to stand and the match was restarted.

The next day's back page of the *Sheffield Star* screamed, 'YOU KANU BE SERIOUS!'

Arsenal were horrified by what had transpired and how they'd seemingly won so unfairly. After discussions between manager Arsène Wenger and chairman David Dein they offered to replay the game. Sheffield United accepted their proposal, the FA sanctioned the rematch which took place at Highbury ten days later, and the result of the first meeting was wiped from the history books. It was the first time that an FA Cup tie had been replayed under such special circumstances in modern times.

The replayed game also ended in a 2-1 win for Arsenal.

FAILING TO SEE THE FUNNY SIDE 1995

After Rangers midfielder Paul Gascoigne spotted that referee Dougie Smith had dropped his yellow card during his side's 7-0 Scottish Premier Division win over Hibernian on 30 December 1995, he picked it up and ran across to him, jokingly holding it in the air and pretending to book him, before handing it back. Unfortunately, Smith failed to see the funny side and then used the same yellow card to book Gazza.

* * *

Paul Gascoigne's yellow card was harsh but maybe not as harsh as the one handed out to the Roma right-back Alessandro Florenzi after he scored in the Serie A match against Cagliari on 21 September 2014. It was the first time his 82-year-old grandmother had ever visited a stadium to watch him play and, to celebrate his goal, he ran into the crowd to give her a big hug. But the miserable sod of a referee failed to appreciate the tenderness of the moment and showed him a yellow card as soon as he returned to the pitch.

THE DISGRACE OF GIJÓN
1982

West Germany and Austria played in the same group as Algeria and Chile at the 1982 World Cup in Spain.

Chile were hopeless, losing all three games, but not so Algeria, who opened their campaign on 16 June with a surprising 2-1 win over West Germany and finished it eight days later with a narrow 3-2 win over Chile. They had a good chance of causing a major upset by securing second spot in the table and qualifying for the knockout stages but it all depended on what happened in the West Germany-Austria game to be played the following day.

	P	W	D	L	GF	GA	GD	Pts
Austria	2	2	0	0	3	0	3	4
Algeria	3	2	0	1	5	5	0	4
West Germany	2	1	0	1	5	3	2	2
Chile	3	0	0	3	3	8	-5	0

However, Austria and West Germany knew perfectly well that a German win by just one or two goals would see them both finish on the same number of points as Algeria – and still qualify for the knockout stage on goal difference ahead of the African team.

The Germans furiously attacked their opponents straight from the start and took the lead after only ten minutes with a Horst Hrubesch goal. And then nothing else happened for the remaining 80 minutes.

The team in possession just passed the ball around among themselves in their own half and back to their goalkeeper; long balls were booted up the field with no apparent motive; few tackles were made, and all the players from both teams appeared to deliberately miss the few easy goalscoring chances that came their way. It seemed that Austria had renounced the chance to finish as group winners (by winning or drawing the game) against a much stronger

German side in exchange for a guaranteed passage to the knockout stage.

	P	W	D	L	GF	GA	GD	Pts
West Germany	3	2	0	1	6	3	3	4
Austria	3	2	0	1	3	1	2	4
Algeria	3	2	0	1	5	5	0	4
Chile	3	0	0	3	3	8	-5	0

The players from both teams were loudly criticised by the fans, the officials and the spectators in the stadium, and even by the German and Austrian TV commentators, who'd urged their viewers to switch channels. Algerian football officials predictably cried foul and immediately lodged a complaint with FIFA, but both teams denied any collusion and FIFA were forced to admit that no rules had been broken and there was no proof of any attempts at match fixing.

Nobody could prove any wrongdoing but, at the same time, nobody had any doubts that a wrongdoing had occurred.

Despite their ruling, FIFA decided to revise their rules for all future tournaments to avoid similar incidents by insisting that all the final group games kicked off simultaneously.

TRICKY PRONUNCIATION
1996

When German striker Stefan Kuntz was selected in the squad for the 1996 European Championship in England, it left the British TV commentators wondering how they were supposed to pronounce his name without causing offence. They appeared to get around the problem by dropping the T and calling him Stefan Kunz.

SHIPWRECKED
1923

Raith Rovers finished the 1922/23 season in third place behind Celtic and Rangers in Scottish Division One. It was their highest-ever finish and, as a reward for their players, the club splashed the cash for a post-season tour of the Canary Islands.

Thirteen players, five officials and manager James Logan boarded the steamer *Highland Loch* at Tilbury in Essex. The service was operated by the Nelson Line Steam Navigation Company and ran between London and the Argentinian capital Buenos Aires, with the players due to disembark at Vigo in Spain where they would watch a bullfight and stay overnight while the ship was replenished, before continuing their journey to Las Palmas in the Canary Islands.

The voyage was literally plain sailing until the *Highland Loch* rounded Cape Finisterre into the Bay of Biscay on 1 July.

The ship had sailed headlong into a violent storm and the wind, rain and high waves sent it crashing on to rocks. It was early on a Sunday morning and many of the passengers were still in their PJs when they were ordered to grab their life jackets and abandon ship. The players demonstrated remarkable composure and bravery and helped ensure the strict maritime tradition of 'women and children first' was adhered to before abandoning ship themselves. In fact, they were among the last passengers to leave.

Spanish fishermen helped in the rescue and towed the lifeboats into various ports along the coast.

A few of the players were separated from the rest of their team and ended up in a tiny village after five hours at sea where nobody spoke a word of English and nobody could offer them any help, so they had to set off again in a motorboat to reach the port of Vilagarcia de Arousa further along the coast where the rest of the team had gone ashore.

After contacting the Nelson Line agent, the players were told to take a train to Vigo where they would be met by the company's representative who would arrange alternative transport for them. Amazingly, the first ship they saw sitting in the harbour when they arrived was the *Highland Loch*. It had been badly damaged but the crew had somehow managed to re-float it and reach the harbour. So, abandoning ship and embarking on a long hazardous lifeboat journey and then ending up disorientated and starving hungry in the middle of nowhere in a foreign land had all been a gigantic waste of time! They could have just as easily stayed on board.

The passengers were eventually ferried out to the ship by motor launch and allowed to go aboard to retrieve their belongings, with the players managing to rescue most of their luggage and the chests containing their football kits.

The following day everyone boarded the steamer *Darrow* which took them on the rest of their journey to Las Palmas. According to player Tom Jennings, their party was invited to dine at the captain's table as a reward for their bravery during the evacuation of the *Highland Loch*.

A few days later than expected, they finally made it to their destination. Their traumatic experience at sea didn't seem to affect the players too much as they went on to win all of their matches.

To this day Raith Rovers remains the only football team ever to be shipwrecked.

THE MOST BIZARRE PENALTY MISS EVER SEEN
2005

Arsenal's Robert Pires and Thierry Henry managed to produce the most bizarre penalty miss in the history of the Premier League during their 1-0 home win over Manchester City on 22 October 2005.

Arsenal were protecting a slender lead when they were awarded their second penalty of the match after Dennis Bergkamp was brought down in the box by Stephen Jordan late in the second half. Pires had already scored with a penalty in the 61st minute and was keen to make it two out of two when the referee pointed to the spot again.

But instead of just blasting the ball directly at the goal, he decided to try and copy that famous Johan Cruyff and Jesper Olsen penalty routine for Ajax against Helmond Sport from 1982, by passing it sideways for a team-mate to run on to and take the shot. He stood over the ball, took a few steps backwards and then began his run-up.

The idea was to pass the ball to his left where Henry was meant to be running into the box. But that's not how it went down. Pires appeared to take a swing at the ball and miss and then just stood there glued to the spot half-heartedly trying to protect it from the approaching City defenders while Henry ran right past him. He probably went to kick it and realised that his team-mate had started his run too late and wasn't yet in position for him to make the pass – and then had no idea what to do next.

The referee believed that Pires had scuffed his first kick and had then touched the ball again so he just awarded a free kick the other way.

Check it out on YouTube.

THE SUNDAY LEAGUE CHANCER 1996

Ali Dia surely ranks as the worst footballer ever to play in the Premier League.

After the Southampton manager Graeme Souness received a phone call purporting to be from the legendary ex-AC Milan player George Weah touting his cousin Ali Dia as the next big thing, he agreed to give the ex-Paris Saint-Germain striker a trial.

Souness must have been thrilled about such an exciting young footballer playing for Southampton and even though he'd never heard of him or seen him play, he justified his decision to sign Dia by smugly announcing to the press, 'When someone like that [George Weah] gives you a recommendation you tend to sit up and take notice.'

Dia was originally due to make his debut playing for the reserve team in a midweek fixture against Arsenal but that game was rained off and then a first-team injury crisis forced Souness to give him a one-month contract and include him in the squad for their next Premier League match against Leeds United on 23 November 1996. He made his debut as a substitute for the injured Matthew Le Tissier in the 32nd minute – and was then substituted himself in the 85th minute because he was so totally hopeless. Many years later, Le Tissier remarked, 'He ran around the pitch like Bambi on ice; it was very embarrassing to watch.' According to Le Tissier, Dia seemed to be running around anywhere that was nowhere near the ball, perhaps in the vain hope that if he never touched it, then nobody would realise just how bad he was.

Souness had clearly been duped. Dia never played for Southampton again and was released from his contract just two weeks later. It soon became apparent that it hadn't been George Weah on the phone; he didn't even have a cousin called Ali Dia, and the guy they'd signed had certainly never played for Paris Saint-Germain.

Dia had played a handful of games for a few lower-league teams in France, Finland and Germany before they realised just how crap he was and let him go. He'd then moved to England in 1996 and played once for non-league team Blyth Spartans before Southampton rushed to sign him. It later emerged that other English clubs had been contacted by the fake George Weah touting the services of his fake cousin but only poor Graeme Souness had been daft enough to fall for it.

Ali Dia then made a few more uneventful appearances for a few more English non-league teams before disappearing from the pages of Wikipedia forever!

THE TEN-GOAL BONANZA
1936

Three separate goalscoring records were set in 121 days in the 1935/36 English season.

In the Division One match on 14 December 1935, Ted Drake scored all seven of Arsenal's goals in their 7-1 away victory over Aston Villa. According to the match reports, he scored with each of his first six shots on goal and in the end failed to convert only one effort, which hit the bar. To this day his seven-goal haul remains a record for any top-flight English fixture.

Twelve days later another player scored nine goals.

Back then, clubs used to play each other home and away on Christmas Day and Boxing Day. On 25 December Oldham beat Tranmere 4-1 at Boundary Park in a Division Three North fixture but the following day they were thrashed 13-4 in the return match at Prenton Park with Robert 'Bunny' Bell getting nine of the goals. He could have got ten but missed a penalty. According to the *Liverpool Daily Post*, the crowd invaded the pitch at full time to carry Bunny Bell towards the dressing room and then waited outside singing 'For He's a Jolly Good Fellow' before carrying him shoulder-high to a room where the directors of both clubs presented him with the match ball.

But it was the Luton Town midfielder Joe Payne who became the first player to score ten goals in a league game in England.

He'd never really impressed anyone and had been loaned out to non-league Biggleswade Town (where he still failed to impress anyone), only making four league appearances for Luton that season, mainly in defence. He was a utility player, more suited to the reserves than the first team, and often criticised by his own fans for seemingly not taking the game seriously enough. Even though Luton's three first-choice strikers were injured for their Division Three South match against Bristol Rovers on Easter Monday in 1936, he was still as surprised as anyone to be handed the number nine shirt and told to go out there and win them the game.

After 20 minutes the match was still goalless. The breakthrough finally came in the 23rd minute after Payne latched on to a long ball and slotted it past goalkeeper Jack Ellis. After his team-mate Fred Roberts got a second goal on 32 minutes, Payne struck again in the 40th and 43rd minutes to bag his hat-trick before half-time. The dressing-room banter centred on Payne and it was jokingly suggested that he had a chance of beating Bunny Bell's record of nine goals.

It seemed that Payne could do no wrong that afternoon and the other players were instructed to pass him the ball as much as possible in the hope of scoring more goals. In the 49th minute he scored again – then carried on, slotting home his final goal in the 86th minute after taking a wild swing at the ball and deflecting his shot past the wrong-footed Ellis. His team-mates and the crowd had been willing him on to beat Bunny Bell's record but at this stage in the match he'd only scored nine goals. Luton did score again in the last minute but it was his team-mate George Martin who hit the back of the net and not Payne – even though he, and everyone else in the ground, probably wished it had been.

Although Luton had resurrected their chances of promotion with such an emphatic win, Payne walked off the pitch rueing the chances he'd missed that would have made him a record breaker.

However, after the match, the referee reported that Luton's sixth goal, which everyone had credited to Martin, had already crossed the line before he'd bundled it into the net, and so Payne was actually the goalscorer. He'd got his ten goals after all, although everyone in the country had to wait until the next day's newspapers were published to know it.

Payne picked up a £2 bonus on top of his £4 weekly wages for his efforts. He also received the match ball as a souvenir and, on the Wednesday after the match, a congratulatory telegram arrived from Robert 'Bunny' Bell. Poor Bunny had only revelled in his record-breaking performance for a few months, while Payne's record remains unbeaten to this day.

Luton missed out on promotion that year by just one point but Payne became a first-team regular after his stunning performance that day. The following season he scored 55 goals in 39 matches which secured the Division Three South championship for the Hatters.

RED CARD FOR TACKLING A STREAKER
2011

Dorchester Town player-manager Ashley Vickers decided to do everyone a favour when he rugby-tackled a streaker in the 70th minute of their Conference South match at Havant & Waterlooville on 7 March 2011 – but was then sent off by the referee for violent conduct.

The idiot pitch invader, dressed only in a lime green-coloured thong and a curly black wig, had given the out-of-shape stewards the slip for at least 30 seconds, much to the amusement of the crowd, running around the field and generally making an arse of himself, before Vickers decided to take matters into his own hands by running across the field and pulling him down to the ground with a shuddering neck-high rugby tackle. Despite doing the right thing, and the stewards thanking him, and players from both sides pleading with the referee not to dismiss him, he was still shown a red card.

The streaker's motive for the stunt was all too familiar. He'd made a bet with his mates down the pub.

Sigh.

THE WORLD CHAMPIONS FROM COUNTY DURHAM

1909

Before the first official FIFA World Cup in 1930, the English businessman Thomas Lipton invited the best club teams from Italy, Germany, Switzerland and England to compete for the Sir Thomas Lipton Trophy, an inter-club competition to be held in Turin. The first three countries duly complied with his request and sent their strongest teams but the old farts at the FA refused to have anything to do with his little competition and declined his request to take part. Not wishing to see England excluded, however, Sir Thomas then asked West Auckland, an amateur side from County Durham playing in the Northern League, to represent their country.

Why they should have got the invite, nobody really knows.

The part-time players of West Auckland were mostly coal miners and struggled to raise the funds for their journey to Italy with many of them forced to pawn their own possessions to find the money. Most of them had never been out of County Durham before, let alone the country, so the journey itself was already a fairly daunting experience for them. They crossed the English Channel and then took a train through France to Turin, where they were greeted by the tournament organisers who believed they were Woolwich Arsenal. They'd been expecting a big club to arrive from England and had been told that WAFC were on their way, so when the players eventually turned up, it was just assumed they'd be from the more famous north London club. Nobody had been expecting a bunch of part-time Geordie miners. The tournament organisers were disappointed but still had to let them play. What kind of a football competition would it be without a representative from the country that invented the sport?

West Auckland met their opponents and then watched a few of their training sessions, but they came away feeling pretty downbeat about their chances as all the other teams seemed more prepared, more skilful and much fitter than them.

But all that nervousness and self-doubt soon disappeared when they started playing football.

On 11 April 1909 they met their first opponents, Sportfreunde Stuttgart of Germany, and secured a fairly comfortable 2-0 victory. They'd started slowly but grew in confidence after scoring an early goal in the tenth minute. Their second goal came two minutes before the final whistle when their goalkeeper James Dickenson converted a spot kick to secure the team's place in the final.

The final was played the very next day, against the Swiss champions and tournament favourites FC Winterthur who had just beaten a Torino XI in the other semi-final. It was expected to be a pretty easy game for them but things didn't work out that way because the boys from County Durham beat them 2-0 too.

Tiny West Auckland were suddenly the first and the most unlikeliest champions of the world.

As the cup holders, West Auckland were invited back to Italy again in 1911 to defend their title. They beat FC Red Star of Switzerland 2-0 and then met Italian giants Juventus in the final on 17 April 1911. This time they won 6-1 and were awarded the Sir Thomas Lipton Trophy outright. It's difficult to believe that a bunch of poorly equipped and underfunded coal miners had just beaten the mighty Juventus team to become champions of the world for the second time.

However, they didn't hold on to the championship for very long. They had serious financial problems after all their gallivanting around Europe and they were forced to pawn the trophy to pay off a £40 debt to the landlady of a local pub. The trophy remained in her possession for almost 50 years until the club were able to buy it back from her for

£100 in 1960. Then, in 1994, the trophy was stolen. Despite an extensive police investigation and the club offering a substantial reward for its safe return, it has never been recovered.

TRANSFER HIJACK
1997

Ponytailed Frenchman Emmanuel Petit had travelled to north London for a meeting with Tottenham chairman Alan Sugar to discuss a move from Monaco. Meanwhile, Arsenal manager Arsène Wenger got to hear about his plan and sent word not to sign anything until he'd heard his proposal for joining the Gunners instead.

Petit had a tour around White Hart Lane and a productive meeting with Mr Sugar. Tottenham even offered him a contract there and then but he asked for a little more time to think about the deal, promising an answer within a few days. He then jumped in a cab and everyone at the club just assumed he was heading back to his hotel. But instead, he diverted the cab to Wenger's house where he and Arsenal vice-chairman David Dein were waiting for him.

He then signed for Arsenal that afternoon with Tottenham unwittingly facilitating the move by paying for his £20 cab fare.

BANG ON THE HEAD
1990s

Scotsman John Lambie was the maverick, no-nonsense, cigar-chomping boss at Partick Thistle.

During one particular match, his star striker Colin McGlashan was involved in a clash of heads with an opponent and was led off the field for treatment. On being told by his assistant that the player was concussed and didn't know who he was, John very matter-of-factly replied, 'Tell him he's Pelé and get him back on!'

THE THEFT OF THE JULES RIMET TROPHY
1966

The 'Victory' trophy was the original prize awarded to the winners of the World Cup and was renamed the Jules Rimet Trophy in 1946 after the third FIFA president Jules Rimet, who established the competition back in 1930.

In January 1966, the FA took possession of the trophy in preparation for the finals, due to be held in England later that year. It was usually kept at their HQ in London but occasionally the trophy was loaned out to the organisers of various events. One such event was the Stampex Exhibition at the Central Hall in London, beginning on 19 March, where the stamp dealer Stanley Gibbons Ltd had arranged for it to be displayed on their stall.

There were tight security measures in place with two uniformed police officers guarding the trophy around the clock, backed up during the day by two plain-clothed detectives. However, on 20 March, when the exhibition was closed to the public and the building was being used for Methodist Church services, it soon became apparent that the tight security measures weren't quite as tight as the organisers had hoped. Thieves had forced open the rear doors of the building, calmly removed the padlock from the display case and swiped the trophy. And none of the guards had seen or heard a damn thing.

A short time later, FA chairman Joe Mears received a ransom note demanding £15,000 for the trophy's safe return and then an undercover police officer code-named 'McPhee' arranged to meet a man called 'Jackson' in London's Battersea Park for the pay-off. The fake notes were handed over and Jackson then agreed to get into McPhee's car and lead him to the trophy. At some point during their journey, however, Jackson spotted the police vans following them and jumped out of the car. He made a run for it, McPhee gave chase and eventually caught up with him, at which point he revealed himself to be a police officer and made an arrest. Jackson turned out to be Edward Betchley, a used-car salesman and petty thief from south London. He denied stealing the trophy and claimed that someone he knew only as 'The Pole' had offered him £500 to act as a middleman. He was later convicted of demanding money with menace and sentenced to two years inside. 'The Pole' was never identified and nobody else was ever convicted of the theft.

With just a few months until the start of the tournament, the police were no nearer to catching the thieves. And it didn't look like they were going to catch them anytime soon either, so the FA started drawing up plans to have a duplicate trophy made. At least the teams would have something to play for when the tournament kicked off on 11 July. But nobody could have imagined what happened next.

Step forward a black-and-white collie called Pickles. On his evening walk in Upper Norwood, a suburb of the capital, he spotted something lying under a hedge, wrapped in newspaper and bound with string. His owner, David Corbett, opened the mysterious package and realised immediately that it was the missing Jules Rimet Trophy. Although he took it to the nearest police station and collected the £5,000 reward, it was Pickles who received all the credit and adulation from the public. He became a national hero overnight, he was voted 'Dog of the Year' and appeared on the children's TV show *Blue Peter* before starring in his own big-screen comedy later that year, *The Spy with a Cold Nose*.

Sadly, his fame and fortune didn't last very long. A year later he was strangled to death by his own choke chain after it got snared on a tree branch while he was chasing a cat near his new home in Surrey.

A plaque was unveiled at the very spot in Upper Norwood where Pickles found the trophy in 2018.

* * *

Brazil won the World Cup for the third time in 1970 allowing them to permanently keep the Jules Rimet Trophy. It was subsequently placed inside a bulletproof glass cabinet and displayed at the Confederação Brasileira de Futebol offices in Rio de Janeiro. On 19 December 1983, thieves broke into the building, forced open the case with a crowbar and made off with the trophy. Although four men were later tried and convicted in absentia for the crime, the trophy has never been seen since.

THE PISSED REFEREE
2008

Sergei Shmolik may have enjoyed something a little stronger than a cup of tea during the half-time break in the Belarusian Premier League game between Vitebsk and Naftan Novopolotsk on 5 July 2008.

In fact, he was so drunk that he couldn't even run around the pitch and spent most of the second half just staggering around in the centre circle, blowing his whistle erratically and officiating the game with meaningless hand gestures. As he was helped off the pitch at the end of the game, he waved to the crowd and seemed totally oblivious to what was happening around him.

At first everyone thought he was suffering from back pain but a blood test later confirmed that he was just pissed out of his head. And to think, only the year before, he'd been voted the best referee in Belarus!

THE BLINDFOLDED BOY
1954

Spain and Turkey were the only two nations drawn in qualifying Group 6, with the top-placed team reaching the 1954 World Cup in Switzerland.

They met each other twice, with Spain winning 4-1 in Madrid and Turkey winning 1-0 in Istanbul. Both teams had won one game each but as penalty shoot-outs or goal difference or away goals or anything else weren't considered as deciding factors to determine tied group places back then, a play-off was hastily arranged at a neutral venue, the Stadio Olimpico in Rome on 17 March. Which was all very well and good but that match ended in a 2-2 draw and the problem of which team should progress to the finals in Switzerland remained.

The winner was eventually decided by Luigi Franco Gemma, a 14-year-old Italian schoolboy whose father worked at the stadium. After the game had ended, he was bundled into a backroom somewhere inside the Stadio Olimpico by a group of overexcited FIFA officials, blindfolded and ordered to pick a team name out of a pot. Little Luigi stuck his hand in, swirled around a couple of bits of paper, like he was about to pick a winning raffle ticket, and finally pulled out the one with TURKEY written on it.

Despite Spain being the better team and winning 6-4 on aggregate across the three games, it was Turkey who got to go to Switzerland.

* * *

The drawing of lots was used for a second time during the 1990 World Cup in Italy. Group F had featured England, the Republic of Ireland, the Netherlands and Egypt and produced some of the most boring and uninspiring games in the tournament's history with only one win and seven goals, and with none of the teams managing to score more than once in any of the six games. England finished top, but tied in second place were Ireland and the Netherlands, having both finished the group stage with three points and scoring and conceding the same number of goals.

Although they had already qualified for the knockout stage, which of them went through in second and third place still needed to be decided, and so a needlessly long and elaborate ceremony was held by FIFA immediately after the final games were played on 21 June. Two orange balls containing the country names and two yellow balls containing the numbers two and three were placed in a couple of goldfish bowls by the FIFA president Sepp Blatter, and then two anonymous assistants who were standing next to him on the stage were invited to pull them out of the bowls again. Ireland got lucky and bagged the runners-up spot.

They then met Romania, winning on penalties, and the Netherlands were beaten 2-1 by eventual winners West Germany.

THE DELIBERATE OWN GOAL
1994

The Caribbean Cup group match between Barbados and Grenada on 27 January 1994 was possibly the most bizarre match ever played.

The organisers of the 1994 Caribbean Cup had imposed an unusual rule which required all matches to have a winner. Extra time would be added in the event of a draw with golden goals (each counting as a double goal) deciding the outcome. This would mean the winner always being awarded a two-goal margin of victory.

Barbados and Grenada were drawn with Puerto Rico in Group 1. Barbados lost 1-0 to Puerto Rico in the first match, on 23 January, and then two days later Grenada defeated Puerto Rico 2-0 with a deciding golden goal, sending them to the top of the group with three points and a superior goal difference of +2, meaning that Barbados had to beat Grenada by at least two clear goals in the final game if they were to finish as group winners and advance to the finals.

	P	W	L	GF	GA	GD	Pts
Grenada	1	1	0	2	0	2	3
Puerto Rico	2	1	1	1	2	-1	3
Barbados	1	0	1	0	1	-1	0

The match started routinely enough with Barbados scoring the two goals they needed to establish a winning margin but then Grenada clawed one back in the 83rd minute to make it 2-1, which would take them through to the finals unless Barbados could score again. Although Barbados attacked and tried to get another goal, time was running out, so they decided to adopt a quite different strategy.

In the 87th minute they stopped attacking altogether. Instead, goalkeeper Horace Stoute and defender Terry Sealey just started passing the ball around between themselves, before Sealey intentionally blasted it into his own net. They'd realised that it would be easier to try and get a winning goal in the half an hour of extra time than in the remaining three minutes of normal time and had deliberately forfeited a goal to make it 2-2. However, the Grenadians weren't daft because they'd cottoned on to their little plan.

If anything, they were even smarter than their opponents after quickly figuring out that they could advance in the tournament by scoring in either goal. Even if they lost by one, they'd still have the same number of points as Barbados but a better goal difference. Obviously, it was a lot easier to score an own goal so that's what they attempted to do – and the Barbados players then started defending the Grenada goal. For the last three minutes of the game, the fans were treated to the unprecedented sight of Grenada trying to score at either end of the pitch and Barbados defending both ends of the pitch.

Ultimately, Barbados managed to hold off Grenada and at full time the score was still 2-2 with the game then going to extra time where a winning goal would count as double. Trevor Thorne eventually got the winner to make it 3-2, which was recorded therefore as 4-2, and Barbados progressed to the finals.

	P	W	L	GF	GA	GD	Pts
Barbados	2	1	1	4	3	1	3
Grenada	2	1	1	4	4	0	3
Puerto Rico	2	1	1	1	2	-1	3

In a press conference after the game, Grenada manager James Clarkson commented, 'I feel cheated. The person who came up with these rules must be a candidate for the madhouse ... The game should never be played with so many players running around the field confused. Our players didn't even know which direction to attack: our goal or their goal. I have never seen this happen before.'

None of the players were sanctioned by FIFA – after all, they were only following the rules – but unsurprisingly the golden double goal rule was never used again, in any tournament, anywhere in the world.

WHEN THE FA CUP WAS STOLEN
1895

Aston Villa won the FA Cup after beating West Bromwich Albion 1-0 on 20 April 1895 at Crystal Palace Park in London.

The FA Cup was still English football's biggest prize at that time and the FA generously allowed the winning team to keep the trophy for a year until the winners of the following season's final took possession.

William Shillcock was a shoemaker and sportswear retailer who'd supplied the winning Villa team with their boots. He was also a lifelong fan, so when he'd asked for their permission to display the FA Cup in the window of his Birmingham shop, the club readily agreed to his request. The trophy attracted huge crowds and no doubt resulted in a lot of extra business for Shillcock too.

After locking up his shop at around 9.15pm on 11 September 1895, he returned the following day at 8am only to discover that he'd been burgled overnight. Although the till had been emptied, the two safes and many other valuables remained untouched. It was only when he checked the window display that he discovered the true reason for the break-in. To his horror the FA Cup had been stolen.

Shillcock informed the police and distributed handbills around the city offering a £10 reward for the trophy's safe return. However, it was ultimately Aston Villa who were responsible for the cup's safety and they were ordered by the FA to pay for a replacement. The police never solved the crime, the FA Cup was never recovered and a replica trophy had to be used until 1911.

Fast forward 63 years and in an exclusive interview with the *Sunday Pictorial* published on 23 February 1958 under the headline 'I STOLE THE FA CUP', an 80-year-old career criminal called Harry Burge claimed to have stolen the trophy with two of his mates. According to Burge, they'd broken into the shop, snatched the cup and then calmly walked back to his house a few streets away to melt it down and make fake half-crown coins. Ironically, most of these coins were then spent on booze in a city-centre pub owned by the Villa striker Dennis Hodgetts and frequented by many of his team-mates. In the newspaper article, Burge speculated that the players would have almost certainly handled the dud coins not knowing that they were actually holding a bit of the melted-down FA Cup in their hands.

LETTERED SHIRTS
1930

When Bolivia turned up for their first group game at the 1930 World Cup, against Yugoslavia, each player wore a white shirt with a huge letter stitched on to the front which would have spelt out 'VIVA URUGUAY' when they all lined up together. It was intended as a tribute to the host nation but, unfortunately, when they all assembled for the pre-match photograph, the 'VIVA' players knelt in front of the 'URUGUAY' players (instead of the other way around) and a player sporting one of the Us was missing from the line-up, so the message actually read 'URUGAY VIVA'.

The Bolivians were obviously just as crap at football as they were at cheap publicity stunts because they were beaten 4-0.

THE RELUCTANT PENALTY TAKER
1924

Nottingham Forest were losing 1-0 at home to Bolton Wanderers on 26 December 1924 when they were awarded a penalty in the dying minutes of the game. Bolton goalkeeper Dick Pym positioned himself on his line but none of the Forest players stepped forward to take the penalty. Earlier in the game they'd had their regular taker Harry Martin carried off the field on a stretcher and none of his team-mates appeared to want the responsibility of taking the spot kick. Then, the Forest captain Bob Wallace ran off the pitch and into the dressing room.

A few minutes later he reappeared with Martin, having persuaded him to re-enter the match and take the penalty.

The injury to his ankle was so painful that he couldn't walk unaided and so he had to be carried across the pitch by Wallace. From a standing position, Martin took the kick, scored and then collapsed, before being stretchered back to the dressing room again.

THE CURSE OF BENFICA
1962

Hungarian coach Béla Guttmann was in charge of Benfica from 1959 until 1962 and led them to Primeira Divisão title wins in 1960 and 1961, along with back-to-back European Cup victories in 1961 and 1962.

Benfica had beaten Real Madrid 5-3 to win their second European Cup at the Olympisch Stadion in Amsterdam on 2 May 1962. At the end of the match, the Real striker Ferenc Puskás famously handed his shirt to the young Eusébio, a gesture which many commentators believed symbolised the end of Real's supremacy in the competition and the start of a new era dominated by the Portuguese club.

After his team's stunning success, Guttmann felt justified in asking for a pay rise. But his bosses felt differently and weren't prepared to meet his request – which proved to be the biggest mistake the club has ever made. Feeling angry and betrayed, Guttmann immediately resigned and purportedly yelled at the directors, 'Not in a hundred years from now will Benfica ever be European champions!' as he stormed out of the stadium. At the time, it seemed like a pretty harmless threat made in the heat of the moment by a very angry man but in the intervening years his prophecy seems to have had some merit and many people have since interpreted it as a curse.

Benfica have since lost EIGHT European finals, finishing as runners-up in the European Cup in 1963, 1965, 1968, 1988 and 1990 and in the UEFA Cup/Europa League in 1983, 2013 and 2014.

It was reported that before their 1990 European Cup Final match against AC Milan, Eusébio even visited Guttmann's grave and prayed for the curse to be lifted – but to no avail.

To date, the curse remains firmly in place as Benfica still haven't won a damn thing in Europe.

THE GOALSCORING BALL BOY
2006

In the 89th minute of the Copa FPF match between the two Brazilian teams of Santacruzense and Atlético Sorocaba on 12 September 2006, a Santacruzense player narrowly shot wide of the opposition goal and the ball ended up in the side netting. The ball boy standing behind the goal then collected it, but instead of throwing it back to the goalkeeper, he nonchalantly dribbled it on to the pitch and tapped it across the line and into the Sorocaba net. Despite ten seconds elapsing between the ball going out of play and the ball boy's actions, the referee, Silvia Regina de Oliveira, then awarded a goal allowing the home team to draw level at 1-1 amid furious protests from the Sorocaba players.

She'd turned her back on play and had then run back up the field again, but when turning around she'd seen the goalkeeper picking the ball out of the net and had just assumed that a goal had been scored.

When questioned about the incident later in a radio interview, she put all the blame on the linesman.

THE WEMBLEY WIZARDS
1928

England's meeting with Scotland on 31 March 1928 was only their second game at the newly built Wembley Stadium.

Both teams had lost their previous British Home Championship matches, against Wales and Ireland, and met at Wembley in the tournament's final match to decide which team would avoid finishing last.

Many of the regular Scottish-based players had been omitted from the team in favour of the Anglo-Scots plying their trade south of the border because the Scottish Selection Committee believed they had a greater chance of getting a result against a more talented and more physical English side. Nevertheless, both the Scottish public and press were still pessimistic about avoiding a defeat.

On the night before the game, Scotland captain Jimmy McMullan addressed his players, 'The [SFA] president wants us to discuss football but you all know what's expected of you tomorrow. All I've got to say is go to your bed, put your head on your pillow and pray for rain.' It was believed that a sodden, heavy pitch would favour the diminutive Scottish forwards and make it easier for them to run around the bigger English defenders.

Their prayers were answered because it was pissing it down the next day.

Scotland took the lead after only three minutes with an Alex Jackson header but a resolute performance by the English defence denied them another goal until just before half-time when Alex James put them 2-0 up.

The second half was probably the most memorable in Scottish footballing history. They raised their game and dominated the play with their third goal coming 20 minutes after the restart through another Jackson header. Moments later, James made it 4-0 and then Jackson claimed the match ball after completing his hat-trick to make it 5-0 after 85 minutes. Bob Kelly scored a consolation goal for England four minutes later.

When asked for a comment after the game, midfielder James simply smiled and said, 'We could have had ten!' The Scottish press lauded their team with praise, the pubs did a roaring Saturday night trade, and the players who would for ever be known as the 'Wembley Wizards' wrote themselves into the history books with their greatest-ever performance against the auld enemy.

Writing in the *Athletic News*, the former player turned sports journalist Ivan Sharpe commented, 'England were not merely beaten. They were bewildered – run to a standstill, made to appear utterly inferior by a team whose play was as cultured and beautiful as I ever expect to see.'

A GAME OF THREE HALVES
1894

Referee Tom Kirkham was running late to Sunderland's Division One match at home to Derby County on 1 September 1894. He'd missed his train connection and was forced to telegram the ground advising everyone that he wouldn't arrive much before 5pm. As the 9,000 spectators were expecting the game to kick off at the advertised 3.30pm start time, and it was decided unwise to keep them waiting for an hour and a half, the two teams agreed to kick off with a substitute referee taking charge, John Conqueror from Southwark.

Presumably a call had gone out to the crowd for any referees to come forward and Mr Conqueror had answered it.

At half-time, with Sunderland leading 3-0, Mr Kirkham finally turned up.

He wasn't best pleased and ordered the game to be restarted with him as the referee if it was to be counted as a proper league fixture. The first half was declared null and void, and the players kicked off again. Two more halves were played but the decision to start the match again didn't help Derby at all. They were just as poor as they'd been during that cancelled first half with Sunderland scoring three goals in the 'second half' and another five in the 'third half' to win 8-0.

THE RE-GIFTED TROPHY
1902

The British League Cup was a one-off competition held to raise funds for the victims of the Ibrox stadium disaster of 1902. The four teams contesting the trophy were the first- and second-placed clubs in the 1901/02 championships in England and Scotland – Sunderland, Everton, Rangers and Celtic.

Celtic easily beat Sunderland 5-1 at Celtic Park in the first semi-final, on 30 April 1902, and then Rangers eventually defeated Everton 3-2 at the same venue on 3 May after drawing 1-1 at Goodison Park on 1 May to set up a final between the two rival Glasgow clubs at the city's Cathkin Park on 17 June. Celtic won 3-2 with Jimmy Quinn scoring the winning goal in the dying minutes of extra time.

Rangers had organised the competition and had been so confident about winning it that they hadn't bothered to commission a trophy. But they didn't win it and were forced to quickly find a substitute trophy as a prize for the victors, so they just put up their newest cup recently acquired as winners of the 1901 Glasgow International Exhibition Cup.

Notwithstanding the trophy still being inscribed with the words 'Won by Rangers FC', it was then re-gifted to Celtic as the winners of the British League Cup.

Celtic then celebrated beating Rangers in the British League Cup by holding aloft the very same trophy in front of their fans as Rangers had done in front of theirs a year earlier after beating Celtic in the Glasgow International Exhibition Cup.

But then the controversy began.

Rangers later announced that they'd only offered Celtic use of the cup on a temporary basis because they needed something to show their fans and they expected it to be returned to them the following season. They even sent someone to Celtic Park to collect it. Celtic, on the other hand, believed it was theirs to keep, having won it fair and square in an official tournament, so they refused to give it back. The lawyers got involved, threatening letters were exchanged, and then Rangers even proposed staging another tournament to give them the chance of winning it back. But Celtic stubbornly refused to back down: they wouldn't be playing any more tournaments and they were holding on to the trophy. End of story!

Despite the many continued attempts by Rangers to recover the cup in the intervening years, it still remains on display in the Celtic trophy room to this day. Having been captured from their Old Firm rivals in such a contentious way, the British League Cup is probably one of their most prized trophies.

WHEN SCOTLAND BELIEVED THEY COULD WIN THE WORLD CUP
1978

Believe it or not, Scotland and their supporters genuinely believed they could win the 1978 World Cup in Argentina.

But the rest of the world knew perfectly well they didn't stand a cat in hell's chance of walking away with the trophy.

Needless to say, it was the rest of the world who were proved right.

It was supposed to be Scotland's greatest sporting triumph but it soon turned out to be their greatest national humiliation.

They had a good team – but it wasn't that good. Nevertheless, the Scottish FA arranged a grand going-away party at Hampden Park in Glasgow so the fans could turn up and show their support. Around 30,000 of them arrived to listen to pipe bands, belt out songs, wave their little flags, and cheer on the 22 players hoping to do them proud in Argentina. The players were joined by Ally MacLeod, who received the biggest cheer of the afternoon. He was the team's flamboyant manager, the pied piper of Scottish football, the man who'd inspired their unofficial anthem 'Ally's Tartan Army' and the man who had virtually guaranteed them a World Cup triumph.

Talk about putting the cart before the horse; they were just asking for trouble. And they got it.

Scotland had been drawn in Group 4 against Peru, Iran and the Netherlands. Their first game took place in Córdoba against Peru on 3 June. They suffered a crushing 3-1 defeat and then had their star striker Willie Johnston sent home in disgrace after failing a drugs test. Four days later they faced a weak Iran team and only managed a 1-1 draw. Scotland now needed to beat their final group-stage opponents by three clear goals on 11 June in Mendoza to qualify for the second group stage. Unfortunately for them, their next opponents were the Dutch team, who had a starting line-up that featured seven World Cup finalists from 1974 in West Germany, including Johnny Rep and Johan Neeskens, so expectations weren't that high.

Predictably, Scotland battled through the opening stages of the game but it was no surprise to anyone when the Netherlands took the lead through a Rob Rensenbrink penalty after 34 minutes. However, Scotland refused to roll over; Kenny Dalglish pulled one back just before half-time, and the little midfielder Archie Gemmill scored after the break with another penalty. All of a sudden, Scotland were right back in it. They were winning 2-1 now and only needed two more goals to pull off what would be their greatest-ever victory.

Scotland's finest World Cup moment came in the 68th minute when Gemmill won the ball on the edge of the Dutch penalty area. He sprinted into the box, dribbled past three defenders and then thumped the ball into the back of the net. *The Scotsman* called it 'an extraordinary goal and an extraordinary moment'.

Could Scotland get another goal? A nation held its breath – but not for very long. The Dutch ran up the other end of the pitch and just 202 seconds later Rep hit a 30-yard worldie into the top-left corner of the Scotland goal. It was that simple.

Although the game ended with a 3-2 victory to Scotland, they'd failed to qualify for the next stage. While the Dutch went on to reach their second successive World Cup Final, the Scots jumped on the next flight home to Glasgow. Around 30,000 fans had waved them off a month earlier at Hampden Park but fewer than 100 of them turned up at Prestwick Airport to see them slink back into the country again.

At the time of writing, Scotland have played in the finals of a World Cup eight times, including five consecutive tournaments between 1974 and 1990. During the 1954 World Cup in Switzerland they failed to score a single goal and in every tournament they've never won more than just one match. It's no wonder they've failed to make it past the group stage in all eight appearances. Scotland have since been credited by *Guinness World Records* as the team with the most appearances without ever advancing to the knockout stage. Even Wales have managed it once!

THE ANGRY GOALKEEPER
1975

Manchester United goalkeeper Alex Stepney is surely the only player to dislocate his jaw by yelling at his own team-mates! He injured himself at the start of the second half of a Division One game away at Birmingham City on 18 August 1975 after berating his defenders, and then had to be subbed off. There were no other goalies sitting on the bench so United's centre-back Brian Greenhoff had to take his place between the posts.

But at least Alex injured himself in the line of duty. These guys did it a long way from the football pitch:

- Danish goalkeeper Michael Stensgaard dislocated his shoulder when he was setting up an ironing board at home soon after joining Liverpool in 1994. The injury became a recurring ailment requiring surgery and he never played a single first-team game for the club.
- Argentinian midfielder Éver Banega injured himself when he ran over his own foot at a petrol station after forgetting to apply the handbrake of his car.
- Dave Beasant, of Chelsea at the time, was making a sandwich in his kitchen at home when he dropped a big glass bottle of salad cream. The goalkeeper foolishly tried to stop it shattering on the floor with his bare foot, resulting in a severed tendon in his big toe and the end of his career at Stamford Bridge.
- American stopper Kasey Keller knocked out his two front teeth when he tried to remove his golf clubs from the boot of his car.
- Tottenham Hotspur and England midfielder Alan Mullery somehow managed to put his back out while brushing his teeth.

- Welsh international Darren Barnard was out for five months with a torn knee ligament after slipping on a wet kitchen floor.

- England goalkeeper David James had already earned the unfortunate nickname of 'Calamity James' at Liverpool after a series of well-reported blunders and didn't do himself any favours when he pulled a muscle in his back after reaching for the remote control while playing video games.

- Kevin-Prince Boateng of Ghana suffered a series of muscle injuries during his time playing for Italian giants AC Milan. After he was ruled out for another month with a thigh problem in 2012, his girlfriend seemed to offer an explanation for his appalling injury record during an interview with *Vanity Fair*, '[It's] because we have sex seven to ten times a week.'

FAIRY TALE FISTICUFFS
1998

The story of the big bad wolf and the three little pigs has been told many times but a modern reworking of the classic children's fairy tale was played out in a land far, far away called Ashton Gate during the half-time break in a First Division match between Bristol City and Wolverhampton Wanderers on 7 November 1998.

The three little pigs were at the game to promote a local double-glazing firm and at half-time they joined Bristol City's regular mascot City Cat and the Wolves mascot Wolfie for a children's penalty shoot-out competition in one of the goals. Unfortunately, there was a quarrel between the wolf and the pigs about sharing a ball; words were exchanged and, as the pigs pursued the wolf up the field, Wolfie turned around and threw a punch at the nearest pig and dislodged his head. The pig retaliated and the away fans in the crowd started chanting 'Come on, Wolfie!' believing that it was all part of the half-time show.

The two animals continued slugging it out with one of the pigs sustaining a split lip before City Cat and a few of the stewards intervened to drag them apart. The wolf blamed the pigs and the pigs blamed the wolf and both clubs issued official statements on the matter as the threat of police action loomed.

As it turned out, however, the police had better things to do with their time, the mascots escaped prosecution and the matter was soon forgotten about.

Wolfie wasn't the only mascot to find himself in a spot of bother with their club:

- Hercules the Lion – the Aston Villa mascot was sacked after grappling with Miss Aston Villa during the half-time break in the home match against Crystal Palace on 14 March 1998. Hercules grabbed her around the waist and tried to kiss her as thousands of fans looked on but the club didn't see the funny side of their mascot groping the local beauty queen. Despite Hercules protesting that it was just a bit of harmless fun and Miss Aston Villa seemingly taking it all in her stride, Gavin Lucas, the man inside Hercules, was sacked immediately after the incident.

- Cyril the Swan – Swansea City's mascot got his wings clipped after overstepping the mark. During his team's 3-0 FA Cup first-round win against Millwall on 13 November 1998, the 9ft-tall bird ran on to the pitch to join in with the celebrations after Martin Thomas scored their second goal. After dancing about and wrapping his wings around the goalscorer, he then ran back to the touchline. The Football Association of Wales were not amused, banning Cyril from the touchline during games and fining the club £1,000.

- Paisley Panda – the controversial St Mirren mascot was given the boot after he was seen pretending to use their opponents' shirt as toilet paper during the

Scottish First Division home game against Falkirk on 3 October 2003.

THREE YELLOW CARDS
2006

The 2006 World Cup Group F game between Croatia and Australia, which would decide one of the qualifying teams for the knockout stages, was a nasty, bad-tempered affair requiring English referee Graham Poll to issue nine yellow cards and three red cards.

Croatian defender Josip Šimunić was actually yellow-carded THREE times before finally being sent off.

The eventual 2-2 draw wasn't Poll's finest match having denied Australia a penalty in the 75th minute for an obvious handball by Stjepan Tomas and then allowing their 79th-minute equaliser to stand despite scorer Harry Kewell being in an offside position. But despite those two howlers, poor Graham Poll will always be remembered for the three yellow cards he mistakenly awarded to Šimunić.

Šimunić received his first yellow for a foul in the 61st minute and a second for another foul in the 90th, at which point he would have expected to have been dismissed. In fact, he'd already started walking towards the tunnel but then realised that Poll hadn't waved a red card at him and so he remained on the pitch and just carried on playing. Despite his unbelievable good fortune, Šimunić wasn't smart enough to just play out the remaining few minutes and then slink away to the dressing room afterwards unnoticed. Instead, in the 93rd minute, after the final whistle and when it was obvious that Croatia had failed to qualify for the knockout stages, he ran up to Poll, yelled in his face and angrily shoved him away, resulting in a third yellow card and then that elusive red.

Although none of the Australian players had noticed that Šimunić's 90th-minute booking should have resulted in a sending off and all the other match officials seemed equally as clueless, Poll very graciously took all the blame for the oversight after watching the DVD match highlights, 'I was the referee, it was my error and the buck stops with me.' It seems that he'd incorrectly noted down the name of the Australian number three, Craig Moore, for the second yellow-card offence, possibly because Šimunić was Australian-born and spoke English with an Australian accent.

Poll was sent home in disgrace and very wisely retired from officiating any more international matches.

If only Šimunić had done the decent thing and left the field on his own accord, Graham Poll might have had a shot of realising his stated dream of refereeing the World Cup Final. Well done, Josip!

BATTLEFIELD FOOTBALL
1914

On 28 June 1914, the heir presumptive to the throne of the Austro-Hungarian Empire, Franz Ferdinand, was assassinated in Sarajevo by a Serbian nationalist group. A month later, Austria-Hungary declared war on Serbia.

And then on various dates after that, everyone declared war on everyone else with Britain entering the fray on 4 August.

On 7 December, Pope Benedict XV begged both sides to consider a truce, asking 'that the guns may fall silent at least upon the night the angels sang'. The warring governments just ignored him of course, but the soldiers along the Western Front did not and took part in their own unofficial and impromptu ceasefires around Christmas. At first they just shouted greetings and sang carols to each other. Then they began climbing out of the trenches and walking into no man's land to shake hands, exchange food and souvenirs, drink beer and smoke cigars together. Prisoner swaps were agreed and arrangements made to recover the bodies of fallen comrades.

Some of the men also organised football matches. It was reported that kickabouts between the British and German soldiers took place on the frozen ground between the trenches in at least four or five different places along the frontline. Perhaps the most famous of these encounters was the match between an unknown regiment of Scottish soldiers and the German 133rd Royal Saxon Regiment, possibly because of a fictionalised account of the game published by the acclaimed English war poet Robert Graves and this detailed description of the match recounted by one of the German soldiers present, Johannes Niemann:

'The mist was slow to clear and suddenly my orderly threw himself into my dugout to say that both the German and Scottish soldiers had come out of their trenches and were fraternising along the front. I grabbed my binoculars and looking cautiously over the parapet saw the incredible sight of our soldiers exchanging cigarettes, schnapps and chocolate with the enemy. Later a Scottish soldier appeared with a football which seemed to come from nowhere and a few minutes later a real football match got under way.

'The Scots marked their goalmouth with their strange caps and we did the same with ours. It was far from easy to play on the frozen ground, but we continued, keeping rigorously to the rules, despite the fact that it only lasted an hour and that we had no referee. A great many of the passes went wide, but all the amateur footballers, although they must have been very tired, played with huge enthusiasm ... But after an hour's play, when our Commanding Officer heard about it, he sent an order that we must put a stop to it. A little later we drifted back to our trenches and the fraternisation ended.'

The match apparently ended in a 3-2 victory for the Germans.

Other known football games involved the Argyll and Sutherland Highlanders who played against an unidentified

German regiment, the Royal Field Artillery who faced off against 'Prussians and Hanovers' near Ypres in Belgium, and the Lancashire Fusiliers who played in a game near Le Touquet in France, in which they used a tin can as a ball.

It was accepted by all the soldiers that the truce was only temporary and the men duly returned to the trenches at dusk. Fighting broke out again the following day although it was reported from certain sectors of the battlefield that some of the unofficial ceasefires remained in place until the new year.

The British press printed reports of these battlefield truces with favourable editorials. The public reacted positively to the news but the British Army did not, and orders were quickly sent down the chain of command to the men in the trenches prohibiting any future such occurrences. By the following year, however, the frontline troops were no longer amenable to the idea of a ceasefire. The war had become increasingly brutal with the large-scale use of poison gas by German forces resulting in a devastating loss of life. The last thing any of the British forces wanted was another kickabout with the Hun.

WHITE BOOTS
1970

World Cup winner Alan Ball was the first player to wear a pair of non-black boots.

German sportswear company Hummel were looking to break into the UK market and signed up several players to wear their new white boots. First up was Everton captain Ball, who was to wear them during the FA Charity Shield against Chelsea on 8 August 1970, but, unfortunately, Hummel didn't have any white boots that suited him so they just got hold of a pair of the black Adidas boots he usually wore, spray-painted them white and stuck their own distinctive chevron logo on them.

Nobody was any the wiser and the following Monday morning the Hummel sales line was ringing off the hook with callers wanting to order the fancy new white boots they'd seen Alan Ball wearing.

THE ONE-DAY CHAMPIONSHIP
1898

The matches in the inaugural Italian championship were all played in the course of just one day.

The knockout tournament was organised by the recently formed Federazione Italiana Giuoco Calcio and featured just four teams, three from Turin and one from Genoa, with all the games being played at the Velodromo Umberto I in Turin on 8 May 1898.

The first semi-final kicked off at 9am and finished in a 1-0 win for Internazionale FC Torino over FBC Torinese, with Englishman Gordon Thomas Savage scoring the first goal in the history of the Campionato Italiano di Calcio (which would later become Serie A). The other semi-final kicked off at 11am and ended with Genoa Cricket & Football Club defeating Ginnastica Torino 2-1.

After a break for lunch, the two finalists assembled on the pitch at 3pm in front of around 100 spectators. The game finished 1-1 after 90 minutes with another Englishman, Norman Leaver, scoring Genoa's winning goal during the 20 minutes of extra time. Genoa were then crowned the first champions of Italy.

And that was that. All done in a matter of hours!

THE GOALKEEPER MORE HATED THAN ADOLF HITLER
1982

The 1982 World Cup semi-final between West Germany and France is widely regarded as one of the best matches of all time due to its drama, late goals and the excitement of the first ever World Cup penalty shoot-out. It had finished 1-1 at full time with each team then adding two more goals to make it 3-3 after 120 minutes.

The shoot-out began when Alain Giresse converted the first kick. France actually hit the back of the net with their first three penalties but the Germans could only score twice after Uli Stielike had his weak shot blocked by the French keeper Jean-Luc Ettori. As Stielike was the first player to miss a penalty in a World Cup shoot-out, he was also the first player to collapse on the ground with despair; the first to hold his head in his hands and the first to be consoled by his team-mates after wandering back to the centre circle.

The score was later tied again at 3-3 after Didier Six had his soft kick blocked by the German keeper Harald Schumacher. Both teams then successfully converted their last kicks and the shoot-out moved into sudden death. In the sixth and final round, Maxime Bossis watched with horror as Schumacher guessed right and dived to save his shot. Horst Hrubesch then stepped up to the spot. He kicked the ball low and hard into the goal, becoming the first player to decide a World Cup penalty shoot-out.

West Germany were through to the final against Italy.

Although France were devastated by the defeat, their defender Patrick Battiston had more reasons than most to remember the match after being involved in a nasty collision with Schumacher early in the second half. The substitute had only been on the pitch for five minutes when his captain Michel Platini played a beautiful through ball to him and he ran towards the German goal. Schumacher came sprinting out of his area but made no attempt to play the ball. As Battiston eased up in an attempt to lessen the impact of their impending collision, Schumacher appeared to run even faster, flying through the air and turning his hip and forearm into the Frenchman's face. He crashed into him and left poor Patrick lying unconscious on the ground. Seven minutes later, Battiston finally left the field on a stretcher with two missing teeth, three cracked ribs and a damaged vertebrae. Everyone expected the Dutch referee Charles Corver to show Schumacher a red card but he never even pulled out a yellow one! In fact, he didn't give a foul, believing that it had all been an unfortunate accident after the two players had challenged for a 50-50 ball. Platini thought his team-mate was dead when he was stretchered off the field; Battiston looked pale, had no pulse and was being kept alive with oxygen. His injuries were later described as being comparable with a car crash and it took him six months to make a full recovery.

The game was resumed with a goal kick. The fans at the ground booed and whistled every time Schumacher got near the ball after that. He might have saved the final shoot-out penalty but to anyone watching the game outside of West Germany he shouldn't have been on the field. It was probably the only time in history when the neutrals watching the game were cheering for France!

A short time after the game, Harald Schumacher famously beat Adolf Hitler into second place as the most hated man in the world in a French newspaper poll.

THE UNFRIENDLY FRIENDLY MATCH
2019

Somebody in the Mexican judicial system thought it was a good idea to arrange a New Year's Eve match between members of the Gulf and Los Zetas drug cartels at a prison in Cieneguillas, Mexico. Family members, including children, were invited to attend with the match kicking off in the early afternoon. It was supposed to be a great PR opportunity for the prison and a fun occasion for the inmates and their families, but things didn't quite work out that way.

The game was abandoned almost as soon as it started when a fight broke out between the players. The fight led to a three-hour riot – and the three-hour riot led to the deaths of 16 inmates.

The authorities reported that the victims had been shot, stabbed or bludgeoned to death with weapons they believed had been brought into the prison by the families. The local media also reported that the authorities had foiled a prison break during the riot too.

Maybe it wasn't such a good idea after all.

THE ALTERNATIVE WORLD CUP FINAL
2002

The 'Alternative World Cup Final' featured the Asian minnows of Bhutan and the tiny Caribbean islanders of Montserrat, the lowest-placed teams in the FIFA World Rankings (or the two worst teams in the world), and was played on the same day a few hours before the two best teams in the world, Germany and Brazil, met in the 2002 World Cup Final in Yokohama.

The game was organised by two Dutch advertising agency partners, Johan Kramer and Matthijs de Jongh, and filmed for a documentary to be released in 2003, *The Other Final*, with the intention of showing how football crossed all boundaries as a means of bringing people together and how the sport shouldn't always be focused on competition and success.

The game was recognised by FIFA as an official international and was played in front of 15,000 fans, many of whom were schoolchildren dressed in the yellow/orange colours of Bhutan or the green outfits of Montserrat. After an hour-long dance routine showcasing the Buddhist traditions of the host country, English referee Steve Bennett blew for the kick off.

Although Montserrat began well, it was Bhutan who took an early lead after only four minutes with a goal from Wangay Dorji. Bhutan were the better team in the first half but were unable to convert their chances into goals and the scoreline remained unchanged at the interval. It wasn't until the 60th minute that Dorji added another, then their veteran striker Dinesh Chhetri made it 3-0 after 76 minutes, and finally Dorji popped up again two minutes later to complete his hat-trick and seal a decisive 4-0 victory for the home team.

Montserrat had struggled with the rarefied atmosphere as the match was played in a stadium 2,300m above sea level. They had eight of their players out with altitude sickness and were forced to field an understrength team. They'd only arrived in the country on the Monday before Sunday's big game and were clearly at a disadvantage; they rarely troubled the Bhutan keeper, having just one shot on target in the whole game, and their players tired long before the end.

Bhutan had played their first international game in 1982 and this was their first-ever victory. But despite the emphatic scoreline, the teams shared the trophy and then both sets of players sat down together in front of the TV later in the day to watch the 'real' World Cup Final from Japan.

PENALTY CARDS
1970

Englishman Ken Aston was one of the games toughest and most respected referees; he also served on the FIFA Referees Committee between 1966 and 1972, and was appointed as the FIFA representative in charge of overseeing all the referees at the 1966 World Cup.

Ken was busy doing his overseeing thing at Wembley during the quarter-final between England and Argentina on 23 July 1966 when the Argentinian captain Antonio Rattín became the first-ever player to be booked and then sent off in a World Cup finals match.

Rattín had been cautioned by West German referee Rudolf Kreitlein for a foul on Bobby Charlton in the 33rd minute and, just two minutes later, after Luis Artime was booked for not retreating ten yards for an England free kick, he started yelling like a madman and getting in Mr Kreitlein's face, so he was cautioned again, this time for 'violence of the tongue', before being ordered off the field. Rattín refused to walk and the game was halted as he and his manager Juan Carlos Lorenzo argued with Mr Kreitlein. Ken Aston then arrived on the scene in an effort to try and calm the situation but the two volatile Argentinians just started arguing with him instead. Eventually, after an eight-minute delay, Rattín seemed to accept his fate, although even after the game had restarted he could still be seen remonstrating with Aston on the touchline!

Just 20 seconds after the restart, Geoff Hurst went in heavily on Roberto Ferreiro. The Argentinian right-back went down hard, the crowd booed his theatrics, and Hurst unbelievably escaped a booking, fuelling the South Americans' pre-match paranoia that Mr Kreitlein and the England team were in cahoots to knock them out of the competition, and prompting Rattín to remark after the match, 'It was clear that the referee played with an England shirt on.'

Things went from bad to worse when Hurst scored the only goal of the game late in the second half and the Argentinians had their appeals for offside dismissed. Their protests continued after the final whistle when they surrounded Mr Kreitlein, with Roberto Ferreiro getting so carried away that he ripped the official's shirt in all the commotion. England manager Alf Ramsey refused to allow his players to swap shirts with their opponents at full time and labelled them 'animals' in the post-match press conference.

To this day the Argentinians still refer to this match as *El Robo del Siglo* (The Robbery of the Century) because they felt cheated out of a result.

The following morning, Ken Aston read in a newspaper that Bobby Charlton and his brother Jack Charlton had both been booked during the game. But he wasn't aware of these bookings and, as it turned out, neither were the players or anyone else in the England camp. Aston realised immediately that another way had to be found to better inform the players and the spectators what was happening on the pitch.

Sometime later, while driving in his car down Kensington High Street in London, Aston was still mulling over the problem when he stopped at a set of traffic lights. As he sat there watching the lights change, he suddenly thought about using a colour-coded system but more specifically amber (eventually yellow) and red cards as a way of getting around the language barrier and demonstrating to the crowds when a player had been booked or sent off. On arriving home, he explained the concept to his wife and she made him some pocket-sized yellow and red cards so he could easily demonstrate how his system might work for when he presented his idea to the footballing authorities.

The cards were first trialled during the 1970 FIFA World Cup in Mexico when five players were shown yellow cards for the first time. However, it wasn't until four years later in West Germany that the first red card was handed out. The Chilean forward Carlos Caszely was the first player to have one waved at him after hacking down German defender Berti Vogts in the 67th minute of their 1-0 defeat to West Germany on 14 June.

These language-neutral coloured cards have since been adopted by the governing bodies of many other sports, including fencing, water polo, field hockey and volleyball.

HAT-TRICK OF MISSED PENALTIES 1999

On 4 July 1999, Martín Palermo became the first player to miss three penalties in an international match.

With only five minutes gone in Argentina's 3-0 Copa América group-stage defeat to Colombia, the ball was played into the Colombian penalty area where defender Alexander Viveros panicked and punched it clear, resulting in *la Albiceleste* being awarded a penalty. Palermo collected the ball, stepped up to the spot, and blasted it against the crossbar.

Five minutes later it was Colombia's turn to be awarded a penalty. Iván Córdoba made no mistake from the spot and they went into the half-time break with a 1-0 lead. Two minutes after the restart they had the chance to go 2-0 up after winning another penalty but a limp shot from Hámilton Ricard was easily saved by Argentinian goalkeeper Germán Burgos.

After 69 minutes, the Argentinian midfielder Javier Zanetti elbowed Rubiel Quintana in the face and was sent off but, despite their one-man advantage, Colombia sat back and allowed Argentina to press forward. Then, 15 minutes from time, Viveros gave away another penalty after handling the ball in the area again. This guy really should have been a volleyball player! Determined to make amends for his earlier miss, Palermo wrestled the ball away from his team-mates and waited by the penalty spot ready to take the kick. The referee blew his whistle and then the striker booted the ball high over the crossbar and into the stands.

Argentina manager Marcelo Bielsa was losing his shit. He couldn't believe what he was watching, so the referee put him out of his misery by waving a red card at him so he didn't have to watch any more. Which was nice of him.

Colombia won a corner late in the second half and Palermo took up his position in the box ready to defend the near post. The ball fell at his feet, but as he tried to hoof it clear, he missed his kick, and substitute Edwin Congo pounced on the ball to double Colombia's lead. Minutes from time, another substitute, Johnnier Montaño, made it 3-0.

At this point Palermo had missed two penalties and given away a goal so it was difficult to imagine how things could get any worse for him, especially as the match had almost ended.

With 90 minutes already on the clock, he intercepted a slack square pass, cut inside Córdoba and ran towards the last defender and the goal. But Córdoba recovered and gave chase, making contact with him inside the box. The challenge was fairly innocuous but Palermo tumbled to the ground, rolled over and then looked up expectantly at the referee.

For a fifth time, the official had no hesitation in awarding a penalty and, for the third time, Palermo had no hesitation in grabbing the ball and walking towards the spot. This time, at least he did hit the target, but his shot was easily parried away by goalkeeper Miguel Calero and the game finished in a 3-0 defeat for Argentina.

The referee had awarded five penalties in this match, three of them to Argentina. Martín Palermo had taken all three – and missed each one. No wonder the poor guy had to wait another ten years to play for his country again.

A FOOTBALLING CHRISTMAS MIRACLE
1957

Huddersfield Town were the first team to score six goals in a professional match in England and still lose, after their opponents staged one of the most remarkable comebacks ever seen.

After only 17 minutes in the Division Two game away to Charlton Athletic on 21 December 1957, the Charlton captain Derek Ufton left the field and was rushed to hospital with a dislocated shoulder, forcing his team to play on with only ten men for the rest of the game as no substitutes were allowed at that time.

At half-time Charlton were 2-0 down. Their manager Jimmy Trotter then decided to play his right-winger Johnny Summers in the centre-forward role, convinced that it was their best chance of getting a few goals, and asked the other players to feed him the ball as often as possible. The plan seemed like it might have had some merit because Summers scored within two minutes of the restart. However, their good fortune didn't last for very long as Huddersfield then took control of the game and scored another three goals. With only half an hour to play in the second half they were 5-1 up and seemingly coasting to a comfortable win with many of the home fans leaving the ground early rather than see it out to the end.

But then the game turned.

After 63 minutes, Summers passed to another Johnny, Johnny Ryan, who made it 5-2; Summers scored his second goal a minute later, and then completed his hat-trick after 73 minutes.

By now Charlton were only 5-4 down and what remained of the home crowd finally began cheering on their team. After 78 minutes Summers scored his fourth goal, and three minutes later with only nine minutes left to play, he scored a fifth, taking his team into the lead for the first time. Charlton had scored five goals in 18 minutes with the last three by Summers coming in the space of just eight minutes.

Charlton's joy was short-lived, however. Just five minutes later, Stan Howard equalised for Huddersfield after his shot was deflected off Charlton defender John Hewie and into his own goal to make it 6-6. But Charlton weren't done yet and in the last minute Johnny Ryan collected the ball from a throw-in and ran up the field; Huddersfield defender Tony Conwell moved in for the tackle but lost his footing on the muddy pitch, and Ryan ran around him towards the goal. Huddersfield keeper Sandy Kennon managed to get a hand to his shot but only succeeded in deflecting it into the net.

The referee blew the full-time whistle moments later with Charlton securing a famous 7-6 victory.

Johnny Summers had scored five goals and engineered one of the most remarkable comebacks in football history. Cries of 'We want Summers!' echoed around The Valley and then the crowd invaded the pitch to carry Summers and the other Charlton players shoulder-high around the ground.

THE COIN TOSS HAT-TRICK
1958

Hearts pair Willie Bauld and Jimmy Murray both appeared to head the ball into the net after 44 minutes for their team's third goal of the Scottish Division One match at home to Aberdeen on 6 December 1958.

As they'd both claimed a touch and had each scored another two goals during the 5-1 win, it was important to decide which of them should also be awarded the hat-trick, so in the dressing room after the final whistle they tossed a coin to resolve the issue. Bauld must have called it right because he was awarded the three goals and presumably went home with the match ball too.

Although, maybe not. They were pretty strict about just giving away the balls back then.

WHEN IT ALL WENT WRONG FOR LIVERPOOL
1989

Liverpool 0 Arsenal 2, 26 May 1989 at Anfield – the most dramatic title-winning match ever played in the history of English football.

The 1988/89 Division One title race was the closest in the history of the English game. Before the last match of the season, Liverpool were top with 76 points and a goal difference of +39 while Arsenal were in second with 73 points and a goal difference of +35.

Liverpool just needed to win, draw, or lose by only one goal to be crowned champions. Arsenal had the much more difficult task; they had to travel away from home and win by two clear goals – drawing level on points (76), adjusting the goal difference for both teams to +37 but awarding them the title because of their superior number of goals scored. Liverpool hadn't lost by two or more goals at Anfield in three years and Arsenal hadn't won there in 14 years. Liverpool were on a roll, having just won the FA Cup after beating their Merseyside rivals Everton, and were confident of adding 'The Lady' – so known because of the statuette on top of the trophy – to their collection of trophies for that season.

The home side were the overwhelming favourites with the bookies to win the title; only a fool would have bet against them.

It was a fairly uneventful first half as both teams seemed to cancel each other out. Arsenal fielded a defensive formation to stifle their opponents' quick-passing game and only counterattacked with some uninspiring long balls, which were easily picked off by the Liverpool defenders. Neither side built up any momentum or looked like scoring.

Then, seven minutes into the second half, Arsenal broke the deadlock when Alan Smith scored with a header from an indirect free kick taken by Nigel Winterburn. As the ball hit the net, the linesman raised his flag – and then quickly lowered it again. The Liverpool players had spotted the raised flag and appealed to the referee to rule out the goal. They weren't exactly sure why it should be ruled out; some of the players were appealing for offside while others were adamant that Smith had not actually touched the ball (with the goal being scored directly and not indirectly from the free kick).

After consulting with his linesman, the referee finally allowed the goal to stand. Arsenal then adopted a more attacking approach, looking for that all-important second goal.

Liverpool appeared very vulnerable and continually surrendered possession as they struggled to cope with the Arsenal attacks. But as full time approached, the scoreline remained 1-0 to Arsenal, meaning that Liverpool would still win the title. TV cameras picked up the Liverpool midfielder Steve McMahon telling his team-mates that there was only one minute remaining as they started wasting time and passing the ball back and forth to their goalkeeper Bruce Grobbelaar. Then, in the second minute of stoppage time, Arsenal launched their final attack, which began with goalkeeper John Lukic bowling the ball out of defence and ended with midfielder Michael Thomas racing into the penalty area and slipping it past the advancing Grobbelaar to score their crucial second goal.

Only 38 seconds later the referee blew his whistle for full time and the distraught Liverpool players slumped to the ground. Arsenal had won the title with a last-minute stoppage-time goal, denying the Reds the chance to complete their second league and cup double – and it all happened in front of the hugely partisan Anfield crowd and an estimated TV audience of around 12 million people.

	P	W	D	L	GF	GA	GD	Pts
Arsenal	38	22	10	6	73	36	37	76
Liverpool	38	22	10	6	65	28	37	76

It was the most dramatic and unbelievable conclusion to a league season ever played in England. The *Daily Mail* reported, 'Never in the history of English football has the championship been won so late, so improbably, so narrowly or with such glory.'

This match also formed the backdrop for the climax to the 1997 film *Fever Pitch*.

THE TOURNAMENT WITHOUT A FINAL
1950

The 1950 World Cup in Brazil remains the first and only World Cup NOT to be decided by a one-match final.

The new format was proposed by the organisers as a way of increasing the number of games and maximising ticket sales. The 13 competing teams were divided into four groups with the winners progressing to another round of group-stage matches to determine the eventual winner. Whereas the traditional knockout format used in previous tournaments would have resulted in only 16 matches being staged, the new format guaranteed 30 games.

The final group of teams featured Brazil, Spain, Sweden and Uruguay with fixtures played between 9 and 16 July.

Uruguay v Brazil on 16 July at the Estádio do Maracanã in Rio de Janeiro was the last game of the final group stage and is often regarded as the *de facto* final. Brazil led Uruguay by one point going into the match and just needed to avoid defeat to claim the title of world champions. They'd won their previous two games against Spain and Sweden by playing attractive, attacking football whereas Uruguay had struggled, managing just a draw against Spain and a narrow victory over the Swedes. There was such a mood of optimism that the Brazilian newspapers *Gazeta Esportiva* and *O Mundo* were proclaiming victory long before the big game.

O Mundo even printed the Brazilian team line-up on its front cover alongside the headline 'Here are the World Champions', which didn't go down too well with the Uruguayan captain Obdulio Varela. He bought 20 copies, scattered them across a bathroom floor in the hotel where the team were staying and wrote on the mirror 'Trample and urinate on these newspapers', before ordering his team-mates to visit the bathroom and follow his instructions.

On the day of the match, many thousands of fans turned out in the streets of Rio de Janeiro early in the morning to start celebrating the coronation – even though kick off was still a few hours away. In a pre-match speech to the crowds, the mayor of the city, Angelo Mendes de Moraes, declared Brazil the winners, 'You, players, who in less than a few hours will be hailed as champions by millions of compatriots! You, who have no rivals in the entire hemisphere! You, who will overcome any other competitor! You, who I already salute as victors!'

Talk about setting yourself up for a fall.

The game holds the record for the most spectators at any World Cup fixture with *Guinness World Records* claiming an official attendance of 173,850, although it's believed that the real number might have been closer to 200,000.

Brazil took the lead shortly after half-time with a goal from Friaça, with Juan Alberto Schiaffino equalising after 66 minutes and Alcides Ghiggia getting the winning goal for Uruguay with only 11 minutes remaining. As he ran away to celebrate, the mainly Brazilian crowd fell silent with winger Ghiggia later joking, 'Only three people have managed to silence the Maracanã: the Pope, Frank Sinatra, and me.'

The impossible had just happened: Uruguay were the new champions of the world after a result considered one of the biggest upsets in the history of world football.

After the final whistle, the Uruguayan players cried with tears of joy and disbelief and the Brazilian crowd openly wept tears of despair. They were inconsolable with grief and so were the fans in the streets and those crowded into the bars and restaurants all across Brazil. Two people died of a heart attack inside the stadium, such was the shock at what they'd just witnessed, and there were even reports from around the country of people taking their own lives.

Brazil had played in an all-white strip that day and many people in the country thought it was unpatriotic and even suggested that it had contributed to their historic loss. In 1953 the *Correio da Manhã* newspaper held a competition to design a new strip that incorporated the colours of the Brazilian flag; it was won by the 19-year-old writer/illustrator Aldyr Schlee who suggested using yellow shirts with a green trim, blue shorts and white socks. The newly designed kit was first worn against Chile in 1954 and has since become the most iconic uniform in world football. Ironically, Mr Schlee was born in a town near the Uruguayan border and had always supported Uruguay.

To this day Brazil have never again played in an all-white kit.

THE GOALKEEPER SENT OFF FOR HANDLING THE BALL IN THE PENALTY AREA
2001

In the 90th minute of a Bundesliga game between Hansa Rostock and Bayern Munich on 3 March 2001, with Bayern trailing 3-2 , they were awarded a corner, so goalkeeper Oliver Kahn ran the full length of the pitch to join his team-mates in the opposition penalty area. As the ball was swung in, he jumped in the air and punched it into the net, earning an immediate red card. He later joked, 'I thought the goalkeeper was allowed to use his hands in the box.'

THAT MARY POPPINS-INSPIRED HEADLINE
2000

On 8 February 2000, Inverness Caledonian Thistle won 3-1 at Celtic in the third round of the Scottish Cup. This famous *Sun Sport* headline appeared with a match report on one of the biggest upsets in the history of the competition: 'SUPER CALEY GO BALLISTIC, CELTIC ARE ATROCIOUS'. How clever is that?

THE ONE-KICK APPEARANCE
1999

When coming on at the end of Manchester United's 2-1 Premier League win at Arsenal on 22 August 1999, goalkeeper Nick Culkin made the shortest debut in Premier League history.

Raimond van der Gouw was kicked in the face towards the end of injury time in the second half and after a long delay for treatment, he was eventually led off the field as the clock ticked past 100 minutes.

Meanwhile, Culkin had run on to the pitch to make his debut. As soon as he took the resulting free kick, the referee blew his whistle for full time – and Culkin never played for United ever again. His first and final match for the club had lasted only a couple of seconds, or just as long as it had taken him to kick that ball.

MASCOT CAUGHT OFFSIDE
2000

When Oldham Athletic hosted Peterborough United on 26 August 2000 in the Second Division, the linesman appeared to flag home striker Carlo Corazzin offside on the opposite side of the pitch – but as there were three Peterborough defenders between Corazzin and the goal, his decision left everyone in the ground a little baffled. Not least the referee. After a brief consultation with his maverick linesman, it turned out that he'd raised his flag after mistaking Oldham mascot Chaddy the Owl as a player standing in an offside position.

Chaddy had been loitering on the touchline further up the field and he was wearing a replica shirt, so it's understandable how the linesman might have been a little confused. Except that Chaddy was also wearing a big, oversized, furry owl's head – and none of the Oldham players looked particularly furry or birdlike in appearance, so maybe it wasn't quite so understandable after all.

The referee had no choice but to show Chaddy a red card.

Oldham suffered a 4-1 home defeat that day with many in the crowd blaming Chaddy's early touchline ban for such a poor performance.

FAILED TRICKERY
2011

Manchester City were taking part in the pre-season, World Football Challenge tournament featuring nine of the top European, Mexican, US and Canadian teams, and as part of their three-game schedule they met LA Galaxy in Carson, California, on 24 July 2011.

City attacked from the start and after only 18 minutes Micah Richards was flattened in the box and his team-mate Mario Balotelli scored from the spot. Then, in the 28th minute, Balotelli suddenly found himself alone in the LA Galaxy penalty area with only their goalkeeper Josh Saunders to beat, but instead of attempting a conventional shot that would have almost certainly found the back of the net to give City a 2-0 lead, he stopped dead, turned around and tried to back-heel the ball over the line. It was a bold move and it would have been a goal that everyone would have remembered for a very long time if it had come off. But it didn't, the ball went wide, and Balotelli suddenly looked a fool for squandering such an easy goalscoring opportunity. Not only did he get a mouthful of abuse from his striking partner Edin Džeko, but he also incurred the wrath of his manager Roberto Mancini.

Despite Balotelli having already scored the earlier penalty, Mancini was so angry at the Italian's obvious lack of discipline that he took the decision to sub him and four minutes later James Milner took his place on the field. Once on the touchline, Balotelli was ordered straight to the dressing room but he just looked at his manager in disbelief and frustration, did that pinched fingers hand gesture that all Italians seem so fond of before strutting away to sit down on the far side of the bench and start sulking like a big baby.

LA Galaxy equalised in the 53rd minute with a long-range shot from Mike Magee and the game finished in a 1-1 draw with City eventually winning 7-6 in a penalty shoot-out.

Balotelli was a talented footballer who never quite lived up to his early promise. He played for some of the best teams in Europe, including Inter Milan, Manchester City, Liverpool, AC Milan and Marseille, but ultimately became more talked about for his undisciplined and arrogant behaviour on the pitch and his eccentric lifestyle off it.

José Mourinho was his manager at Inter in 2009 and once recounted this story about the 19-year-old striker, 'We went to [Russian club Rubin] Kazan in the Champions League. In that match, all my strikers were injured. No [Diego] Milito, no [Samuel] Eto'o, I was really in trouble and Mario was the only one. Mario gets a yellow card in minute 42. So when I go to the dressing room at half-time, I spend 14 minutes of the 15 speaking only to Mario. I said, "Mario, I cannot change you. I cannot make a change. I don't have a striker on the bench. Don't touch anybody. Play only with the ball. When we lose the ball, no reaction. If somebody provokes you, no reaction. If the referee makes a mistake, no reaction. Mario, please." Minute 46, red card!'

THE FIRST TELEVISED WORLD CUP
1954

The 1954 World Cup in Switzerland established the appeal of football for a mass TV audience.

The European Broadcasting Union was established in 1950 and by 1954 a system of transmitters had been set up around Europe allowing for the Continental Television Exchange (Eurovision) to broadcast live TV pictures across the region. The first pan-European broadcasts were a collection of very dull shows broadcast in mid-1954 which included screenings from a Swiss flower festival, a Danish agricultural show and a German holiday camp. The first Eurovision show was the hour-long *From Switzerland: Fete des Narcisses* (Narcissus Flower Festival) broadcast by the BBC on 6 June 1954 with segments featuring choirs, singers, brass bands, yodellers and no doubt some flowers too.

Mercifully, the schedule also included various matches from the World Cup.

Yugoslavia v France in Group 1, at the Stade Olympique de la Pontaise in Lausanne on 16 June, was the first live World Cup match ever shown on TV.

The BBC only had one commentator covering the entire tournament. Sometimes the first halves were deemed too unimportant to show, and only one semi-final was broadcast, with highlights of the other one being replaced in the schedules by that Danish agricultural show. In total, the BBC transmitted eight matches but had no say in which of them they were allowed to show. On one occasion Hungary v Germany was broadcast instead of England v Switzerland. Viewers only got to see the highlights of that match ... three days later.

THE BATTLE OF OLD TRAFFORD
2003

Manchester United v Arsenal on 21 September 2003 was an ill-tempered Premier League game characterised by a high number of fouls and yellow cards, player fights, a sending off for Arsenal's hardman midfielder Patrick Vieira and a controversial stoppage-time penalty miss from the home side.

The Gunners' Martin Keown was adjudged to have brought down Diego Forlán in the box after trying to head away a cross in the last minute and the referee duly awarded a penalty. Ruud van Nistelrooy stepped up to take it, despite having missed his last two spot kicks, with the Arsenal goalkeeper Jens Lehmann doing everything possible to distract him by jumping up and down and waving his arms in the air. His gamesmanship seemed to pay off because the Dutchman then smashed his shot against the bar and could only stand and watch as the ball bounced back into play.

The Arsenal players had blamed him for getting Vieira sent off after his apparent overreaction to a retaliatory kick from the Frenchman and now it seemed like that particular injustice had finally been righted.

The game ended a minute later with yet another scuffle, resulting in the referee handing out yet more cards. Six Arsenal players and two from Manchester United were later fined and/or banned, and Arsenal themselves received a fine from the FA for 'failing to ensure the proper behaviour of their players'.

If Van Nistelrooy hadn't missed that penalty, Arsenal would have almost certainly lost the game. As it happened, they became the first invincible Premier League team after completing the 2003/04 season without a single defeat with a record of 26 wins and 12 draws.

And to this day the Dutchman still likes to take the credit for that record.

AN UNFORTUNATE CHOICE OF WORDS
1996

Tony Adams spent his entire playing career at Arsenal, making 672 appearances between 1983 and 2003, and winning four Division One/Premier League titles, three FA Cups, two League Cups and one UEFA Cup Winners' Cup.

He was made captain at 21 years old and led the team for 14 years until his retirement. He was a true servant of the club and is now considered one of their greatest players.

Tony also had a chronic drink problem for most of that time too. He battled alcoholism for 12 long years through the late 1980s and early 1990s. He often played when he was hungover, and sometimes when he was drunk; he even did some jail time for a drink-driving offence in 1990, and went on a 44-day bender after captaining England to a defeat against Germany in Euro 96.

The culture of the club at that time did him no favours. Some of the players had formed the infamous 'Tuesday Club' with the aim of organising regular team-bonding exercises (presumably on a Tuesday) but in reality they just met up to get pissed. Their drunken antics occasionally made the headlines, most notably when Ray Parlour was arrested for assault in 1995 on a club tour to Hong Kong after throwing prawn crackers at a taxi driver and then giving him a bit of a slap.

But then in 1996, Adams turned his life around. The bottles went down the sink and he started attending AA meetings. His team-mate Ian Wright had nothing but praise for him when he announced his newfound sobriety, 'It took a lot of bottle for Tony to own up.'

SEX DOLLS IN THE STADIUM
2020

When FC Seoul and Gwangju met in a K League 1 match on 17 May 2020, the fans were all dressed in their team colours; they were all socially distanced and wearing masks in accordance with the local anti-COVID regulations, and they remained silent and seated throughout the game.

And they were all sex dolls.

FC Seoul were fined ₩100m by the Korean Football Association for filling their stadium with adult toys during the spectator-free game after claiming that their actions had caused deep concern among families and female fans when watching the match online.

The club had ordered 30 dummies from a company making mannequins and sex dolls and had received the wrong shipment. They apologised for the *faux pas* but put all the blame on their supplier. According to the authorities, however, FC Seoul had ample time to realise the true nature of the dolls from when they were delivered until kick off time and whacked them with that huge fine.

* * *

Things were a bit different in the Netherlands. The Eredivisie game between SC Heerenveen and FC Emmen on 24 October 2020 was held behind closed doors due to the strict COVID-19 restrictions in place at the time. But instead of filling the seats of the Abe Lenstra Stadion with sex dolls, 15,000 teddy bears were kitted out in the home club's shirt and placed around the ground, setting a new world record for the most teddy bears in a stadium at one time. Who knew there was even a record for that? The Heerenveen fans were later encouraged to buy the bears to raise money for a local child cancer research charity. All 15,000 of them were sold within 24 hours, raising more than €230,000 for the charity.

PLAYING UNDER AN UMBRELLA
1894

Aston Villa's 5-0 Division One win over Sheffield United on 12 November 1894 was played in the freezing rain, and their players did whatever they could to protect themselves from the adverse weather conditions. They occasionally wandered off the pitch for a hot drink; Jack Devey wore an overcoat, and Charlie Athersmith borrowed an umbrella from someone in the crowd to keep himself dry as he ran up and down the right wing.

The Sheffield United players weren't quite so resourceful. There were only six of them left on the field by the end of the game and their goalkeeper William Foulke subsequently needed treatment for frostbite.

THE ABANDONED FINAL
1920

Fifteen teams entered the 1920 Olympic Games football tournament, which began with the first round of games on 28 August and ended five days later with a gold medal final between Belgium and Czechoslovakia.

The match was played in a fairly hostile environment thanks largely to the Belgian press who, before the match, had unfairly portrayed their opponents as first world war aggressors. Much to the delight of the 35,000 partisan Belgian supporters inside the stadium, Robert Coppée scored with a penalty after only six minutes and then Henri Larnoe made it 2-0 after 30 minutes. Things weren't going too well for the Czechs and then they had their left-back Karel Steiner dismissed for violent conduct, at which point captain Karel Pešek led his team off the field in protest. English referee John Lewis requested their return but they refused and Belgium were immediately declared the gold medal winners. In the mayhem that followed, the home crowd, including a large contingent of rowdy Belgian soldiers, invaded the pitch, ripped up a few Czech flags and indulged in a bit of fisticuffs with anyone who looked even slightly eastern European.

Czechoslovakia lodged a protest with the International Olympic Committee seeking a cancellation of the match. In their letter of complaint they claimed that both goals should have been disallowed and accused the referee and his linesmen of not acting impartially after making many biased and/or incorrect decisions which appeared to favour their opponents. They also complained about all those Belgian soldiers in the crowd, claiming their presence around the pitch had been 'provocative and menacing' and had put them off their game. The Czechs then refused to take part in any further matches until they'd received an apology from those nasty soldiers, who they also blamed for initiating the attacks on their flag.

However, it didn't matter two hoots what they wanted or didn't want because their appeal was immediately rejected by the IOC; Belgium were formally declared the winners, and the Czech team were barred from taking part in the silver/bronze medal series of matches.

The history books tell us that it was the only time when a major international football tournament final has been abandoned. Apparently that Intercalated Games match of 1906 doesn't count.

SHARING THE BLAME
1954

Leicester City pair Stanley Milburn and Jack Froggatt are the only players ever to have scored a joint own goal.

They both attempted to clear the ball during Leicester's 3-1 Division One defeat at Chelsea on 18 December 1954, but ended up booting it into their own net instead. Both players then took the blame as they'd kicked the ball at the same time and it couldn't be proved who'd actually had the last touch.

THE TWO-TEAM LEAGUE
1950s

The Isles of Scilly Football League is the world's smallest football league and consists of only two clubs, the Woolpack Wanderers and the Garrison Gunners, who play each other 18 times during a season for the league title, once in the final of the Wholesalers Cup, twice in the two-legged final of the Foredeck Cup and once in a pre-season exhibition game for charity. In total they play each other on the same pitch at the same time every Sunday morning 22 times a season.

The Isles of Scilly is the only place in the world where the football teams are guaranteed at least a runners-up spot in the league and an appearance in two cup finals every year.

The league originally consisted of four teams but by the 1950s an ageing and dwindling population meant only two on the main island of St Mary's survived. They were originally called the Rangers and the Rovers but changed their names in 1984.

It may seem a little predictable but the teams change players every year. Before the start of each new season, the two elected captains follow that age-old school playground tradition of taking it in turns to pick a player for their team. However, the order of selection is kept a secret. With only so many eligible players to choose from, the league organisers can't afford to risk offending anyone. Players can sometimes change teams before a match too. If one team turns up without enough players, one-game loans are quickly arranged to even up the sides.

Being a small island community, it can mean some players being called away mid-match to deal with other issues, especially policemen or firemen who may be playing while on call. On one occasion a farmer had to abandon a game at half-time because he'd received a message that all his cows had escaped!

PLAYER SHOT DEAD AFTER SCORING AN OWN GOAL
1994

Defender Andrés Escobar was nicknamed *El Caballero del Futbol*, the gentleman of football; a quiet and disciplined player known for his calmness and clean style of play on the pitch, and the captain and much-loved leader of the Colombian national side who were expected to do well at the 1994 World Cup in the USA.

Colombia had been drawn in Group A with the hosts, along with Romania and Switzerland. However, they got off to a bad start in their first game on 18 June against Romania after losing 3-1 and then suffered another embarrassing loss against the USA four days later. Although they managed to beat Switzerland 2-0, they still finished bottom of the group and failed to qualify for the knockout stage.

Escobar's fatal own goal came after only 35 minutes in the 2-1 defeat to the USA on 22 June at the Rose Bowl in Pasadena, after he'd tried to block a cross from John Harkes and inadvertently deflected the ball past his own hopelessly wrong-footed goalkeeper to give their opponents a shock 1-0 lead.

Ten days after that match, on 2 July, Escobar was back at home in Medellín and enjoying a night out at a local nightclub with his mates. A group of three or four men began taking the piss out of him about that own goal, so he left and returned to his car; they followed him outside to continue the argument, and then at least one of them produced a handgun and shot him six times, before fleeing the scene and leaving poor Andrés to bleed out. An ambulance was called to the scene but he was declared DOA at the hospital 30 minutes later.

At the time, his murder was widely believed to be a revenge killing by local gangsters for the own goal, after they'd incurred heavy losses betting on the game, although some people involved in the incident have since claimed that Escobar was just in the wrong place at the wrong time.

The grumpy ex-player and TV pundit Alan Hansen was commentating on the game between Argentina and Romania the day after the shooting. After watching some sloppy defensive play by one of the Argentinian players he blurted out, 'The Argentine defender warrants shooting for a mistake like that.' Although it was just an off-the-cuff remark, his timing couldn't have been worse and the BBC was forced to issue an apology.

THE SHIRTLESS STRIKER
2002

Uruguayan striker Diego Forlán was signed by Manchester United in January 2002 and then failed to score a single goal in 23 Premier League matches.

It was one of the most famous goal droughts in British football history and he was consequently dubbed 'Diego Forlorn' by the press. After waiting some eight months, he finally got his maiden goal; a late equaliser in the 1-1 draw with Aston Villa on 26 October 2002. Fortunately for him, he didn't have to wait quite so long for his second. After coming on as a late second-half substitute against Southampton a week later, he scored, having been on the pitch for only six minutes, after picking up the ball on the edge of the box and firing a dipping shot past goalkeeper Antti Niemi.

Overcome with relief and emotion, Forlán whipped off his shirt and ran around the pitch celebrating what would turn out to be the match-winning goal. However, by the restart, he still hadn't put his shirt back on. The challenge of getting re-dressed in time had seemingly proved a greater one for poor Diego than scoring goals and so he was forced to play on half naked. He even managed to tackle James Beattie and win the ball off him before passing it back to his keeper in the minute or so he was running about the pitch topless and clutching his shirt in his hand. Eventually, he ran to the touchline for help and a couple of the United backroom staff helped him put his shirt back on. Apparently, it was something to do with the material used in the Nike shirts that Manchester United were wearing that season which made them a bit tricky to slip on.

It's been rumoured that the FIFA killjoys failed to see the funny side of the incident and that's why they introduced the law which came into effect for the start of the 2004/05 season requiring referees to yellow-card players who take off their shirts as part of a goal celebration.

THE PASTY-EATING GOALKEEPER
2017

When non-league Sutton United hosted Premier League Arsenal in the fifth round of the FA Cup on 20 February 2017, the home crowd were astonished to see their 46-year-old, 23-stone 'roly poly' reserve goalkeeper Wayne Shaw sitting on the bench stuffing his face with a pasty while watching the game.

However, it wasn't quite as innocent as it all seemed. It was true that Shaw hadn't eaten all day, and he'd waited until all three substitutes had been used before downing the pasty, but he'd also been aware of a publicity stunt organised by an online betting company as part of their one-game shirt sponsorship deal with Sutton offering odds of 8/1 on him eating a pie during the game, and had decided to play along with the joke.

Sutton weren't too pleased and an investigation was launched by the FA and the Gambling Commission, although Shaw decided to jump before he was pushed and resigned from the club before their rulings. He was later fined £375 and banned from playing football for two months for breaching the betting rules.

However, it wasn't all bad news for him: the supermarket chain Morrisons had been so impressed by his commitment to pie-eating that they offered him a one-year contract as a taster.

ELECTRIFYING THE FANS
1985

After the shocking scenes of violence at the end of the League Cup semi-final between Chelsea and Sunderland at

Stamford Bridge on 4 March 1985, the FA ordered Chelsea to improve stadium safety and introduce stricter crowd control measures at their ground.

The club's chairman/owner at the time was the controversial businessman Ken Bates, a man who spoke his mind and liked to ruffle a few feathers, and never more so than when he announced his plan to combat hooliganism by erecting a 12ft-high, barbed wire-topped electrified fence around the pitch at Stamford Bridge. The harebrained scheme was over-reactionary and dangerous and attracted almost universal criticism from politicians, the press and the footballing authorities, but nonetheless Bates was determined to press ahead with it, claiming that the vast majority of law-abiding Chelsea fans were behind him.

The fence was shown off to journalists and TV crews with Bates announcing that it would be switched on for the first time at the upcoming London derby against Tottenham on 27 April. However, like everybody else, the Greater London Council weren't quite so keen on the idea. They'd always opposed the use of an electrified fence, arguing that Chelsea weren't allowed to make any alterations to the stadium without their consent, and ordered Bates not to use it or they would be forced to seek a court injunction.

Bates seemed a little confused by the GLC's stance, arguing, 'Why all this sudden compassion for hooligans? Just a few weeks ago the whole nation was up in arms about these thugs attacking innocent people and driving them away from the game. Now there is all this concern that a few soccer hooligans might get their fingers burnt trying to scale the fences at Stamford Bridge.'

He refused to back down and the GLC had no choice but to follow through with their threat of legal action.

Bates appealed against the court injunction but then suddenly gave up the fight later in the year after announcing how well behaved the fans had been recently and the electrified fence was no longer needed. But it was just a poor attempt at saving face. Nobody believed for one moment that the yobbos had suddenly been transformed into the decent, law-abiding citizens he was now describing.

Bates's crackpot scheme to rid the world of football hooliganism was suddenly dead in the water; the electrified fence was soon dismantled and he went back to being his old outspoken, provocative and opinionated self about other things.

* * *

Daft though the idea was of sticking up an electric fence, it wasn't the daftest crowd control measure ever devised by a club to combat hooliganism. In 2003, the Romanian Divizia D (now Liga IV) club Steaua Nicolae Balcescu had been threatened with expulsion from the league after a series of pitch invasions and violent incidents at their ground, so their chairman Alexandra Cringus came up with the idea of digging a moat around the pitch and packing it full of crocodiles, asserting, 'The problem of fans running on to the pitch will be solved once and for all.'

Although the moat would have been far enough away from the pitch to avoid any players and ball boys inadvertently falling in and the crocodiles would have been well looked after (swimming about in heated water and fed with meat from the local abattoirs when there weren't any hooligans to feast on), the scheme failed to get off the ground after the local authorities unsurprisingly refused planning permission.

A MINUTE'S SILENCE DURING THE GAME
1974

The president of Argentina Juan Perón died on 1 July 1974, two days before the final matches in the second group stage of the World Cup were due to be played.

About ten minutes into the Group B game between Poland and hosts West Germany, which kicked off at 4.30pm on 3 July 1974, just as Uli Hoeneß was about to take a throw-in, the referee blew his whistle and the 22 players on the field suddenly remained rooted to the spot, as if they were taking part in some children's game, to observe a minute's silence for the deceased politician.

And then a minute later, the referee blew his whistle again and everyone's attention reverted back to Hoeneß – who was still standing on the touchline waiting to take that throw-in.

The same odd spectacle was repeated later that day in the three other games, which kicked off at 7.30pm: Netherlands v Brazil and Argentina v East Germany in Group A (the latter probably the only game where a minute's silence might have been expected), and Yugoslavia v Sweden in Group B.

The FIFA bigwigs had clearly felt the death of an Argentinian president should be marked with a traditional minute's silence but nobody had expected them to arrange it during the actual games.

THE REFEREE WHO DISALLOWED A PERFECTLY GOOD GOAL, MISSED A BLATANT PENALTY AND WAVED PLAY ON
1993

Partick Thistle's 4-0 Scottish Premier Division defeat at home to Dundee United on 13 February 1993 saw perhaps one of Scottish football's most bizarre incidents.

After 43 minutes, Paddy Connolly appeared to have put Dundee United 2-0 up when he drilled his shot into the Partick net. However, the ball had hit the goal's stanchion on its way in and then bounced straight back out again – and into the arms of the Partick defender Martin Clark, who just calmly handed it to his goalkeeper Andy Murdoch to restart play.

Not only did referee Leslie Mottram fail to spot the obvious goal, he also failed to spot the equally as obvious handball and didn't award a penalty. If he was going to disallow the goal, then he should have at least awarded a spot kick, but he did neither. Instead, he just ran back up the pitch through a crowd of protesting Dundee United players and waved play on.

THE GREATEST MATCH NEVER SEEN
1945

The league champions of the Soviet Union, Dynamo Moscow, embarked on a three-nation, four-game mini tour of Britain in 1945 to promote a spirit of camaraderie between the two countries after the Allied victory in the Second World War.

They first played Chelsea at Stamford Bridge on 13 November, bemusing the crowd by running out on to the pitch 15 minutes early for a pre-match warm-up – which was something the British public had never seen before and which led many to believe that they were needlessly wasting all their energy – and then confusing the Chelsea players by presenting them all with a bunch of flowers instead of just returning the cold, limp handshakes they'd been offered by their opponents. Chelsea were outplayed for most of the match as they struggled to cope with Dynamo Moscow's elegant and quick-passing style of play. The crowd were totally enthralled by their football and they actually began cheering for them late in the second half when they were 3-2 down. The referee allowed a late equalising goal to stand despite a Soviet player being offside and the game ended in a very diplomatic 3-3 draw. When the final whistle sounded, the crowd streamed on to the pitch to pick up some of the Soviet players and carry them shoulder-high to the tunnel.

Next up were Cardiff City on 17 November. The Soviets handed over their bouquets and in return all their players were presented with a miner's lamp. Very Welsh but also a little bit weird! Memories of those pre-match pleasantries soon faded, however, as Dynamo took control of the game. Cardiff were 3-0 down after only 25 minutes and in the second half they conceded five goals in eight minutes on their way to a 10-1 trouncing and the record for the heaviest loss ever incurred by a British club team to foreign opposition.

The Soviets then travelled back to London for their biggest game of the tour, against the famous Arsenal team. Unusually, it was played at Tottenham's White Hart Lane ground as Highbury was still being used for wartime purposes.

Arsenal were missing a few players who were still doing their bit for king and country around the world so they drafted in a few 'guests' like Stanley Matthews of Stoke City and Stan Mortensen of Blackpool to bolster their weakened team. The Soviets complained that, in effect, they were being asked to play an England side – which was a bit rich considering they were already using four players in their own team from other Soviet clubs.

Over 50,000 fans turned up to see the mysterious Soviet team that had given Chelsea such a hard time and convinced every Welshman that they were better off sticking to rugby. But seeing them proved more difficult than anyone could have imagined.

A thick blanket of fog had rolled over the ground before kick off; a nasty yellow pea-souper that smelt like rotten eggs and could kill off plants and blacken buildings which then stubbornly hung over White Hart Lane for the whole of the match. The fans had started queuing the night before, the gates had been opened at 10.30am long before the fog had arrived and there were already 40,000 people inside the ground two hours before kick off, so it was impossible for the authorities to cancel the match.

Kick off went ahead at 2.15pm, as scheduled, but the players, fans and match officials couldn't see a damn thing! Just to add to the confusion, the Russian referee couldn't speak English and both his linesmen, who were English, couldn't speak a word of Russian.

Dynamo took the lead after only 33 seconds before Arsenal had even touched the ball, although the Gunners did draw level shortly afterwards. There were three further goals in four minutes late in the first half with Arsenal going into the break leading 3-2. Matthews had been targeted with some heavy lunging tackles which went unseen by the referee, and the Arsenal goalkeeper Wyn Griffiths was kicked in the head so many times that he had to be replaced at half-time by Queens Park Rangers' goalie Harry Brown who'd only been at the game as a spectator.

In the second half it seemed that both teams were keen to exploit the worsening metrological conditions.

Dynamo restored parity early on with a goal that was blatantly offside and then Arsenal had a penalty appeal turned down. After about 20 minutes, the Arsenal players suddenly realised that their opponents had 12 men on the pitch; they'd made an early substitution, brought another player on but had conveniently forgotten to take a man off. The game was eventually stopped and a Dynamo player ordered back to the dugout.

After the game, some of the fans in the crowd claimed that Dynamo had as many as 15 players on the pitch.

That's not to say that Arsenal didn't use the fog to their advantage too. Their inside-forward George Drury had thrown a punch and had been sent off but had then sneaked back on to the pitch again sometime later to carry on playing.

Arsenal had a perfectly good goal disallowed. Ronnie Rooke picked up the ball 40 yards out and ran towards the opposition goal but the Dynamo captain Mikhail Semichastny tried to rugby-tackle him to the ground, leaving him with a huge gash on his head. Rooke somehow managed to elbow Semichastny out of the way (giving him a black eye in the process) before hitting a 25-yard shot into the net. But then the referee blew his whistle for a foul, disallowing the goal and awarding Dynamo a free kick where the original collision had occurred.

Dynamo eventually won 4-3 with another offside goal. Understandably, the Arsenal players later accused the referee of being biased towards the Soviet team with their captain Cliff Bastin commenting, 'So long as the Dynamos got the ball in the net, even if they carried it there, the referee was going to award them a goal.'

The majority of the crowd had no idea what the final score was and had to wait until they'd read the match report in the following day's newspaper. The *Daily Mail* reported, 'It was one of the most exciting games 54,000 people never saw.'

Dynamo Moscow finished off their UK tour in Glasgow with a 2-2 draw against Rangers a week later on 28 November 1945 in front of 90,000 spectators at Ibrox. The crowd laughed their little socks off when their hardman captain Jock Shaw was presented with a bunch of flowers but they were soon silenced when the Soviets opened the scoring after just two minutes and then continued running rings around the home team with their classy play. During the second half both teams made substitutions with the Soviets seemingly up to their old tricks again by forgetting to take a player off. It was only after Rangers' Torry Gillick ran around the pitch doing a quick head count and then alerted the referee to the fact that he'd counted 12 Dynamo players that one of them reluctantly left the field.

Dynamo returned to the Soviet Union unbeaten and were welcomed home as heroes. Their tour was hailed as a great success with the British public falling head over heels in love with their electric style of football. Unfortunately, the Brits continued with their own style for many years afterwards and it wasn't until the so-called 'Match of the Century' in 1953 when England were thrashed 6-3 by Hungary at Wembley that a review of training practices and tactics persuaded the clubs to copy the European way of doing things.

THE HOMEMADE TROPHY
1964

Liverpool clinched their sixth Division One title three matches from the end of the 1963/64 season with an easy 5-0 home win over Arsenal on 18 April.

However, the Anfield fans would be denied the chance to see their team presented with the trophy because those remaining games were all away from home and the Football League rules at the time didn't allow for the trophy to be sent to any stadium in anticipation of a title win. Everton were the 1962/63 winners and had very kindly offered to courier the trophy across to Anfield by the end of the match should Liverpool be winning. However, the Football League bosses refused permission, insisting that the trophy could only be presented to them at their next game, away to Birmingham four days later.

Knowing that their beloved team wouldn't have a trophy to parade around the ground after their expected win against Arsenal, two local lads, Ted and Terry Curlett, made their own from an old vase. They painted it red and white, stuck a few newspaper photos of their favourite players around the side and added a wooden cap from a staircase banister as a lid. Then they contacted the club and asked them if they wanted to use their 'Curlett Cup' for the expected post-match celebrations. To their surprise, they received a reply from the manager Bill Shankly, inviting them to Anfield to watch the game as his guests and telling them to bring along their cup.

The slightly tacky homemade trophy was presented to the players straight after the final whistle; they ran around the pitch with it, danced with it and held it up to the adoring fans like it was the real thing. The fans didn't know it was a fake trophy and the players didn't seem to care as they held it aloft and celebrated their championship win.

Unbelievably, the same trophy was used again at the end of the 1965/66 season when Liverpool secured their seventh league title with a 2-1 win over Chelsea at Anfield on 30 April 1966 in their penultimate game of the season.

And then it was never seen again for more than 40 years.

In the meantime, the 'Curlett Cup' had become a cherished family heirloom; carefully wrapped and stored in an attic somewhere, and only brought out on special occasions, until Terry's youngest son contacted Liverpool in 2006 and offered it to their museum. The paint is fading a bit now but the trophy remains on display in the club museum to this day alongside the other more recognisable medals and trophies won by Liverpool.

A SOUTH AMERICAN HORROR STORY
1967

The Intercontinental Cup, featuring representative clubs from UEFA and CONMEBOL, was first played in 1960.

The first British team to compete for the trophy was Celtic in 1967. They'd won the European Cup earlier that year and faced the Copa Libertadores winners Racing Club of Argentina. Celtic won 1-0 in the first leg at Hampden Park on 18 October but then lost the return game in Avellaneda 2-1 on 1 November. With the aggregate score tied at 2-2, a play-off was quickly arranged at a neutral ground in Montevideo, Uruguay, on 4 November.

The game was marred by Racing Club's cynical fouling, kicking, spitting and continual provocation, Celtic's complete loss of composure and an incompetent Paraguayan referee who was completely out of his depth and should never have been placed in charge of such an important game. Riot police had to intervene on the pitch several times, with six players being sent off: four from Celtic and two from Racing Club.

The two teams spent more time kicking each other than the ball. A 14th-minute tackle on the Celtic winger Jimmy Johnstone by Juan Carlos Rulli left him writhing on the ground in agony and resulted in a mass brawl and the appearance of riot police on the field to try and quell the violence. At one stage, John Clark was seen approaching Rulli and Alfio Basile with his fists up, striking a pose reminiscent of a bare-knuckle boxer. After five minutes of complete mayhem, the referee finally appeared to have gained control of the match and then sent off Basile and Celtic's Bobby Lennox. As the players appeared innocent of any offence, it was assumed at the time that the referee had made a mistake but it later transpired that he'd previously warned both players that they'd be dismissed for the next serious offence committed by their respective sides, even if they weren't actually involved. Understandably, Celtic manager Jock Stein attempted to keep Lennox on the pitch but he was eventually escorted off the field by a sword-wielding policeman. The referee was just making up the rules as he went along but there wasn't a single thing anyone could do about it.

After 48 minutes, Johnstone was being held back by Rulli again and was sent off after lashing out at him; six minutes later another Juan Carlos, Juan Carlos Cárdenas, scored for Racing Club with a superb 25-yard shot, and after 74 minutes John Hughes was dismissed for kicking the opposition goalkeeper Agustín Cejas when he was lying on the ground. Rulli was finally dismissed shortly afterwards for punching Clark.

Two minutes from full time another scuffle broke out, resulting in another intervention by the Uruguayan riot police. Bertie Auld was also sent off but refused to leave the field and just played out the remaining time; by now, the referee was totally irrelevant. In all the confusion Tommy Gemmell took his revenge on Humberto Maschio – who'd earlier spat at him – by kicking him in the balls.

The game ended in a 1-0 victory to Racing Club, making them the first Argentinian winners of the Intercontinental Cup. Jock Stein later commented, 'I would not bring a team to South America again for all the money in the world.'

Reuters described the play-off as 'a bar-room brawl with soccer skills abandoned for swinging fists, flying boots and blatant body checking'. It was a sentiment seemingly shared by Celtic chairman Robert Kelly, and the club's board of directors, as they fined every player £250 for their shameful behaviour. In Argentina, however, the mood was quite different. Racing Club were applauded for their victory, even by rival clubs and their supporters, and their players all received huge cash bonuses and a new car.

This match also cost Jock Stein a knighthood. He was originally due to receive the honour after Celtic's European Cup win in 1967 but a letter from the Scottish Office to the prime minister Harold Wilson, unearthed in 2007, recommended downgrading his award to a CBE in the New Year Honours List due to 'the unfortunate events in South America'.

* * *

Subsequent Intercontinental Cup matches would also descend into violence. The following year's clash between Manchester United and Estudiantes de La Plata, also of Argentina, was marred by cynical and violent play by the South Americans. In 1969, Estudiantes met AC Milan, which was probably the most violent of all the Intercontinental Cup clashes. AC Milan striker Pierino Prati was knocked unconscious and his team-mate Néstor Combin had his nose and cheekbone broken before being dragged semi-conscious from the pitch and then arrested by the Argentinian police on some trumped-up draft-dodging charges (having been born in Argentina but then moving to Europe and later playing for France). The violent play by the South American teams led some of their European counterparts to boycott the Intercontinental Cup. Ajax flatly refused to play in 1971 and 1973 and so did Bayern Munich in 1974 and Liverpool in 1977 and 1978.

SCHEIDT ON THE PITCH
1999

The Brazilian defender Rafael Scheidt was signed by Celtic for £4.8m from his homeland club of Grêmio in 1999.

He never really settled in Scotland, he was plagued by injury and he wasn't particularly good at playing football either. Celtic had bought him based solely on one cleverly edited highlights reel so they only had themselves to blame! Then it was revealed that his surname was actually pronounced 'shite'. Which probably didn't come as much of a surprise to anyone who'd seen him play.

Celtic quickly rebranded him 'Rafael'. But it didn't matter what the name was on the back of his shirt or what the TV commentators were instructed to call him, he was still Scheidt on the pitch. He only played a handful of games for Celtic before being sent back to Brazil, out on loan to Corinthians. In 2002 he threatened to return, but luckily for Celtic he no longer had a valid UK work permit, and so they just paid off the remainder of his contract.

THAT FAMOUS BEACH-BALL GOAL
2009

Darren Bent bagged one of the craziest goals ever scored in English football as Sunderland beat Liverpool 1-0 in the Premier League on 17 October 2009.

His innocuous shot was heading straight towards the goalkeeper Pepe Reina for an easy save but the ball then took an unexpected deflection off a beach ball and flew into the net.

The beach ball had been thrown on to the pitch by a Liverpool fan before the game and nobody had thought to remove it before kick off. Five minutes in, Andy Reid skipped past Fábio Aurélio and found Bent on the far side of the box with his cross. The English striker hit his shot towards the goal as Glen Johnson stuck out a leg to try and block it but the football hit the beach ball; the football went one way and into the net, and the beach ball went the other way with the wrong-footed Reina appearing confused enough to try and save it.

Football's laws clearly state that if an 'outside agent' makes its way on to the pitch then the game should be stopped and the object/person removed. Unfortunately for the referee, he'd completely forgotten about that particular rule and instead of restarting the game with a drop ball, he foolishly let the goal stand. He was later demoted to officiating Championship games; the fan was roundly castigated by other Liverpool supporters for costing them the game and even received death threats on social media, and Darren Bent became famous solely for that one goal despite being a '100 Club' member after scoring another 105 of them in his long Premier League career.

GUNFIRE AND RIOTING IN PARADISE
1912

The ongoing political turmoil over Irish Home Rule had resulted in an increase in sectarian violence on the streets of Belfast during the months prior to the match between the Protestant club of Linfield FC and their local Catholic rivals Belfast Celtic on 14 September 1912. Despite this serious deterioration in inter-community relations, nobody ever thought to postpone the game and the two teams met at Belfast Celtic's ground in Donegall Road, colloquially known as 'Paradise', in front of a record 16,000 crowd.

The first half was evenly contested although the away team went into the break leading 1-0.

No sooner had the teams walked off the pitch than a group of Celtic fans charged towards the Linfield end, taunting the supporters by waving nationalist flags and banners, and throwing rocks and stones at them. The away fans retaliated, scuffles broke out on the terraces and on the pitch, and the few police officers on duty that afternoon struggled to maintain order as they baton-charged the hooligans.

Suddenly, shots fired from the home end rang out amid all the chaos. As many of the fans then ran for the exits, the shooter fired off several more rounds into the retreating crowd.

Meanwhile, the English referee and his linesmen were enjoying their half-time cup of tea and blissfully unaware of the rioting taking place outside – until a rock came flying through the window and landed at their feet. They were understandably shocked to discover what was happening outside, and even more shocked to discover that both teams still wanted to play the second half. It was only the sound of gunfire and the sight of the wounded laid out by the side of the pitch that had apparently persuaded them otherwise.

The fighting spilled out on to the streets. For a full 15 minutes the rival factions slugged it out with their fists and whatever else they could find to throw at each other as more gunshots rang out around them. It was only when police reinforcements arrived and began dispersing the fans in different directions that some kind of order was restored. Sixty people were ferried to hospital, some with very serious injuries, including five people with gunshot wounds and a policeman who'd lost an eye.

The local and national press reported the incident in great detail with some of the British papers concluding that the violence was a direct response to the Home Rule crisis.

Many of the rioters were arrested and prosecuted, although the shooter was never apprehended.

One victim of the violence was Linfield fan Robert McGuicken. During a subsequent court case he recounted how he'd encountered three Celtic supporters on the tram before the game who'd threatened him and, at half-time, he was unlucky enough to encounter them again when they punched and kicked him to the ground before stabbing him in the head.

Both clubs released statements condemning the violence and the game was replayed on 16 October 1912, ending in a rather dull 0-0 draw with little or no drama being reported on or off the pitch.

* * *

Belfast Celtic played their very last league game on 21 April 1949 against Cliftonville FC after permanently resigning from the Irish League following the crowd violence at their traditional Boxing Day match at home to Linfield at Windsor Park in 1948. Celtic had been winning for most of the match but after Linfield equalised in the final minute, their ecstatic fans invaded the pitch and began attacking the Celtic players. Most famously, Celtic's young striker Jimmy Jones was chased across the running track and on to the terraces where a mob stamped on him and broke his leg. The vicious assault was reported worldwide; the public outcry forced Linfield to issue an apology, and the Irish FA penalised them by closing their ground for the next two games. Everyone believed it was a totally inadequate punishment for such a serious violent offence. Realising that their club's vicious rivalry with Linfield was a political issue rather than a footballing one, and there was nothing they could do to resolve it, Belfast Celtic took the unusual step of announcing their withdrawal from the league at the end of the 1948/49 season.

THE EUROPEAN JINX
1960-1999

Italian club Fiorentina may have won the inaugural European Cup Winners' Cup after beating Rangers 4-1 on aggregate in the two-legged final on 17 and 27 May 1961, but they also became the first victim of the tournament's jinx.

In the competition's 39-season history, no club has ever won the cup and then retained it the following year. The so-called jinx affected every winning club who made it through to the final again the following year: on eight separate occasions the previous year's winner was defeated.

The jinx began after Fiorentina were beaten 3-0 by Atlético Madrid in 1962. A similar fate then befell the Spanish team when they lost 5-1 to Tottenham in the 1963 final. The jinx continued with AC Milan (1973, 1974), Anderlecht (1976, 1977), Ajax (1987, 1988), Parma (1993, 1994) and Paris Saint-Germain (1996, 1997). The only British victims were Arsenal in 1995. On 4 May 1994 they'd beaten Parma 1-0 and then a year later they got through to the final again, this time against Zaragoza, but the jinx kicked in and they lost 2-1 in the last moments of extra time.

TOO MUCH RED IN THE STADIUM
2021

The first time that a team has blamed the colour of the seat coverings in their own stadium for their poor performance.

Twenty-five years after Manchester United manager Alex Ferguson famously ordered his players to change out of their light grey shirts at half-time in the Premier League match against Southampton on 13 April 1996 because they were having difficulty in picking each other out on the pitch, during the spring of 2021 their latest manager, Ole Gunnar Solskjær, claimed that a similar issue was the reason behind his team's recent poor performances.

. During the COVID-19 pandemic when crowds were banned from attending matches, most of the big clubs covered the terraces with huge banners displaying team logos and adverts to hide the empty seats and make the stadiums seem a little more cheerful than they actually were without the fans.

As Manchester United played in red shirts and the club had chosen to cover the red seats of Old Trafford with red banners, Solskjær had the cheek to suggest that his players were sometimes blinded by the colour red and unable to distinguish between the banners, the seats and the shirts when making a quick pass.

Of course, he was talking complete nonsense but, after his comments, all the red banners were suddenly replaced with black ones.

Not that it did them much good: they still only won two of their remaining five home matches.

THE MIRACLE OF ISTANBUL
2005

The 2005 Champions League Final will always be remembered for one of football's all-time great comebacks.

AC Milan were regarded as the favourites to win the match and claim their seventh trophy, and after just one minute in Istanbul's Atatürk Olympic Stadium their captain Paolo Maldini volleyed home their first goal. The Italians completely outplayed Liverpool in the first half and enjoyed a 3-0 lead at the break after Hernán Crespo scored two further goals after 39 and 44 minutes. As the teams walked off the pitch, some of the Liverpool supporters were already walking out of the stadium.

However, they should have had a little more faith in their team; their manager Rafael Benítez must have given them one hell of a bollocking at half-time. Whatever he said to them had the desired effect because shortly after the restart, Liverpool scored three goals in six minutes through Steven Gerrard, Vladimir Šmicer and Xabi Alonso to level 3-3.

After the usual 30 minutes of extra time, there had been no further goals and the teams began the dreaded penalty shoot-out. This was the second time in three years that the final was going to be decided in this way, with the Italians having been victorious against fellow Serie A club Juventus in 2003.

First up were AC Milan but Serginho shot high over the crossbar. Liverpool's first penalty taker was Dietmar Hamann, and despite playing with a broken toe, he still managed to hit the back of the net. Andrea Pirlo then saw his penalty saved by Jerzy Dudek, before Djibril Cissé scored Liverpool's second to put them 2-0 up. Milan finally got off the mark after Jon Dahl Tomasson slotted home their third kick to make it 2-1. John Arne Riise was next up for Liverpool but his penalty was saved by Dida; Kaká slotted away the next kick to level at 2-2, and then Vladimir Šmicer scored with Liverpool's fourth penalty to restore their one-goal advantage. Milan striker and reigning Ballon d'Or holder Andriy Shevchenko stepped up to the spot. He was arguably one of the most proficient goalscorers of the time and had to successfully convert his penalty otherwise Liverpool would win. He hit the ball straight down the middle of the goal and Dudek went to his right – but just managed to block the shot with his left hand.

Liverpool had won the penalty shoot-out 3-2 to snatch the win, and their fifth European Cup/Champions League.

The crowd of 69,600 and an estimated TV audience of over 100 million had just witnessed what would later become known as the 'Miracle of Istanbul'. The TV pundit and ex-Liverpool player Alan Hansen later commented, 'It wasn't just the best comeback in a European Cup Final; it wasn't just the best comeback I've seen in football; it was the best comeback I've seen in sport anywhere in the world.' Of course, it was his team, so he might have been a little biased.

The Italians had somehow managed to throw away a 3-0 lead and lose the biggest game in world club football. In his autobiography *I Think Therefore I Play* (2013), Andrea Pirlo wrote about that night, '[Afterwards] we sat like a bunch of half-wits in the dressing room ... We couldn't speak, we couldn't move. They had mentally destroyed us. Insomnia, rage, depression, a sense of nothingness. We'd invented a new disease with multiple symptoms: Istanbul Syndrome.'

REFUSAL TO LEAVE THE FIELD
1915

Oldham were challenging for the Division One title in 1915 but for whatever reason they were having a bit of an off-day on 3 April at Middlesbrough after quickly conceding three first-half goals.

Ten minutes into the second half Boro were awarded a penalty after Billy Cook brought down Jackie Carr in the box. Cook was booked and Walter Tinsley completed his hat-trick after scoring from the spot to give Middlesbrough a 4-1 lead. Seconds later, Cook hacked down Carr again and was sent off.

But Cook was having none of it; he wasn't going anywhere. He refused to leave the field, so the referee walked off instead. He had no option but to abandon the game and after 55 minutes all the players and match officials returned to their dressing rooms.

A few days later the FA decided to let the result stand. Oldham were fined £350 and Billy Cook was suspended for 12 months.

THE POINTLESS PENALTY SHOOT-OUT
1971

A thrilling first-half display in the first leg of the Cup Winners' Cup second round against Sporting at Ibrox on 20 October 1971 resulted in Rangers taking a 3-2 lead into the second leg two weeks later.

At the Estádio José Alvalade, Héctor Yazalde put the hosts ahead after 25 minutes but Colin Stein equalised just a minute later. Sporting took the lead again with a João Laranjeira goal in the 38th minute but again Stein stepped up to level with another goal at the start of the second half. With Rangers on course to claim a stunning 5-4 aggregate victory, up popped Pedro Gomes in the 87th minute to spoil the party and take the tie into extra time with the aggregate score tied at 5-5. Willie Henderson made it 3-3 on the night after 100 minutes but again Sporting clawed a goal back late in the game to win 4-3 and draw level at 6-6 on aggregate.

What happened next must be one of the most bizarre incidents in the history of all the European tournaments: Dutch referee Laurens van Ravens ordered the two teams to prepare for a penalty shoot-out having seemingly forgotten all about the away goals rule. Rangers had scored three of them over the two games compared to Sporting's two and should have automatically won the tie but it seemed that Mr Van Ravens had other ideas about how a winner should be determined.

The Rangers players tried to point out his mistake but he was convinced that the rule didn't apply if extra time was played. In his mind the teams were still level at 6-6 and the winner hadn't yet been decided. The players were understandably upset by his decision but what could they do? Nobody could convince him he was wrong so they just had to go ahead with the shoot-out as ordered – but Rangers then missed three out of their four spot kicks, handing the tie to Sporting. The home fans went crazy, cheering and screaming, climbing over the barriers, and carrying their heroic goalkeeper Vítor Damas shoulder-high around the pitch.

Meanwhile, the Rangers players had retreated to their dressing room and were sitting in silence feeling sorry for themselves when John Fairgrieve, a reporter from the Scottish press, appeared at the door clutching a copy of the UEFA rule book. He confirmed that they were right and the referee was wrong. The penalty shoot-out should never have happened because Rangers had already won the tie. It later transpired that he and Rangers manager Willie Waddell had gone to track down and confront the senior UEFA official present at the game to try and get the result overturned.

The official probably didn't need much persuasion as Rangers were immediately awarded the tie on the away goals rule and the mood in the two dressing rooms suddenly changed. Now it was the turn of the Rangers players to celebrate and the Sporting players to sit in silence, shake their heads and wonder where it had all gone wrong.

The referee never did apologise for his error and neither did anyone at UEFA.

Rangers then went on to beat Torino and Bayern Munich to reach the final on 24 May 1972 against Dynamo Moscow. And then they beat them 3-2 to pick up their first – and so far only – European trophy, but if it hadn't been for that smart-arse reporter, they would have ended up with bugger all.

SNIFFING THE LINE
1999

Opposition fans had long taunted Liverpool striker Robbie Fowler about his alleged drug habit. There was no evidence to suggest that he took any illegal substances but the joke had persisted for a few years, especially among the Everton supporters, who seemed to assume that the nasal strip he wore to aid his breathing during a game also meant that he had a passion for snorting cocaine.

After equalising from the penalty spot in the second Merseyside derby of the 1998/99 Premier League season, Fowler played up to the jibes by running towards the away end, getting down on all fours, and pretending to sniff the goal line as if it was one giant line of cocaine.

He later apologised for his inappropriate celebration but the FA hit him with a £32,000 fine and a four-match ban.

THE TEAM WITH TWO NUMBER NINES
1998

Chilean striker Iván Zamorano had a glittering career for Real Madrid (1992–1996) and Inter Milan (1996–2001), making 322 appearances and scoring 118 league goals for the two clubs.

At Inter he wore the number nine shirt and for the 1997/98 season was partnered up front with Brazilian marksman Ronaldo, who more regularly wore nine but took ten after his move from Barcelona.

Then in the summer of 1998 Inter signed Roberto Baggio from Bologna, who insisted on wearing his usual number ten shirt, so the club reassigned it to him and gave Zamorano's favoured nine to Ronaldo. This didn't sit well with Zamorano who was now obliged to wear some anonymous squad number.

He knew what number nine meant in terms of prestige and refused to give it up, instead wearing a shirt with 1+8 on the back. The numbers were the regulation size but inserted between them was a slightly smaller + sign.

Officially he was Inter's number 18 but unofficially he was still their number nine.

MORE EUROPEAN TROPHIES THAN DOMESTIC LEAGUE TITLES
1980

'I wouldn't say I was the best manager in the business. But I was in the top one,' Brian Clough once claimed.

Nottingham Forest had been lying 13th in Division Two when the flamboyant Yorkshireman was appointed as their manager on 6 January 1975. At the end of the following season they finished eighth, and on 16 July 1976 Peter Taylor re-joined his old boss as the club's assistant manager. Together they had won the Division One title with Derby County in 1971/72 and now hoped to replicate that success at the City Ground.

Their first trophy together was the short-lived and much-maligned Anglo-Scottish Cup after beating Leyton Orient 5-1 on aggregate in the two-legged final. At the end of the 1976/77 season, Forest finished third and were promoted to Division One. Then they won the League Cup, followed by their first Division One title after ending the season seven points clear of second-placed Liverpool

Brian Clough became only the second manager to win the top-flight league title at two different clubs.

The 1978/79 season began on 12 August 1978 with a 5-0 thrashing of Ipswich Town to win the FA Charity Shield, and on 9 February 1979 they signed Britain's first £1m player when they bought Trevor Francis from Birmingham City. They also retained the League Cup and finished as runners-up in Division One. However, their greatest achievement occurred at the end of that season when they beat Malmö 1-0 in the final of the European Cup at the Olympiastadion in Munich to win the trophy for the first time.

They beat Barcelona 1-0 to win the European Super Cup and then in May 1980 they beat Hamburg by the same scoreline to retain the European Cup and become the first British club to have won the tournament without first winning their own domestic league.

It was also the first time that any club had won more European Cups than domestic championships.

In the space of just five short years, Brian Clough and Peter Taylor had turned a struggling Division Two club fighting off relegation with an unlikely assortment of free transfers, bargain buys and misfit players into a two-time European Cup-winning side of exceptionally gifted footballers.

MAKING IT PERSONAL
2001

On 27 September 1997, Manchester United played a Premier League game against rivals Leeds United at Elland Road. Roy Keane was in their team that day and struggled to contain the Leeds midfielder Alf-Inge Haaland. The big Norwegian had given him the runaround for most of the match and Keane was not best pleased. Five minutes from time, he decided to get even and landed a crunching tackle on Haaland – but injured himself in the process! He'd snapped a cruciate ligament in his left leg and as he lay incapacitated on the ground, Haaland stood over him and accused the fiery Irishman of feigning injury to gain a penalty. Keane was stretchered off and didn't play again until a year later.

The two men met again on the pitch many times after that without incident and then in 2000 Haaland left Leeds to join Manchester City.

But Keane hadn't forgotten about that incident at Elland Road. He still wanted his revenge. It had been eating away at him and, in his mind, the only way of exorcising those demons and putting an end to their feud was to cause Haaland a lot of pain. Towards the end of the derby at Old Trafford on 21 April 2001, he caught Haaland with a horrendous studs-up, knee-high tackle which left him rolling about on the ground in agony. Keane screamed at him, 'Don't ever stand over me again sneering about fake injuries,' before being sent off. He then calmly walked away towards the tunnel completely unfazed by the distress he'd just caused.

Keane later received a three-match suspension and a £5,000 fine from the FA for his moment of madness. No doubt he thought it was well worth it.

A year later he released a book, *Keane: The Autobiography*, in which he recounted his feud with Alf-Inge Haaland and how he'd intentionally tried to hurt him. His admission that the tackle was premeditated led the FA to ban him for another five matches and fine him a further £150,000 for bringing the game into disrepute.

The original foul was bad enough but to then brag about it in a book was taking things too far.

THE REMAINING BIT OF A LEAGUE GAME TACKED ON TO THE END OF A CUP GAME
1996

The Danish Superliga game between Aalborg and Brøndby at the Aalborg Stadion on 1 September 1995 was suspended after 73 minutes and 53 seconds when Brøndby took a 2-0 lead and their overly exuberant fans let off some flares in celebration. The smoke would have cleared eventually but the pernickety referee wasn't in the mood to hang around and decided to abandon the game there and then.

As the possession and use of flares at Danish football grounds wasn't actually illegal at that time, there was no rule that the Dansk Boldspil-Union could use to award the game to the home team and so it remained unfinished with Brøndby leading 2-0 for another six months and five days until the teams met again on 6 April 1996 in the DBU

Pokalen (Danish Cup) and it was decided just to play the remaining 16 minutes and seven seconds of the outstanding league game after the cup tie had ended.

Brøndby won the cup match and then added another goal to their tally in the league match to finish as 3-0 winners.

THE WORST SHITHOUSERY EVER SEEN
1989

Brazil v Chile at the Maracanã on 3 September 1989 in a World Cup qualifier is possibly the most shameful match ever played.

The two teams were drawn with Venezuela in CONMEBOL Group 3 with only one of three qualifying for the finals in Italy. As Venezuela were just making up the numbers and were considered the whipping boys of the group, goal difference was always going to be an important factor in deciding which of the other two teams would qualify. Brazil had beaten them 10-0 over their two matches but Chile had only managed an overall score of 8-1.

The first meeting between Chile and Brazil, on 13 August 1989 at the Estadio Nacional in Santiago, ended in a 1-1 draw.

The second encounter, on 3 September, was the last group game to be played. Brazil had the better goal difference and only needed to avoid defeat to qualify for the finals. However, Chile were upbeat about their chances; they had a fairly decent team, and had finished as runners-up in the 1987 Copa América. Much of their recent success was down to their charismatic goalkeeper Roberto Rojas, nicknamed *El Condor* by his adoring fans, who'd made his name with Colo-Colo in Chile before signing for Brazilian giants São Paulo and eventually becoming one of the best goalkeepers in the world.

After a goalless first half, however, it was the Brazilians who broke the deadlock with a goal after 49 minutes from Careca.

With just over 20 minutes left Brazil were still 1-0 up and looking likely to qualify, especially as a draw would be good enough to take them through. But then, in the 67th minute, all hell broke loose.

The game was stopped after Rojas appeared to have been hit in the face by a flare thrown from the crowd. He was rolling around on the ground and the flare was lying nearby still fizzing and belching out smoke, as his team-mates rushed towards him and beckoned over their medical staff. He was eventually carried to the dressing room with blood gushing from his head as 130,000 partisan Brazilian fans booed him off the pitch. The Chilean players, led by their captain Fernando Astengo, then refused to continue playing and the referee had no choice but to abandon the game and award a victory to Brazil.

However, Brazil never really celebrated their win. They knew perfectly well that Chile would appeal the decision and, in all probability, they'd win it. It was obvious to everyone that the flare had been launched from a section of the crowd packed with Brazilian fans and there was a very real possibility that if Brazil were punished for the incident, they could face elimination from the World Cup altogether.

The Chilean players were welcomed home as heroes. Their newspapers were full of photos of a bloody Rojas, inflammatory headlines like 'THE WAR STARTED HERE' and demands for Chile to be awarded the World Cup spot.

FIFA immediately began an investigation into the incident but it soon became apparent that everything was not as it seemed.

El Condor appeared strangely evasive about the incident and his injuries weren't at all consistent with being hit by a burning object. There were no TV images of the flare hitting him and it was believed that none of the pitchside paparazzi had captured the moment either; until the Argentinian photographer Ricardo Alfieri stepped forward. He'd been covering the game for some obscure Japanese magazine and was the only one of the 200 or so photographers to record exactly what had happened, after taking a sequence of around 15 shots showing the flare falling and landing – about two metres away from Rojas. Which was a little strange because he was seen immediately afterwards lying bleeding on the pitch and clutching his head.

With the damning photographs being widely circulated in the Brazilian media, Rojas finally confessed in an interview with the Chilean newspaper *La Tercera* to having faked his injuries. He admitted hiding a razor blade in his glove and when the dream of reaching the World Cup finals seemed to be slipping away, he decided to cut his head with it in the hope that the referee would abandon the game.

FIFA's punishment was harsh. Brazil were awarded the result and, just for the hell of it, FIFA added on an extra goal, with the final score being recorded as a 2-0 victory; Roberto Rojas received a lifetime ban from playing professional football, and Chile were banned from taking part in not just one but two World Cup tournaments. They were thrown out of the 1990 scompetition and told not to bother trying to qualify for the 1994 finals either. Everyone else on the team involved in the deception also received a sanction; the manager, the captain, the team doctor and his assistant: and even the kit man, who'd sewn a little pocket into Rojas's gloves to hide the razor blade.

Meanwhile, the Brazilian police had identified 24-year-old Rosenery Mello do Nascimento as the fan who threw the flare. She became known as the *Fogueteira do Maracanã* (Firecracker of Maracanã) and enjoyed her 15 minutes of fame by appearing on the front cover of the November 1989 edition of *Playboy* magazine.

TWO GOALS WITHOUT THE OTHER TEAM TOUCHING THE BALL
2000

Wycombe Wanderers entered the record books on 23 September 2000 after scoring two goals within nine seconds without the opposition touching the ball.

Jamie Bates blasted home a free kick from just outside the box two minutes into first-half stoppage time to open the scoring in a Second Division encounter at home to Peterborough United; the referee then decided there was no more time to restart the game and blew his whistle for half-time. After the break, Wycombe kicked off; the ball was laid off to Jermaine McSporran who ran through the opposition defence before striking the ball past the Peterborough keeper Mark Tyler and into the back of the net.

The game finished with a 2-0 win for Wycombe and soon afterwards it was confirmed that they had also set a new world record for the shortest time for one side to score two goals.

LOSING A BODY PART WHEN CELEBRATING A GOAL
2004

Servette midfielder Paulo Diogo jumped on to the perimeter fencing to celebrate setting up his team's third goal for Jean Beausejour in the 87th minute of their 4-1 away win at Schaffhausen in the Swiss Super League match on 5 December 2004. Unfortunately, as he jumped back down again a few seconds later, he caught his wedding ring on the fencing, tearing it off his finger – and tearing his finger off his hand. Despite screaming in pain and clutching his bloodied left hand, the referee still showed him a yellow card for time-wasting!

The stewards searched for the missing digit and later that evening surgeons tried to reattach it but without success.

THE GREATEST MARGIN OF VICTORY

2001

Australia's 31-0 win over American Samoa in an Oceana Football Confederation World Cup qualifier on 11 April 2001 set a new record for the biggest biggest victory in any international match.

Striker Archie Thompson also broke the record for the most goals scored by any one player in an international.

Australia fielded a B team with many of their regular players rested or omitted from the squad through injury. American Samoa, who had just joined FIFA and were playing in their first World Cup qualifying campaign, only had one regular senior player available to them due to passport issues. They couldn't even call up any of their under-20 squad because they were all back home swatting for their high-school exams, so they were forced to draft in youth players, including three 15-year-olds, to make up the team.

The game was still goalless after ten minutes but then Con Boutsianis opened the scoring and Thompson added a second two minutes later. By half-time Australia were already 16-0 up with Thompson getting eight of the goals. Australia then added 15 more in the second half with Thompson getting his name on the scoresheet another five times. Needless to say, he also won the man of the match award.

This 31-0 scoreline broke the record for the largest winning margin in any international match, which was already held by Australia after their 22-0 thrashing of Tonga in another World Cup qualifying game at the same stadium just two days earlier!

Australia inevitably finished top of OFC Group 1 with 12 points, a +66 goal difference and without conceding a goal while American Samoa finished bottom with no points, a -57 goal difference and without ever scoring a goal.

This match and the other one-sided games in both of the two OFC qualifying groups contributed to the re-introduction of preliminary rounds for the smaller teams for the 2006 World Cup.

At the end of 2005, Australia withdrew from the OFC and joined the more competitive Asian Football Confederation.

THE BURNDEN PARK DISASTER
1946

The second leg of Bolton Wanderers' FA Cup quarter-final against Stoke City on 9 March 1946 still went ahead with dead bodies lying by the side of the pitch.

The FA had decided to increase the number of matches to boost the income of the clubs during the 1945/46 tournament by playing every game from the first round to the sixth round (quarter finals) over two legs. It was the first and only time that this alternative format has been used.

Bolton had won the first leg 2-0 away at the Victoria Ground in Stoke on 2 March 1946. The authorities were expecting a crowd of around 55,000 to attend the second leg at their 70,000-capacity Burnden Park stadium but it's since been estimated that as many as 85,000 fans managed to find their way into the ground that day. Although the turnstiles had been shut at 2.40pm, it didn't stop supporters from jumping over them, climbing fences or gaining access through an open gate in the Railway End stand.

Shortly after the match began, many of the spectators from the Railway End spilled on to the pitch with play being temporarily suspended to clear them. It was soon restarted but then the barriers on the terracing collapsed and the fans standing behind them surged forward, with many people being crushed or trampled to death in the stampede. After a policeman came on to the pitch to inform the referee of the tragedy, he called the two captains together to explain that he was suspending the game again and then led the teams off the field.

Rather surprisingly, it restarted again just half an hour later with the dead bodies covered with coats still laid out by the side of the pitch. Some accounts of the tragedy have even stated that the corpses were so close to the pitch that a new touchline had to be marked out in sawdust before the match could begin!

TWO FOR THE PRICE OF ONE
1921

The FA had closed Stockport County's Edgeley Park ground as a punishment for the crowd trouble during a home game against The Wednesday (later Sheffield Wednesday) on 2 April 1921. However, those nice people at Manchester United agreed to help them out by letting them play their last home game of the season, against Leicester City on 7 May, at Old Trafford at 6.30pm after their own match against Derby County had ended.

Only 13 people turned up to watch the Stockport-Leicester game, which was the lowest number ever recorded for any English or Scottish league game.

However, it wasn't quite as bad as it seemed because a few thousand fans who'd watched the earlier match, which had kicked off at 3pm, had then stayed on to watch the Division Two fixture. Only 13 people were daft enough to pay the entrance fee between games just to watch second-tier football rather than take advantage of the two-for-the-price-of-one offer and the chance to watch top-flight football as well.

THE FIRST MANAGER
1886–1926

One day in 1876, the former Glasgow Rovers and Druids player George Ramsay stumbled across the Aston Villa team in the middle of a training session in a Birmingham park and was asked to make up the numbers for a practice match.

Apparently, the Villa players were so impressed by his ball skills that they invited him there and then to join the club.

Ramsay was soon appointed team captain and took charge of training; abandoning the outdated dribbling style of football which he later described as just 'a dash at the man and a big kick at the ball' and introducing his team-mates to the more refined passing game already being practiced in Scotland. In 1880, he led the club to their first trophy – the Birmingham Senior Cup. Unfortunately, a serious injury then forced him to retire from playing in 1882.

In 1885, Aston Villa renounced their amateur status and became a professional club with a notice soon appearing in the local papers advertising for a manager, 'Wanted: manager for Aston Villa Football Club, who will be required to devote his whole time under direction of the committee. Salary £100 per annum. Applications with reference must be made not later than June 23rd to Chairman of the Committee, Aston Villa Club House, 6 Witton Road, Aston.'

They received 150 applications but, in the end, the best man for the job seemed to be George Ramsay. He took up his role as the world's first professional football manager on 26 June 1886 and led Villa to six Division One titles and six FA Cup victories during the team's 'Golden Age' between 1893 and 1920. He stayed in the job for almost 42 years until 1926 to become the third-longest serving English or Scottish league manager. In total, his association with Aston Villa lasted 59 years as a player, manager and, later after his retirement, as an advisor and vice-president.

And to think, it all came about after a chance meeting in a Birmingham park.

THE SHOWMAN
1957

Back in the day, when a player scored a goal he was just expected to shake the hand of his nearest team-mate and sprint back into position for the restart. So it wasn't all that surprising when the young Portsmouth striker Derek Dougan was criticised for daring to raise his arms above his head in celebration after scoring his first career league goal, for Portsmouth against Wolverhampton Wanderers on 9 November 1957. One journalist commented on his inappropriate behaviour and asked his manager Eddie Lever what he thought about it. Lever replied, 'It was the natural elation of a youngster scoring his first goal for his club. He's a bit of a showman!'

Since then, we've gone from a simple handshake and a couple of raised arms to lots of kissing and cuddling, a run around the field, a knee slide across the wet grass, giving the corner flag a good kicking, or even a quick gymnastics display or choreographed dance routine.

And this:

- Muangthong United midfielder Mario Gjurovski pulling off his shorts, wrapping them around his head and dancing around the pitch in 2013.

- Atlético Mineiro player Edmilson Ferreira whipping a carrot out of his sock and eating it in front of the opposing América Mineiro fans in 1998 – because the nickname for their club was 'The Rabbits'.

- In Finland in 2011, Hangö IK striker Marcello Matrone running to the touchline, slipping on a curly blond wig (hidden behind an advertising board) and then performing a rendition of the Colombian pop star Shakira's 2010 hit, 'Waka Waka'.

- Hidetoshi Wakui arranging his Nõmme Kalju team-mates into a tenpin bowling formation before knocking them over with the match ball in 2014.

- Antoine Griezmann of Atlético Madrid jumping behind the wheel of a car parked at the side of the pitch and beeping the horn in 2010.

- Roma striker Francesco Totti taking a selfie in front of the Lazio fans during a Serie A derby in 2015.

- FC Nordsjælland striker Bajram Fetai launching into a spectacularly staged fake fight in 2010, pretending to punch out his team-mates one by one after scoring against his old club Silkeborg IF, who had previously kicked him out for fighting.

- The players of Icelandic club Stjarnan FC choreographing no end of bizarre and very elaborate goal celebrations that have gone viral on social media – everything from ballroom dancing and catching a fish to giving birth, pirates walking the plank and a Rambo-style shooting spree. They've also formed human bicycles, rowboats, bobsleighs and even a toilet (with three players twisting their bodies to make the actual shape of the WC and the goalscorer acting the part of the toilet-goer by pulling up the seat, having a dump while reading his newspaper and then flushing before running away to restart the game).

How times have changed!

JUMPING THE GUN
2013

It looked certain that Nigerian striker Peter Odemwingie would make the move from West Bromwich Albion to

Queens Park Rangers on transfer deadline day in 2013. So much so that he drove down from the Midlands to London to complete his medical after assuming that it was just a few i's and t's that needed dotting and crossing on the contract to make things official. But when he arrived outside QPR's Loftus Road ground, he was refused entry after being told that the deal hadn't yet been finalised. Peter waited in his car, signing autographs and even giving an interview to Sky Sports to say how much he was looking forward to this new chapter in his career.

Then word reached him that the deal was off and so he just drove the 125 miles back to Birmingham again.

As if spending the whole evening sitting in a car park and making an arse of himself in full view of the TV cameras wasn't embarrassing enough, he was then disciplined by West Brom for his unprofessional behaviour and didn't start another game for them all season.

SOUND AND VISION
1901
FILM FOOTAGE

The 1901 FA Cup Final was played out between Sheffield United and Tottenham at Crystal Palace Park in London on 20 April 1901 but ended in a 2-2 draw, with the two teams meeting again a week later at Bolton Wanderers' Burnden Park for the replay.

Film catalogues seem to suggest that the 1898 FA Cup Final may have been the first football match to be filmed; however, the two grainy film clips which have since been dubbed *Entry of the Teams* and *Play in Progress* of the 1901 replay on 27 April are the oldest-surviving pieces of film.

The 1901 FA Cup Final was also famous for proving what everyone already knew: referees make mistakes.

The first match was played in front of a world-record crowd of 110,820. Within ten minutes of the start, Fred

Priest rather predictably put pre-match favourites Sheffield United ahead. However, the Tottenham striker Sandy Brown levelled 13 minutes later, becoming the first player to score in every round of the FA Cup in a single season, and it remained 1-1 until half-time. Brown then scored again just after the restart to give Tottenham a shock 2-1 lead.

However, their unexpected advantage lasted for less than 60 seconds as, with a little help from the referee, the game was suddenly level at 2-2 after 52 minutes.

It's unclear exactly what happened but it seems that the Tottenham goalkeeper George Clawley went to catch a shot from Bert Lipsham but fumbled it, the ball dropped behind him, Clawley spun around and was barged by Walter Bennett just as he kicked the ball away. The linesman signalled a corner, believing that the ball had gone out of play and the keeper had been the last to touch it, but the referee Arthur Kingscott overruled him and awarded a goal. He never bothered to consult with his linesman and was too far up the field to see clearly what had actually happened in the goalmouth scramble; nonetheless, he seemed convinced that the ball had crossed the line before being cleared by Clawley and ran off towards the centre circle for the restart. However, the Pathé News film cameras captured all the action and the footage clearly showed that the ball had gone nowhere near the goal line, never mind over it.

Poor Arthur Kingscott couldn't have been more wrong. Unfortunately for him, he was the first match official to have his incompetence captured on film. But despite his obvious lapse of judgement, he was then called upon to referee the replay!

MOVIE
The first football-themed movie was 1911's *Harry the Footballer*, a silent film drama starring Hay Plumb as a footballer kidnapped by the fans of an opposing team.

However, their dastardly plot is foiled by his gutsy girlfriend, played by Gladys Sylvani, and he's rescued just in time to play in the big match and score the winning goal.

The plot of *Harry the Footballer* was repeated three years later in *The Cup Final Mystery* but this time it was the goalkeeper rather than the striker who was kidnapped before the big match. It seems that every screenwriter's imagination was limited to producing scripts involving footballers and abduction plots at that time because *The Rival Captains* hit the big screen in 1916 and this time it was the turn of the team captain to be kidnapped and his girlfriend's dog to do the rescuing!

The first feature-length box-office hit was *The Ball of Fortune* (1926), directed by Hugh Croise and based on the novel of the same name by Sydney Horler. Much of the film's success was most likely due to a guest appearance by the Manchester United striker Billy Meredith, playing himself in the lead role of a football coach, and a plot that didn't involve anyone being kidnapped!

The Great Game (1930) was the first football-themed 'talkie' and featured John Batten as Dickie Brown, an aspiring young footballer for Manningford FC who romances the chairman's daughter, breaks into the first team and wins the FA Cup. It was mainly shot at Stamford Bridge and featured a few guest appearances from some of the famous footballers of the day.

The Arsenal Stadium Mystery (1939), directed by Thorold Dickinson, is probably the most famous of all the early footie films and the first to actually use a real team in its storyline. The low-budget flick based on a novel by Leonard Gribble revolves around a friendly between Arsenal and the fictitious amateur side The Trojans. After one of the Trojan players drops down dead during the match, Inspector Slade of Scotland Yard, played by Leslie Banks, is called in to investigate what appears to be a murder. The film was partially shot on location at Highbury and features the Arsenal players of the time and their manager George Allison, who was afforded a speaking role. The match footage was constructed from film of Arsenal's last official league game before the outbreak of the Second World War, against Brentford on 6 May 1939, and a specially arranged mock-up game between Oxford University students for the close-up shots.

RADIO

The world's very first live radio broadcast of a football match came on 15 January 1927 when Arsenal and Sheffield United drew 1-1 at Highbury in Division One. The ex-rugby union player Teddy Wakelam commented for the BBC, with *The Times* reporting that his description of the play was 'notably vivid and impressive'.

The *Radio Times* had published a grid of the pitch to accompany the broadcast. The grid was divided into eight squares to help listeners understand where the ball was as the match progressed. The expression 'back to square one' is thought likely to have originated from these early radio broadcasts.

TELEVISION

The specially arranged match between Arsenal's first team and their reserves at Highbury on 16 September 1937 was broadcast live by the BBC for just 15 minutes at 3.40pm. The brief television coverage ended at 3.55pm to make way for a cartoon before the station ended transmission for the afternoon at 4pm.

The BBCs decision to feature Arsenal was a simple matter of geography and convenience. Highbury was the nearest ground to their Alexandra Palace studios and they had a ready-made gantry for the TV cameras in the East Stand. Three cameras were used: one positioned on the gantry that gave a comprehensive view of the field, and another two near to the goals to capture the pre-match presentation of the players by manager George Allison and close-up shots of the play during the match.

The first full live match shown on TV was in the British Home Championship match when England met Scotland at Wembley on 9 April 1938. The BBC were keen to show the FA Cup Final later that month and had negotiated with the FA to transmit this match more as a test broadcast in preparation for the much bigger and more important occasion to come.

The first live televised league game shown anywhere in the world was Barnet v Wealdstone in the Athenian League on 19 October 1946. The *Radio Times* listed the match as *Amateur Soccer* with the promise that 'viewers will see part of the first half and the whole of the second half.' However, the BBC's coverage consisted of only 35 minutes of the second half because it became too dark to continue broadcasting. The half-time break was filled by a ten-minute show featuring Murray, the famous Australian escapologist wriggling his way out of a straitjacket while suspended upside down from the roof of Alexandra Palace.

It wasn't until 1960 that the TV companies had another go at broadcasting live league football. This time it was ITV but things didn't turn out much better for them. On 10 September 1960 they broadcast the Division One match between Blackpool and Bolton, but it was all a bit dull: Stanley Matthews didn't play, it was only partially covered live (kicking off at 6.50pm but with coverage not beginning until 7.30pm) and the viewing figures were considered poor for such a big showcase event. Due to its spectacular lack of success, other clubs suddenly had second thoughts about allowing the TV cameras into their grounds and so ITV were forced to abandon their plans to show any more matches.

The next televised league game wasn't until 23 years later when ITV screened the Division One clash between Tottenham and Nottingham Forest on 2 October 1983.

BRAKE CLUBS
1880s

The Brake Clubs, the first organised away supporters' clubs in football, were so named after the horse-drawn wagons (or brakes) that Glasgow-based fans owned or hired to travel around Scotland to away games. The wagons were often adorned with colourful banners, bunting and paintings of favourite players, and packed with up to 25 fans, who were often rowdy and usually drunk, yelling at passersby and blowing trumpets, as they made their way to the grounds. The fans were notoriously loud and were frequently heard long before they were seen.

The wagons were really only suited to getting to matches within the city and a few neighbouring areas of Dunbartonshire, Lanarkshire and Renfrewshire, but despite these restrictions they changed the way fans were allowed to support their clubs. Up until the Brake Clubs were formed they'd really only attended home games but now they had a cheap and fairly reliable way of getting to away games too.

The first Brake Clubs were mostly formed from temperance groups within Glasgow's Catholic parishes. The Sarsfield Brake Club founded by Celtic fans and named after the famous Irish soldier Patrick Sarsfield, 1st Earl of Lucan, was possibly the most famous, with even some of the Celtic players of the time rumoured to have hopped on board to and from their matches. Although the original Brake Clubs would raise generous amounts of money for charity, in later years their reputation was tarnished by drunkenness and hooliganism. Rather ironic since they were formed by the very people who liked nothing better than preaching about the evils of drink.

The Brake Club fans from Celtic and Rangers became more and more boisterous and their partisan support for a particular club often led to skirmishes with rival supporters and the police, as they deliberately chose the most provocative and incendiary routes through opposition heartlands, singing sectarian songs and throwing stones and bottles from the wagons.

Despite their increasing unpopularity with the authorities and the general public, it was only the wider use of motor cars and the railways in the early part of the 20th century which eventually led to their demise.

By the early 1920s they had disappeared from the streets of Glasgow for ever.

THE CANCELLED DOUBLE HAT-TRICK
1961

On 28 January 1961, after only 69 minutes, Manchester City were 6-2 up in the FA Cup fourth round match away to Luton Town with Denis Law having scored all six goals. A minute later, however, the heavens opened and the match was abandoned because of a waterlogged pitch – meaning all of his goals would be struck from the record books.

The match was replayed four days later and, although Law scored another goal, City lost 3-1 and went out of the cup; he never scored another double hat-trick in his career, and those six cancelled goals meant missing out on becoming the FA Cup's top goalscorer of the 20th century with only 41 goals against 44 from Ian Rush playing for Liverpool and Newcastle United.

MATCH OF THE CENTURY
1953

The two most famous games played at Wembley resulted in the two most famous defeats for England. In only their second match at the new stadium they lost 5-1 to Scotland's 'Wembley Wizards' in the British Home Championship on 31 March 1928, and then on 25 November 1953 in the so-called 'Match of the Century' they got well and truly stuffed 6-3 by the 'Mighty Magyars' of Hungary who were ranked number one in the world and unbeaten for 24 games since May 1950.

England had only lost once before to foreign opposition, a 2-0 defeat to Ireland on 21 September 1949, but that match was played at Goodison Park and not on the hallowed turf of Wembley.

The FA had always very arrogantly assumed that since football was invented in England, then the English players must be the best in the world; their Selection Committee, who seemingly knew nothing about the game, continued to pick the team, and they quite happily ignored all the coaching and technical developments pioneered on the continent by insisting that the England team continue playing the outdated WM formation.

The match was played in front of around 105,000 spectators with some of them still finding their seats when Nándor Hidegkuti put the visitors ahead inside the first minute. Although Jackie Sewell clawed a goal back for England after 15 minutes, Hidegkuti got a second to make it 2-1 five minutes later and then the great Ferenc Puskás made it 3-1 four minutes after that. He scored his second goal after 27 minutes and then Stan Mortensen pulled another one back for England in the 38th minute.

Hungary went into the break leading 4-2.

The second half was much the same as the first: Hungary dominating the play with the England players constantly being outclassed by their trickery. József Bozsik added another goal after 52 minutes and Hidegkuti completed his hat-trick three minutes later. Alf Ramsay got one back from the spot after 57 minutes and the match ended with a 6-3 victory to Hungary.

The result barely reflected Hungary's complete dominance: they'd had 35 shots on goal to England's five, a perfectly good goal was ruled offside, and they pretty much eased up after an hour until the final whistle.

The magnitude of the defeat by the Hungarians and the brilliance of their players stunned the British public and, as a result, the FA ordered a review of the training, tactics and strategies employed by the England team, which eventually led to them and many club teams in England subsequently adopting the classier continental system of play and abandoning the moribund WM formation.

On 23 May the following year, England travelled to Budapest intent on revenge – but this time they lost 7-1 ... which still ranks as their heaviest defeat.

THE HERO OF SEVILLE
1986

Steaua Bucureşti had never progressed beyond the first round of the European Cup in their six previous appearances in the tournament, but all that changed during the 1985/86 season.

Their progress through the intermediary rounds was relatively comfortable after aggregate victories over Vejle Boldklub of Denmark, Hungary's Budapest Honvéd, Finland's FC Kuusysi and RSC Anderlecht of Belgium before meeting Barcelona in the final in Seville.

The match was a dull and scrappy affair with few chances for either side and inevitably it became the first European Cup Final to finish goalless after 120 minutes, with a penalty shoot-out then needed to decide a winner.

Things got off to a pretty poor start for everyone. Barcelona keeper Javier Urruticoechea easily saved a weak shot from Mihail Majearu but then José Ramón Alexanko missed Barcelona's first penalty too. Steaua's goalkeeper Helmut Duckadam had correctly guessed that he would shoot to his right and dived to palm the ball away. Unbelievably, László Bölöni then missed Steaua's second penalty of the night with everyone in the stadium beginning to wonder if they'd ever see a goal.

Duckadam then saved again after assuming that Ángel Pedraza wouldn't expect him to dive to his right again. Sure enough he hit his shot hard and low towards the bottom left-hand corner of the goal but Duckadam dived that way too and deflected the ball away with a one-handed save.

After four penalties the score was still 0-0, then the deadlock was finally broken with the fifth spot kick of the night after Marius Lăcătuș hammered the ball into the net via the underside of the crossbar to put Steaua 1-0 up. Barcelona's third attempt was a weak shot towards the left side of the goal from Pichi Alonso which was easily caught by Duckadam as he again guessed correctly and dived to his right. After kicking the ball in the air he then fell to his knees in celebration having saved three out of three penalties.

Steaua were on the brink of a famous victory, and a successful kick from Gavril Balint brought them even closer to glory. Next up was Marcos Alonso to try and save the day for Barcelona.

Everyone knew that Duckadam had saved three penalties by diving to his right and that he'd probably made up his mind to go that way even before the shoot-out had begun. Duckadam knew that Alonso would be thinking the same thing so this time he dived the opposite way. It was a pretty lame shot with no power behind it and it was placed too near to the centre of the goal. Duckadam easily blocked the shot and then ran towards his team-mates to celebrate. He'd just kept a clean sheet in a penalty shoot-out in Europe's most prestigious club competition.

It was the first time that the UEFA European Cup had been won by any club from an Eastern Bloc communist country, and Duckadam was later dubbed 'The Hero of Seville' for his spot kick heroics. But little did he know that the game would turn out to be his last for the club.

As Steaua București were administered by Valentin Ceaușescu, the son of Romania's hard-line leader, it's probably fair to say that he wielded a great deal of power and influence over the Federația Română de Fotbal and the other clubs to ensure his team always had the best players and the best chance of success. A few weeks after the final, Duckadam was told to play in a game that was fixed to allow their team's striker to score a lot of goals so he could win the Divizia A Golden Boot award. However, he didn't want to be involved in anything underhand and refused to play, so he was banned from the training ground, dropped from the team and, as Steaua were an army team, he also had to endure a military trial presided over by the dictator's brother Ilie Ceaușescu which resulted in him being fined the equivalent of two months' wages. Just when he thought all of his troubles were over after eventually being allowed back into the team again, the club doctors discovered an aneurysm in his right arm and he was advised not to play football again as it was too dangerous.

Ilie Ceaușescu then kicked him out of the army too. If he couldn't play football, then he was no use to anyone.

THE BEST AND THE WORST OF THE MAN
1986

The 1986 World Cup quarter-final between Argentina and England was famous for two second-half goals scored by the diminutive forward Diego Maradona.

Argentina had more possession and the majority of chances in front of goal but the game remained goalless at half-time. However, shortly after the break their flamboyant and controversial little captain killed the game with the 'Hand of God' goal and the 'Goal of the Century' before Gary Lineker scored a late consolation goal for England after 81 minutes.

Six minutes into the second half, after a run through the midfield, Maradona tried to play a one-two with Jorge

Valdano through the English defence. Steve Hodge, who had dropped back to help defend, then tried to clear the ball but instead of booting it up the field and out of danger, he miskicked it towards his own goal and right into the path of Maradona, who had continued his run. Goalkeeper Peter Shilton came off his line to punch the ball clear but Maradona got there first. As he leapt into the air in an attempt to head the ball towards the goal, he stuck out his left arm and punched it into the empty net instead.

The Tunisian referee Ali Bin Nasser failed to spot the blatant handball and awarded the goal.

Instead of admitting his complete lack of sportsmanship and maybe offering an apology, Maradona chose to boast about his deceit after the game by stating that the goal had been scored 'a little with the head of Maradona and a little with the hand of God' and many years later he even claimed that it had been some kind of karma for his country's defeat in the Falklands War in 1982.

Then what many people believe was the greatest individual goal of all time came just four minutes later.

Maradona received the ball from Héctor Enrique inside his own half and then began a 60-yard run towards the England goal, skipping past Peter Beardsley, Peter Reid, Terry Butcher and Terry Fenwick, before dribbling around Shilton and slotting the ball into an empty net to give Argentina a 2-0 lead. The goal was voted 'Goal of the Century' in an online FIFA poll in 2002.

In Argentina, the match result was generally seen as payback for the Falklands War and even their country's 1-0 defeat in that infamous *El Robo del Siglo* game of 1966, with their ex-player Roberto Perfumo remarking, 'Winning the game against England was enough. Winning the World Cup was secondary to us [Argentina beat West Germany 3-2 in the final]. Beating England was our real aim.' The splendour of that second goal and the notoriety of the first prompted the French sports newspaper *L'Équipe* to describe Diego Maradona as 'half-angel, half-devil'.

In 2015, he had the cheek to visit referee Bin Nasser at his home in Tunisia, calling him his 'eternal friend' and presenting him with a signed shirt. Someone else who got a shirt off Maradona was Steve Hodge. They'd swapped shirts at the end of the match and when it was put up for auction in 2022, it fetched over £7m, a new record at the time for any item of sports memorabilia.

THE KHAKI FINAL
1915

A few of the more famous FA Cup finals are better known by a name such as 'The White Horse Final' of 1923, 1930's 'Zeppelin Final' and 'The Matthews Final' from 1953. The first of these matches was Sheffield United's 3-0 win over Chelsea in 'The Khaki Final' in 1915, which was the drabbest and most downbeat final in the history of the competition.

It was the last FA Cup Final to be staged before all professional football in Britain was suspended for the duration of the First World War and so called due to the many thousands of wounded and on-leave soldiers dressed in their khaki uniforms present in the crowd that day.

Before the game a public debate had raged as to whether it should go ahead. Many were angry that football was distracting young men from signing up to fight, with one speaker at a protest meeting in Manchester even suggesting that professional football was 'the greatest hindrance to recruiting in the United Kingdom'. The newspapers reported how wrong it would be to continue playing when war raged across Europe. On the same day as the final, British soldiers were fighting in the Second Battle of Ypres, now noted for the first mass use of poison gas by Germany.

But the match did go ahead. It was played at Old Trafford instead of Crystal Palace Park, which had been requisitioned for military use. The muted crowd was much smaller than normal due to the wartime travel restrictions; it was a bleak and rainy day and the game itself was a fairly dull affair. In the second half, a thick fog fell over the stadium, preventing the crowd from seeing what was happening on the other side of the pitch, though *The Times* later reported that they weren't missing much because there was nothing much to miss.

Sheffield United were the pre-match favourites and won quite easily. Despite their emphatic victory there was none of the usual festivities afterwards; there was no victory parade and no celebratory dinner, and the players were even told not to smile for the official photographs. Instead, the team sneaked back to Sheffield after dark with the police given strict orders to disperse any misguided fans stupid enough to try and welcome them home.

Although the game was known as 'The Khaki Final' due to the great number of soldiers in attendance, *The Guardian* later reported that there was still a large section of the crowd who appeared to be 'young men of military age and not conspicuously unfit for service' and this may have been what prompted Edward Stanley, 17th Earl of Derby, to remark when addressing the 50,000 crowd after presenting the trophy that anyone not in uniform should step up and play 'a sterner game for England'.

AN ORIGINAL PIECE OF FOOTBALL IMPUDENCE
1970

In the 80th minute of Coventry's 3-1 win over Everton on 3 October 1970, Willie Carr took a free kick on the edge of the Everton penalty area, but instead of crossing the ball into the box hoping for the usual deflection, he gripped it between his ankles and flicked it into the air for the onrushing Ernie Hunt to volley the ball over the wall and past the goalkeeper into the top-right corner of the net.

Coventry coach Bill Asprey has been credited with developing what became known as the 'donkey kick'. After practising it in pre-season training with the two players, this was probably the first and only time that the move actually paid off in a competitive match. Luckily, the *Match of the Day* cameras were at Highfield Road that day to capture one of the most ingenious goals in the history of the sport, with the TV commentator John Motson calling it 'an original piece of football impudence'.

The jaw-dropping move was so controversial that FIFA immediately banned it.

FOOTBALL AT THE PALACE
2013

The first time that a competitive football match was staged at Buckingham Palace came on 7 October 2013.

Civil Service FC, the only surviving team from the 11 that formed the FA on 26 October 1863, were invited by HRH Prince William to play a fixture in the palace gardens as part of the FA's 150th-anniversary celebrations. They in turn selected another historic team, the Chiswick-based Southern Amateur League club Polytechnic FC as their opponents.

Wembley groundsmen and the royal household gardeners marked out the pitch in the 39-acre garden and the former Premier League and FIFA referee Howard Webb was chosen to officiate.

Before the game, around 150 volunteers, mainly coaches, referees and local officials who dedicated their free time to supporting amateur football causes were honoured in a special ceremony presided over by Prince William, who also addressed the players, 'Today we will be playing football on my grandmother's lawn. One warning, though – if anyone breaks a window, you can answer to her!' He then apologised for the Queen's absence but added, 'At least it means there will be no corgis invading the pitch!'

To add a little extra pomp and ceremony to the royal occasion, the half-time refreshments of water, orange slices and chocolate bars were served to the players from silver platters by palace footmen dressed in tailcoats.

THE POOLS PANEL
1963

With many matches being abandoned and many more postponed during the winter of 1962/63, the three big pools companies of Vernons, Zetters and Littlewoods established a committee called the Pools Promoters' Association Pools Panel to predict the match results in an attempt to better manage the loss of revenue incurred by all the fixture cancellations.

The first panel included the ex-players Tom Finney, Tommy Lawton, Ted Drake and George Young, along with the former referee Arthur Ellis, who sat behind closed doors in the swanky surroundings of the Grand Connaught Rooms in Holborn, London, on 26 January 1963 to decide the outcome of the 38 cancelled matches for that Saturday.

Using ex-players and others involved in football made sense – but rather bizarrely there was also a space on the first panel for people from outside the sport too. The Second World War flying ace Douglas Bader and the flamboyant Conservative MP Gerald Nabarro were also invited to attend, as was Britain's first aviator John Moore-Brabazon, 1st Baron Brabazon of Tara, who, at the meeting, actually described the whole idea of forecasting the results as 'a farce'.

PUTTING MONEY BACK INTO THE COMMUNITY
2002

Jamie Carragher was hit by a coin thrown from the crowd during Liverpool's FA Cup tie at Arsenal on 27 January 2002, but instead of falling to the ground and pretending to be close to death like any other player would have done, he just picked up the coin and hurled it back into the crowd.

The referee was not impressed and sent him off.

Carragher later received a police warning about his conduct, a £40,000 fine from his club and a three-match ban from the FA.

MIDNIGHT MADNESS
2003

The midweek La Liga match between Barcelona and Sevilla was originally scheduled for the evening of Wednesday, 3 September 2003, on the same day as the Spanish clubs were obliged to release their players for international duty in time for the upcoming weekend of fixtures. Not wishing to play with a weakened team, Barcelona appealed to the Real Federación Española de Fútbol to have the match brought forward to the Tuesday, but without success.

Barcelona no longer had a say over the day but they still had control over the kick off time – so they decided that it should kick off at 00.05am on the Wednesday! They could still field a full-strength team and their players would still get a good night's sleep before joining their international squads later in the day.

The club were a little worried that the fans wouldn't turn up at such a ridiculous hour, so they reduced the ticket prices, extended the Camp Nou museum's opening hours, laid on some live music and gave away lots of free snacks. But they needn't have worried; the novelty of the occasion, the party atmosphere, and the free Kit Kats, Doritos and cups of gazpacho attracted 80,237 fans to the stadium. The fact that it was also the home debut of their new Brazilian superstar striker Ronaldinho, who they'd signed earlier in the summer, probably helped a bit too.

GRABBING ALL THE HEADLINES
1976

Aston Villa defender Chris Nicholl seemed intent on grabbing all the headlines after he scored all four goals in his team's 2-2 Division One draw at Leicester City on 20 March 1976.

Twice he put Leicester ahead and then twice he equalised for Villa. He has since gone on record as saying that his third goal of the match – his second own goal – was the best he'd ever scored in his 19-year career. After hitting his first 'hat-trick' he asked the referee if he could keep the match ball but the official said no: it was the final game of his own career and he was keeping it for himself.

SORE LOSER
2011

Liverpool's Ryan Babel became the first player to be fined for a social media post.

He wasn't best pleased by referee Howard Webb awarding Manchester United a penalty after only two minutes of their FA Cup tie at Old Trafford on 9 January 2011, from which Ryan Giggs scored the winning goal, and then red-carding his team-mate Steven Gerrard for serious foul play after 31 minutes. After the game, he posted a doctored photo of Mr Webb wearing a Manchester United shirt with the caption, 'And they call him one of the best referees? That's a joke. SMH [Shaking My Head].' Babel later admitted to an FA charge of improper conduct and was fined £10,000.

BAD GOALKEEPERS
1993

Colchester United were the first Football League club to have two goalkeepers sent off in the same match.

John Keeley was dismissed in the 43rd minute of their 5-0 defeat at Hereford United on 16 October 1993 after hacking down a Hereford player; Roy McDonough replaced him in goal until half-time and then their substitute goalkeeper Nathan Munson came on for the second half. Except, he was sent off in the 68th minute and poor old Roy McDonough had to go back between the posts again.

Chris Pike scored a hat-trick against three different goalkeepers that day. His first goal, after 28 minutes, was against Keeley, his second was a 43rd-minute penalty against McDonough and his third came after 51 minutes against Munson.

THE BATTLE OF NUREMBERG
2006

Portugal's 1-0 last-16 victory over the Netherlands in 2006 was the most violent World Cup match ever played.

Hard-line Russian referee Valentin Ivanov set a new record for issuing cards in a finals game. In total he showed 16 yellow cards – including nine to just one team – and four red cards.

Dutch defender Mark van Bommel started it all as early as the second minute when he picked up a yellow for hacking down Portugal's star striker Cristiano Ronaldo, and his team-mate Giovanni van Bronckhorst ended it all in the fifth minute of stoppage time when he was shown a second yellow and then a red for a petulant trip on Tiago Mendes.

Ronaldo was still recovering from that first foul when Khalid Boulahrouz went in hard on him just four minutes later in what was a cynical and brutal attempt to kick him out of the game. Despite the viciousness of his studs-up tackle, he only received a yellow card and played on until the 63rd minute when he then elbowed Luís Figo in the face and was finally sent off after receiving another yellow card.

Portugal's first yellow card was issued to Maniche in the 20th minute and then three minutes later he scored the only goal of the game. Another ten minutes on, Costinha levelled the bookings at two apiece after a rash sliding tackle on Phillip Cocu and then earned the honour of becoming the game's first red-carded player after deliberately sticking out his arm to block a pass in first-half stoppage time.

The half-time break seemed to subdue the players a little. Petit picked up a fairly tame yellow in the 50th minute after pulling back Van Bommel but most of the unsporting behaviour, dissent, brutal tackling and persistent fouling of the first half had disappeared and the players were now passing the ball around, running into space and actually firing off shots.

It stayed that way until the hour mark and then a further nine bookings were awarded in just 20 minutes.

A mistimed tackle from Van Bronckhorst on Deco resulted in a bit of fisticuffs with many of the players squaring up to each other and Figo head-butting the ever-present Van Bommel. He went down like he'd just been hit by a truck, clutching his face, rolling around on the ground and using all his limited acting skills to get a second Portuguese player sent off. But perhaps he overdid it a bit because Figo only got a yellow.

Boulahrouz then decided to exact his own revenge on Figo by elbowing him in the face as he attempted to win the ball off him. The referee didn't take too kindly to his vigilante-style tactics and re-established numerical parity between the teams in the 63rd minute by showing him a second yellow card and then ordering him off.

Things went from bad to worse after 73 minutes when another flare-up saw another three players booked – Dutch duo Wesley Sneijder and Rafael van der Vaart, along with Deco. Deco had bundled over John Heitinga who was then yelled at by some Portuguese players for his overreaction to the foul. The two Dutchmen rushed to his aid and set upon the Portuguese players doing all the yelling before Mr

Ivanov intervened to break up the latest handbags-at-dawn moment by showing them all a yellow card.

Not to be left out, Portuguese goalkeeper Ricardo then got himself booked for a bit of time-wasting a couple of minutes later.

A needless foul by Nuno Valente added another yellow card to Portugal's tally after 76 minutes before a stupid handball from Deco earned him a second yellow and his team's second red card of the game two minutes later.

Nine-man Portugal somehow managed to hang on to their slim 1-0 lead for the remaining ten minutes.

FIFA president Sepp Blatter blamed the referee for such a shameful game, commenting that he should have shown himself a yellow card for his poor performance. Although Blatter later regretted these words and promised to apologise, poor Valentin Ivanov was never picked to referee another World Cup match ever again.

THE CRAZY ONE
1995

Colombian goalkeeper René Higuita was nicknamed *El Loco* (The Crazy One) for his unorthodox, high-risk, sweeper-keeper-style of play. He was well known for his flair and composure on the ball, often acting as an extra defender, running out of his area to challenge strikers, and even going on individual runs up the field and trying to dribble past opposition players to set up an attack.

The otherwise unremarkable friendly between England and Colombia on 6 September 1995 is only remembered for one particular moment of brilliance (or madness) when he pulled off one of the most audacious saves ever made by a goalkeeper.

Jamie Redknapp misfired a cross into the box and the ball floated towards the goal but, instead of just catching it like any normal keeper might have done, Higuita performed what would later be called a 'scorpion kick' – jumping forward with his back arched while positioning both legs over his head and kicking the ball away with his heels.

Although he was best known for his unconventional playing style and for inventing the scorpion kick, Higuita had a pretty eventful life off the field too. In 1993, he was imprisoned for seven months before being released without charge for his part in a kidnapping plot. He'd delivered the ransom money and ensured the victim's safe release but he'd also received a $64,000 reward for his services, therefore breaking the law by profiting from a kidnapping.

Commenting on the case, he later said, 'I'm a footballer. I didn't know anything about kidnapping laws.'

A DOG NAMED BRYN
1987

A German Shepherd police dog called Bryn inadvertently saved Torquay United from relegation in 1987.

It was the final day of the 1986/87 season and Torquay were second from bottom place in Division Four with 47 points, sandwiched between Burnley (46) and Lincoln (48). The year before, it wouldn't have mattered one jot who finished last but this was the first season when relegation to the Conference was automatic for the bottom team and so there was still everything to play for going into the last match.

Torquay could avoid the drop if they picked up some points against Crewe and one or both of their relegation rivals dropped points – Burnley were up against Leyton Orient and Lincoln faced Swansea.

At half-time Torquay were losing 2-0 and things were beginning to look a bit bleak. However, two minutes into the second half, centre-half Jim McNichol made it 2-1 when he blasted the ball home following a free kick. After that, Torquay continued attacking but seemed destined never to get that equaliser. They hit the crossbar and had a few near misses but time was running out, and that fairy tale ending was looking more and more unlikely.

Then, seven minutes from full time, a rather bizarre incident proved to be the catalyst for their Football League survival. As McNichol sprinted across to the touchline to take a quick throw-in, , the aforementioned police dog mistook him for someone about to attack his handler; he broke free from his leash and ran towards McNichol, locked his jaws around the player's thigh and sank his teeth into him.

At that time, teams were only allowed one substitute and Torquay had already used theirs. After a lengthy stoppage in which McNichol was patched up and sent back on to the pitch, the Torquay players were all told of the results in the other games, and knew they still had a chance to avoid relegation if they could just get one more goal. The referee was prepared to play an extra four minutes of added time and it was in the dying seconds of those additional four minutes that striker Paul Dobson pounced on a defensive mistake by Crewe and drilled the ball into the back of the net to make it 2-2.

Seconds later, the referee blew his whistle and the home supporters swarmed on to the pitch to celebrate their Football League survival.

McNichol later commented, 'I don't remember much, I was hobbling around. I didn't see any of the celebrations. I was off getting all sorts of injections and I had all the tetanus checks and tests. Then I went home and went to bed.'

Burnley beat Leyton Orient 2-1 to climb off the bottom and save themselves but Lincoln had lost 2-0 to Swansea, so although they'd finished on the same number of points as Torquay, it was the Imps who were relegated on goal difference.

A Devon & Cornwall Police spokesperson later commented that the biting incident was most unfortunate but Bryn was only doing his job.

But if it hadn't been for Bryn, Torquay wouldn't have had those extra four minutes to save themselves.

INTERNATIONAL FOOTBALL
1870

Between 1870 and 1872, the Wanderers player and FA secretary Charles W. Alcock organised a series of five representative football matches between England and Scotland. Despite being referred to as international games at the time, they have never been recognised as such by FIFA.

All of these unofficial matches took place at the Kennington Oval with the first one kicking off at 3.15pm on 5 March 1870 in front of 500–600 spectators. The English XI lost the coin toss and found themselves playing against a strong wind. Both teams appeared evenly matched with the play rather tame and monotonous due to the slippery conditions; Scotland were unable to take advantage of the wind at their backs, and at half-time it was still goalless.

England were considered the better team and with the wind advantage in the second half they dominated play. Only some quite brilliant defending and a heroic display from the Scottish keeper Alexander Morten denied them a goal. Surprisingly, it was Scotland who took the lead, against the run of play, after 75 minutes. Alcock, who was captaining the England team, had foolishly decided to move their keeper forward in support of the strikers, leaving their goal completely unguarded. When Robert Copland-Crawford got the ball, he just shot from distance at the empty net and scored with what the *Sporting Gazette* sarcastically described as 'a rather lucky kick'. Despite the setback, however, England continued pressing forward and were finally rewarded with a late goal after 89 minutes from Alfred Baker to level.

Four more England XI-Scotland XI games were played over the next year with England winning the series 3-0.

There was widespread resentment in Scotland that only London-based players had been considered for inclusion in the Scotland team. But Alcock dismissed the protests, vigorously defending his decision to include only 'London Scotchmen' and insisting that the invitation had been open to 'every Scotchman whether his lines were cast north or south of the Tweed' and it wasn't his fault that nobody north of the border had replied to the adverts he'd placed in the Scottish newspapers for players to come forward for selection.

The next match between England and Scotland took place later that same year on 30 November 1872 is officially recognised by FIFA as the first international football match ever played.

It had been proposed by Charles W. Alcock as a continuation of the series of games played earlier in the year and was viewed as an opportunity to further promote the playing of Association Rules football in Scotland. At this time, some of the Scottish teams were still playing by their own set of rules and appeared reluctant to adopt the new ones invented by the English.

Although the Scottish Football Association hadn't yet been formed, the Glasgow club Queen's Park accepted the invitation to play England and the match was subsequently arranged for 30 November 1872 at the Hamilton Cricket Ground in Glasgow.

A photographer had been hired for the occasion but when he was told that there was no guarantee of the Scottish team paying for any of the prints, he just upped and left. The only pictorial record of the match is an illustration by the Glaswegian artist William Ralston, later published in *The Graphic* newspaper on 14 December 1872, which showed nine separate scenes of the game.

The English players were selected by Alcock from nine different clubs although he didn't play himself due to injury. The Scottish team had hoped to secure the services of Wanderers' Arthur Kinnaird and Henry Renny-Tailyour of Royal Engineers, but both men were unavailable, so all 11 players selected by captain Robert Gardner came from his own club, Queen's Park.

The match kicked off 20 minutes late at 2.20pm in front of around 2,500 spectators (with ladies admitted free of charge). The pitch was heavy after three days of almost continuous rain and the smaller and lighter Scots were clearly the better side for most of the match, having a goal disallowed and a shot by Robert Leckie hitting the tape. But despite their home advantage, a Scottish referee, a superior passing game and playing a 2-2-6 formation, they failed to break the deadlock and the match finished in a rather disappointing 0-0 draw. England did play a little better in the second half; they had eight forwards on the pitch but they couldn't manage a goal either.

Though it was a goalless draw, the quality of play was widely praised, with *The Field* defining it 'as spirited and as pleasant as can possibly be imagined' and the *Aberdeen Journal* describing the game as the best ever seen in Scotland.

* * *

Before the formation of any leagues and long before the rest of the world started playing football, Scotland were the best team in the world – between 1874 and 1887 they won ten and drew three of their 14 games, thrashing England 6-1 (1881), 5-1 (1882) and 7-2 (1878) and inflicting even heavier defeats on Wales and Ireland in the same period. In the early internationals, the Scots were already playing their 'Scottish style' passing game with everyone else still practicing the outdated dribbling-focused style of play which meant they rarely had possession of the ball. Then everyone else started copying them. They got better and Scotland just got worse. And they've been pretty dire ever since!

* * *

The oldest football shirt known to exist is the England jersey worn by the Oxford University player Arnold Kirke Smith when he played his one and only game for his country, against Scotland on 30 November 1872. The shirt is now on display at the National Football Museum in Manchester.

FIGHTING TEAM-MATES
2005

Lee Bowyer and Kieron Dyer of Newcastle United were the first players in the Premier League from the same team to be sent off after fighting with each other, both seeing red during a home defeat to Aston Villa on 2 April 2005.

Juan Pablo Ángel opened the scoring for Villa after only five minutes; Gareth Barry made it 2-0 from the penalty spot in the 73rd minute after Steven Taylor was red-carded for deliberately handling the ball, and then 3-0 in the 80th minute from another penalty after Darius Vassell was bodychecked in the area.

But nobody remembers any of that; they just remember what happened in the 81st minute.

The home team were three goals and one man down and, as if things weren't already bad enough, two of their players then started fighting among themselves. With no chance of a comeback, Bowyer and Dyer decided to take out their frustration on each other.

Bowyer confronted his team-mate and accused him of never passing the ball. Dyer responded by telling him that he never passed the ball because he was such a shit player. Bowyer walked menacingly towards him, pushing his head towards Dyer's face; they grappled, Dyer tried to shove him away, which prompted Bowyer to throw a couple of punches in retaliation. Just as Dyer was about to fight back, players from both sides rushed to intervene and break up the scuffle with Bowyer eventually being dragged away with his shirt ripped at the neck. Both players were dismissed but continued their spat in the tunnel and had to be separated by team officials.

In the dressing room after the game, their manager Graeme Souness reportedly invited both players to have a proper fight if they were such tough guys but they refused and instead they were whisked into a hastily arranged press conference to apologise for their actions. They both sat shamefaced either side of the manager and said sorry to all the usual suspects – the fans, the chairman and the staff, the other players, families and friends, and anybody else who'd witnessed their little catfight.

The FA handed down a three-match ban to both players and Newcastle fined Bowyer a record six weeks' wages as he was perceived to have thrown the first punch. The FA later increased his ban by three more matches and fined him an additional £30,000, and then Northumbria Police charged him with offences under the Public Order Act. He eventually pleaded guilty to a lesser charge of using threatening behaviour and was fined £600 plus £1,000 costs.

MIX UP WITH THE MEDALS
1992

Liverpool's 2-0 victory over Sunderland on 9 May 1992 saw the first FA Cup Final where the losing team were invited to collect their medals ahead of the winners.

Sunderland's players had been first to climb the 39 steps to Wembley's Royal Box to collect the little blue boxes containing their medals. The Liverpool squad then followed and walked away with their little red boxes.

Except it should have been the other way around as the blue boxes contained the winners' medals and the red boxes contained the losers' prizes. After an awkward few minutes when all the players just stood around on the pitch looking a little confused and questioning whether they'd actually won or lost the match, they began swapping the boxes among themselves.

Presumably someone forgot to tell the dignitaries what was going to happen and which medals were in which boxes.

THAT NOTORIOUS SPITTING INCIDENT
1990

No doubt there have been a few times when one player has spat at another player during a match. It's not pleasant and it's rightly condemned. Thank goodness it rarely happens. But when it does, it's always going to make the headlines.

The incident involving Frank Rijkaard of the Netherlands and West Germany's Rudi Völler during a 1990 World Cup last-16 match is certainly the most famous, thanks largely to the close-up TV images.

Everyone was expecting a volatile game due to the fierce long-standing rivalry between the Germans and the Dutch – and they weren't disappointed.

In the 21st minute, Rijkaard received a yellow card for a harsh tackle on Völler. It was his second caution of the tournament, meaning he'd miss the quarter-final should the Dutch progress. Clearly maddened by what he believed was an unjust punishment, he spat at Völler as he ran past him to take up his position for the free kick. The little goblet of mucus flew through the air and landed in the striker's immaculately coiffured mullet; Völler complained to the referee, inviting him to inspect the spittle in his hair, but the official was having none of it, and booked him as well.

The free kick was floated into the area by Andreas Brehme, and the Dutch keeper Hans van Breukelen raced off his line to grab it. But Völler also contested the ball and the two players inevitably clattered into one another despite Völler seemingly doing all he could to avoid a collision. Rijkaard was the only Dutch player who overreacted; walking across to Völler, getting in his face and pinching his ear like a petulant little child. Players from both sides, notably Van

Breukelen and German striker Jürgen Klinsmann, then intervened to drag them apart.

The referee brandished a red card at Rijkaard and then turned around and did the same to Völler. The German was dumbfounded by the decision to dismiss him and as he stood there rooted to the spot, pondering the injustice of it all, Rijkaard walked past him, conjured up another mouthful of phlegm from the back of his throat, took aim and landed another direct hit on Völler's flowing blond locks.

Völler was still rooted to the spot but now he was rooted to the spot with a big goblet of phlegm dangling from the back of his head.

As Rijkaard was escorted off the field by Dutch team officials, Völler broke into a little jog – and the world held its breath. It looked like he might attack his saliva-spewing assailant, prompting another, much bigger and much more exciting brawl. But rather disappointingly, he chose to be the bigger man and just continued jogging right past Rijkaard without so much as a mumbled insult or a sideways glance.

Unsurprisingly, Rijkaard later earned the nickname of 'Llama' in the German press.

WHITE BALLS
1927

A white ball was first trialled as an alternative to the traditional brown leather ball in a pre-season game between the Arsenal first and second teams at Highbury on 13 August 1927, but it wasn't until many years later that they were regularly used in competitive matches.

The idea of using a white-painted ball wasn't entirely new as they'd already been used in Europe, but it was a Mr E.L. Roberts of Shrewsbury in a letter published by the *Athletic News* who first alerted the FA to the desirability of using them in English matches. His proposal was accompanied by a front-page editorial endorsement written by the examateur footballer and Olympic Games gold medallist Ivan Sharpe, arguing that the white balls would indeed be a welcome innovation because spectators found it difficult to see a brown ball being kicked around a brown, muddy field on the gloomiest days of a British winter.

A few club managers were sufficiently intrigued to test the white balls during their pre-season matches in the summer of 1927, although it seems that all the players and match officials involved in the experiment were left pretty unimpressed, claiming they'd lost sight of the balls in the air and that they were often too slippery to control. Sometimes the white paint was so poorly applied that it rubbed off the ball and by the end of the match the teams were back to playing with a brown ball again anyway.

The *Burnley News* triumphantly declared that the use of these white balls was dead in the water, 'The experiment has met with a chorus of condemnation, and we may take it for granted that the white ball has been kicked for the last time.'

It wasn't until 1951 that the Football League finally allowed the use of white balls, although their appearance was fairly infrequent at first with most games continuing to start with the traditional brown ball and then switching to a white one only if the weather got a bit murky. By now the manufacturing process for the white balls had improved considerably with a first layer of white paint being protected by a second layer of cellulose, which also guarded against the ball absorbing water. Some of the old brown leather balls increased in weight by as much as 20 per cent on a wet day! The new lighter balls aided smaller players, favoured the short passing game and were a lot easier to hoof around the pitch than some sodden old leather ball.

In 1953, the FA recommended using white balls from the start of a match or not at all and, in the following years, more and more teams chose to play with the lighter, more modern white footballs. By the time they were used at the 1958 World Cup in Sweden they were no longer considered a novelty.

Everybody was using them now. Except when it snowed, and then they used the orange balls.

WHEN A FOOTBALL MATCH STARTED A WAR
1969

Honduras and El Salvador were paired together in Group 2 for the second-round of CONCACAF qualification matches for the 1970 World Cup.

The first game was held in Tegucigalpa, Honduras, on 8 June 1969, with the home team winning 1-0. The Salvadoran team had been harassed by the Honduran fans at their hotel the night before the game and then, afterwards, the Salvadoran supporters reportedly set fires in the stadium. The return took place in San Salvador on 15 June, won 3-0 by El Salvador. Before the match, the Salvadorians had rioted outside their opponents' hotel and a dirty rag had been flown at the stadium instead of the Honduran flag; then, after the game, anti-Salvadorian riots took place all across Honduras, forcing many Salvadorian immigrants to flee the country.

With the matches tied at one win each, the two teams then had to meet again to decide the Group 2 winner. A play-off took place in Mexico City on 27 June which El Salvador eventually won 3-2 after extra time.

The night before this match, El Salvador had cut all diplomatic ties with Honduras, claiming that 12,000 of their countrymen had been forced to flee Honduras following those anti-Salvadorian riots, and that the Honduran government had failed to punish the perpetrators or offer the victims any reparations.

Following a series of border skirmishes, war broke out between the two countries on 14 July 1969 when Salvadorian forces launched a military attack against Honduras.

Although the hostilities only lasted for a few days, there were still many killed and injured on both sides before a peace agreement brokered by the Organization of American States came into effect on 18 July.

The war has since been dubbed 'The 100 Hour War' (because of its brevity) or 'The Soccer War' because the sparks which ignited the flames occurred in the football stadiums of Tegucigalpa and San Salvador.

THE LORD OF MILAN
1899

After playing for his local church team and then amateur club Notts Olympic, Herbert Kilpin moved to Turin in Italy to work in a textile factory owned by the Italian industrialist Edoardo Bosio.

Bosio had spent some time in England and had become a big football fan, so on his return to his homeland he formed the first-ever Italian club, Torino Football & Cricket Club, in 1887. Four years later they merged with another local club, Nobili Torino, to become Internazionale Torino.

Kilpin played for Internazionale Torino from 1891 until 1899, becoming the first Brit to play football abroad, and during his time at the club he took part in the first two seasons of the Campionato Italiano di Calcio.

In 1899, Kilpin travelled east to Milan where he and his expat friend Alfred Edwards decided to form their own football club, Milan Foot-Ball and Cricket Club (later renamed AC Milan), claiming, 'We will be a team of devils. Our colours will be red like fire and black like the fear we will invoke in our opponents.'

He also served as the team's first player-manager, making a total of 23 appearances in nine seasons, and leading the club to three league championship wins, in 1901, 1906 and 1907. He wasn't a particularly good player but he was still the club founder and presumably got a game easy enough whenever he felt the need to slip on his boots. Apparently, he was famed for his boozy antics and even kept a bottle of whisky behind the goal to soften the blow when the opposition scored.

In honour of the club's English origins the club are still called AC Milan instead of the more obvious AC Milano.

SUNDAY FOOTBALL
1974

In 1974, Britain was in the midst of an energy crisis owing to industrial action by the coal miners and railway workers, resulting in the government imposing a three-day working week for businesses and public services from 1 January in an effort to conserve coal stocks and reduce the nation's electricity consumption.

With the football clubs also looking at ways of saving energy, floodlit games were suspended and matches were scheduled to be played on Sundays to cope with the fixture backlog. It proved to be a popular innovation and attendances on Sundays were generally higher than average. The law at the time prevented an admission fee being collected for any events held on a Sunday but the clubs got around that little obstacle by making every fan buy a programme before entering the ground.

Four FA Cup third-round matches were scheduled for Sunday, 6 January with Cambridge United v Oldham Athletic at the Abbey Stadium being the first due to its 11am kick off time. The first Sunday league games were played two weeks later.

Swindon Town's Scottish goalkeeper Jimmy Allan was the first player who refused to play on the Sabbath due to his devout religious beliefs. His manager Les Allen was quoted at the time as saying how much he fully respected his position – and then dropped him from the team! He never got his place back for another two years.

A GREAT NOISE IN THE CITY – THE ETON FIELD GAME
Masters vs. Old Etonians (1905)

HALF-TIME TEAM TALK ON THE PITCH
The Hull City manager Phil Brown ripping his players a new one in front of everyone during the half-time break in the Premier League match against Manchester City on 26 December 2008.

THE FAT BASTARD PIE-EATING GOALKEEPER
William 'Fatty' Foulke appearing front and centre in a Chelsea team photograph of 1905.

THE THEFT OF THE JULES RIMET TROPHY
Pickles posing for photographers near to the spot where he found the stolen Jules Rimet trophy.

LETTERED SHIRTS
The Bolivian World Cup team proudly sporting their lettered shirts paying tribute to the host nation of Uruguay in a photograph taken prior to their opening game against Yugoslavia on 17 July 1930.

THE WEMBLEY WIZARDS
The Scottish captain Jimmy McMullan leading out his 'Wembley Wizards' team for the British Home Championship match against England at Wembley Stadium on 31 March 1928.

WHEN SCOTLAND BELIEVED THEY COULD WIN THE WORLD CUP
Archie Gemmill scoring Scotland's third goal in their 3-2 win over the Netherlands at the World Cup finals in Argentina on 11 June 1978.

ELECTRIFYING THE FANS
The Chelsea chairman Ken Bates showing off the newly installed electric fencing at Stamford Bridge on 25 April 1985.

A SOUTH AMERICAN HORROR STORY
Police intervening to escort the Racing Club player Alfio Basile off the pitch in the Intercontinental Cup game against Celtic on 4 November 1967.

SNIFFING THE LINE
The Liverpool striker Robbie Fowler celebrating a goal against Everton in a Premier League game on 3 April 1999.

THE TEAM WITH TWO NUMBER NINES
The Inter Milan striker Iván Zamorano wearing his unique number 9 shirt during a Serie A game against Napoli on 14 October 2000.

MORE EUROPEAN TROPHIES THAN DOMESTIC LEAGUE TITLES
Captain John McGovern lifting the European Cup after Nottingham Forest's shock win over Malmo on 30 May 1979.

SOUND & VISION
Poster for the film The Arsenal Stadium Mystery *(1939).*

THE HERO OF SEVILLE
Fans of FCSB (Steaua Bucureşti) displaying a tifo in honour of Helmut Duckadam (1959–2024) before the UEFA Europa League game against Manchester United at the National Arena, Bucharest (Romania) on 30 January 2025.

THE BEST AND THE WORST OF THE MAN
The Argentinian striker Diego Maradona scoring his controversial 'Hand of God' goal in the World Cup quarter-final match against England on 22 June 1986.

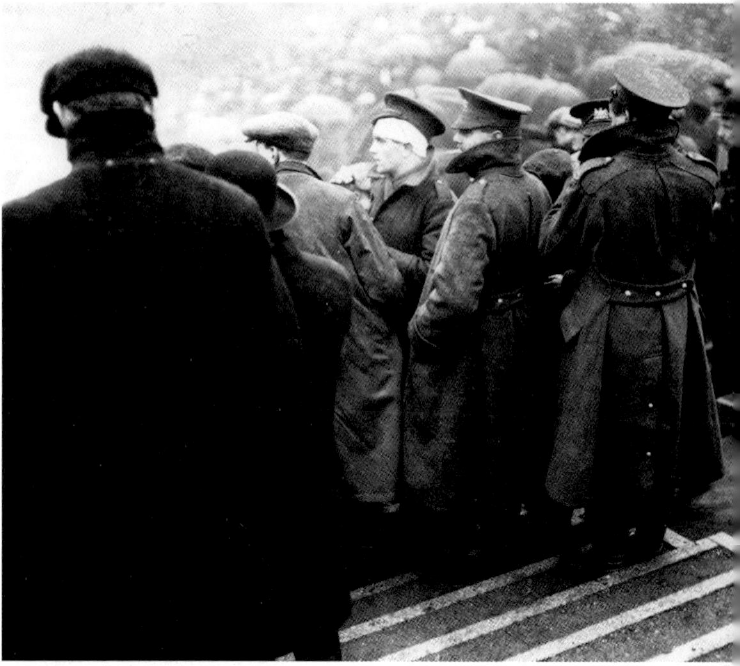

THE KHAKI FINAL
Soldiers dressed in their khaki uniforms attending the FA Cup Final on 24 April 1915.

TED DRAKE · ARTHUR ELLIS · TOM FINNEY · TOMMY LAWTON · GEORGE YOUNG

THE POOLS PANEL
First meeting of the pools panel held on 26 January 1963.

INTERNATIONAL FOOTBALL
Scenes from the first international football match played between Scotland and England on 30 November 1872 drawn by the Glaswegian artist William Ralston (1848–1911) and first published in The Graphic *newspaper on 14 December 1872.*

HAT NOTORIOUS SPITTING INCIDENT
ank Rijkaard spitting at Rudi
ller during the West Germany vs
etherlands World Cup finals match
24 June 1990.

WOMEN'S FOOTBALL
Artist's impression of the first British Ladies' FC match played on 23 March 1895.

THE MOST STUPID, APPALLING, DISGUSTING AND DISGRACEFUL EXHIBITION OF FOOTBALL
The Italian midfielder Giorgio Ferrini being escorted from the pitch by armed policemen during a World Cup finals match between Chile and Italy on 2 June 1962.

FLYING OBJECTS ABOVE THE STADIUM
The Graf Zeppelin airship passing low over Wembley Stadium during the FA Cup Final on 26 April 1930.

THE MASTER OF THE DARK ARTS
Luis Suárez deliberately handling the ball in Uruguay's World Cup finals match against Ghana on 2 July 2010.

THE ON-FIELD MARRIAGE PROPOSAL
2022

In the 85th minute of the Belarusian First League match between FK Smorgon and Volna Pinsk, the Smorgon defender Vladislav Shubovich converted a penalty to seal a 2-0 win for the home team. After accepting all the usual hugs and kisses from his team-mates, he then ran across to the stand where his girlfriend was sitting, got down on one knee and produced a ring. However, he didn't expect an overzealous steward to intervene and ruin his big moment.

As Shubovich's partner approached the pitch, the steward thought she was an overenthusiastic fan, stepped in between her and Vladislav and violently shoved her back towards the stand. Shubovich then jumped to his feet and shoved the steward and, for a brief moment, it looked like things were going to get a bit ugly, as his team-mates (and even the referee) all encircled the idiot steward to do a bit of shoving of their own. Fair play to the guy: after realising his mistake, he appeared to apologise before hastily making his retreat.

As the steward faded away into the background, the girlfriend was then beckoned forward to the touchline again.

Shubovich got back down on one knee as his applauding team-mates rallied around him, she finally said yes, they hugged and kissed, and then an anonymous woman who'd been standing nearby clutching a giant bouquet of flowers handed them to Vladislav, who then gave them to his new fiancée.

Love had triumphed in the end.

WOMEN'S FOOTBALL
1881
MRS GRAHAM'S XI

Mrs Graham's XI was formed in 1881 by the Scottish artist/suffragette Helen Matthews using the pseudonym of Mrs

Graham. Their first match, on 7 May 1881, was against a team of English suffragettes which was billed as a Scotland v England international. It was played in front of around 1,000 spectators at the original home ground of Hibernian, with the *Glasgow Herald* noting that the Scottish women were kitted out in 'blue jerseys, white knickerbockers, red belts and high heeled boots'.

Scotland won 3-0 with Lily St Clair getting the first goal in the history of women's football.

On 20 May the teams played each other again, this time in front of 5,000 in Glasgow, but the match was abandoned after only 55 minutes when the crowd invaded the pitch. The women were jostled and chased out of the ground by an angry mob and had to make their escape in a horse-drawn bus.

After further violence at other matches, women's football was outlawed in Scotland shortly afterwards, and Helen Matthews moved south to England to play for British Ladies' Football Club.

In 2018 Helen Graham was inducted into the Scottish Women in Sport Hall of Fame for having pioneered women's team football in Scotland.

BRITISH LADIES' FOOTBALL CLUB

British Ladies' FC was formed on 1 January 1895 by Mary Hutson, under the pseudonym of Nettie Honeyball. In 1894, Nettie had placed an advertisement in the *Daily Graphic* seeking like-minded ladies interested in playing football. The ad attracted about 30 replies and the women soon began training under the tutelage of the Tottenham wing-half Bill Julian.

In an interview for the *Daily Sketch* in 1895, Nettie explained that she'd founded BLFC 'with the fixed resolve of proving to the world that women are not the ornamental and useless creatures men have pictured'.

Their first match took place on 23 March 1895 in front of 10,000 spectators at the Crouch End Athletic Ground in London, with the women organised into two teams representing north and south London. It lasted for 60 minutes with the north winning 7-1. Newspaper coverage was extensive but also fairly derisive and unsupportive of the women, with the *Manchester Guardian* commenting, 'When the novelty has worn off, I do not think women's football will attract the crowds.'

The *Daily Sketch* was probably the most scathing in its criticism, 'The first few minutes were sufficient to show that football by women, if the British Ladies be taken as a criterion, is totally out of the question. A footballer requires speed, judgement, skill and pluck. Not one of these four qualities was apparent on Saturday. For the most part the ladies wandered aimlessly over the field at an ungraceful jog-trot.'

The women no longer had to wear corsets or high-heeled boots like Mrs Graham's XI did back in 1881, although they did wear bonnets and the game had to be paused sometimes when a player headed the ball and dislodged it. Play was only resumed once any hairpins had been adjusted or replaced and the bonnet re-tied back into position.

The women were often heckled, insulted and laughed at by the crowds but, despite this aggression towards them, they still played over 100 north v south exhibition matches all around the country in the next two years and raised many thousands of pounds for charity.

By late 1896, however, the strain of playing so many fixtures was taking its toll; finances were in a bit of a mess, player numbers were dwindling and by the following year the club had folded.

The first great women's player was probably BLFC midfielder Daisy Allen, who played in the north team alongside Nettie Honeyball. She was only 11 years old and about 4ft tall but the *Bristol Times* noted that she was 'a brave young girl that [led] her team-mates with great courage'.

DICK, KERR LADIES

Perhaps the most famous of all the early women's football teams were the Dick, Kerr Ladies formed in 1917.

Women replaced the men in the factories during the First World War and many of them formed football teams. The Dick, Kerr Ladies team was named after the engineering company, Dick, Kerr & Co. in Preston, where most of the players worked, and they soon became the most successful women's team of the time, playing over 800 games between 1917 and 1965. Their first match was a 4-0 win against the Coulthard's Foundry Ladies played in front of around 10,000 spectators at Preston North End's Deepdale ground on Christmas Day 1917 to raise money for the wounded soldiers being treated at the town's Moor Park Hospital.

Alfred Frankland was a clerk at the company; he'd originally suggested forming a works team to play charity matches and eventually became their manager, organising the matches and arranging for the women to train at the company's Ashton Park sports ground with the help of several members of the Preston North End coaching staff.

Frankland believed that they were a good enough team to represent England and contacted the Fédération des Sociétés Féminines Sportives de France, which promoted women's sport in France, to arrange a series of games against their best players. The FSFSF accepted the challenge and four matches were scheduled to take place in Preston, Stockport, Manchester and London. The first of these unofficial England v France fixtures was played at Deepdale on 30 April 1920. England won 2-0 with goals from Florrie Redford and Jennie Harris.

Dick, Kerr Ladies won their second match 5-2, drew the third 1-1 and then lost 2-1 in the last outing. This game, at Stamford Bridge, caused a bit of a stir in the newspapers after the two captains Alice Kell and Madeleine Bracquemond kissed each other following the final whistle.

The team embarked on a tour of their own later that same year to France, playing another four games against the same French XI in Paris, Roubaix, Havre and Rouen between 31 October and 7 November. Although the first game ended in a draw, the Dick, Kerr Ladies emerged as 2-0, 6-0 and 2-0 winners in the other three.

THE NAZI COLLABORATOR
1940

The Algerian-born midfielder Alex Villaplane was the first footballer of north African origin to play for France. He won the first of his 25 caps in 1926 against Belgium and was appointed the team captain just before the 1930 World Cup in Uruguay.

He led his team to a 4-1 victory over Mexico in the inaugural World Cup match on 13 July 1930, which he later described as 'the happiest day of my life', and 14 years later, on 27 December 1944, he was executed by firing squad for being one of the most despicable traitors in the history of France – which was probably the worst day of his life.

Villaplane was a high-energy, tough-tackling player, hailed as the best header of the ball in France, and one of the most perceptive passers. He made his name at Nimes from 1927 to 1929 but it wasn't until he moved to Racing Club de Paris that his career really took off. He was well paid for his services and was often seen living it up in the city's fashionable bars and nightclubs or at the horse track splashing the cash and hanging out with gangsters and other lowlife criminals. In 1932 he moved to FC Antibes and helped them win the championship – but then it emerged that the crucial play-off against SC Fives Lille had been fixed. Antibes were stripped of the title with their manager getting the blame, although it was widely believed that Villaplane and a couple of his dodgy team-mates were the real instigators behind the scam. Antibes soon got rid of him, then he popped up at Nice in 1933 – and they got rid of him too. By this point he was slow and out of shape and totally disinterested in playing football. After a brief spell at lower-division club Hispano-Bastidienne he ended up in prison for his part in some crooked scheme to fix a few horse races.

After his release, Villaplane got involved in every shady money-making scheme imaginable – even gold smuggling. At some point, after the Germans occupied France in 1940, he hooked up with the Parisian mobster Henri Lafont and became part of the French Gestapo. They would regularly track down Jews, resistance fighters and other enemies of the Third Reich and in return the Nazis would turn a blind eye to their criminal activities. Villaplane soon acquired a liking for the violence and impressed his Nazi overlords with his commitment to their cause. In 1944, his loyalty was rewarded with the go-ahead to set up his own unit made up of north African immigrants which he called the Brigade Nord Africain. The BNA soon gained a reputation for cruelty with Villaplane ordering his men to rape, murder and burn their prisoners alive. He himself was accused of pulling the trigger when 11 resistance fighters were captured and executed in the French village of Mussidan on 11 June 1944.

When he realised that Germany wasn't going to win the war, Villaplane attempted to gain favour with people by staging very public acts of mercy or allowing a few of his captives to escape. But all this sudden compassion came at a price. He was still an evil bastard and would only save lives if he was going to make some money from it.

In August 1944, with the Allied forces approaching Paris, the Parisians rose up against their oppressors. Punishment for any suspected collaborators was swift and very bloody.

Villaplane was hunted down, put on trial and sentenced to death. He was then executed along with his old BFF Henri Lafont at Ford de Montrouge in Paris on 27 December 1944.

THE FASTEST RED
2000

Lee Todd picked up the quickest red card ever recorded during a Sunday league clash, between Cross Farm Park Celtic and Taunton East Reach Wanderers on 31 October 2000.

Just before kick off the referee had warned all the players that he wouldn't tolerate any bad language – then he blew his whistle to signal the start of the game. Unfortunately for Todd, the full-time builder and part-time striker for Cross Farm Park, the official was standing next to him and blew the whistle right in his ear. He instinctively blurted out, 'Fuck me, Ref. That was loud!' and two seconds later he was being ordered to leave the field for an early bath (although it's doubtful if he actually needed one). Todd asked the referee if he was taking the piss and he confirmed that he wasn't. He'd warned everyone about swearing and Todd had just sworn, so he was off. Todd's team-mates had a good laugh as he trudged back to the dressing room, seemingly unconcerned about playing the whole match with just ten men. Presumably they knew their opponents were so bad they could have put out a five-a-side team and still won; it finished 11-2 in their favour.

Todd was later fined £27 and banned from playing football for 35 days. The red card remains the fastest-ever recorded at two seconds.

THE FAKE TEAM
2010

A week after Bahrain's apparent 3-0 friendly victory over Togo on 7 September 2010, the Togo FA announced that they hadn't sent a team to play in Bahrain.

Sports minister Christophe Tchao seemed to confirm this during an interview with *Jeune Afrique* magazine when he said that nobody in Togo had 'ever been informed of such a game'. It seems that the Bahrain FA had employed the services of some dodgy match fixer from Singapore and he'd just rounded up a group of random African players and called them Togo. Every player was an imposter. Apparently, the real Togo team had been on a bus travelling back from Botswana at the same time as they were supposed to be playing in Bahrain.

Bahrain manager Josef Hickersberger told the *Gulf Daily News* that the match had been a complete waste of time, 'They were not fit enough to play 90 minutes. The match was very boring.'

SHORTEST TIME IN THE JOB
2007

Fred Everiss holds the record for the longest managerial career at any British club. He led West Bromwich Albion for 46 years between 1902 and 1948, winning a Division One title in 1919/20 and an FA Cup in 1931. In contrast, Leroy Rosenior was in a managerial job for the shortest period of time. He was appointed as head coach of Torquay United on 17 May 2007. A press conference was quickly arranged to make the announcement but unfortunately for Rosenior, by the time it had ended, the club had been sold and the new owner had decided to appoint somebody else.

He'd been in the job for just ten minutes!

THE MOST STUPID, APPALLING, DISGUSTING AND DISGRACEFUL EXHIBITION OF FOOTBALL
1962

The Battle of Santiago – possibly the ugliest and most violent game of football ever played in the ugliest and most violent

World Cup ever staged. In the eight fixtures prior to this infamous match it seemed like everyone had forgotten about playing football, with dirty tricks and brutal fouls dominating the games, resulting in players leaving the field injured with cracked ribs, fractured ankles and broken legs, or being sent off by the referees with almost as much regularity as they were being booked.

Chile's 2-0 group-stage victory over Italy did nothing to break that cycle of violence.

Shortly before the 1962 tournament, the Chileans got to hear about a series of inflammatory articles written about their country in the Italian newspapers *La Nazione* and *Corriere della Sera*. The journalists believed it was 'pure madness' to stage the tournament in such a country 'proudly miserable and backwards' and claimed Santiago was a city where 'the phones don't work, taxis are as rare as faithful husbands, a cable to Europe costs an arm and a leg and a letter takes five days to turn up', where 'entire neighbourhoods are given over to open prostitution' and 'the people are prone to malnutrition, illiteracy, alcoholism and poverty'.

The Chilean newspapers retaliated by describing all Italians as oversexed, drug-addicted fascists, and tensions were already running high even before the kick off on 2 June.

The *Daily Mirror* reported, 'The pitch quickly became a battlefield as players forgot the ball and concentrated on kicking the nearest opponent.' The first foul was committed after only 12 seconds and the first dismissal came after eight minutes, Italy's Giorgio Ferrini after a foul on Honorino Landa – but he refused to leave, until armed policemen were called on to the pitch to drag him off.

The two teams continued spitting, kicking and provoking each other with the police being called upon to intervene on three further occasions.

Chilean forward Leonel Sánchez had a particularly busy game. In all the commotion that surrounded the dismissal of Ferrini, he swung a left hook at Italy's captain Humberto Maschio and broke his nose. Then, in the 38th minute, he landed another punch on the Italian defender Mario David in retaliation for being fouled by him seconds earlier. English referee Ken Aston missed both incidents but when David attempted to kick Sánchez in the head a few minutes later, he was sent off, leaving Italy with nine men.

It was also Sánchez who took the free kick which led to Jaime Ramírez heading the opening goal after 73 minutes. Jorge Toro then added a second after 87 minutes with a long-range shot.

The bad feeling between the two countries inevitably continued after the game. In Italy, Chilean immigrants suddenly found themselves banned from bars and restaurants and the army was dispatched to guard Chile's embassy in Rome. In Chile, the Italian training camp was placed under armed guard and then Jorge Pica, a senior member of the Federación de Fútbol de Chile, caused further controversy by alleging that the Italian players had all been doped up to the eyeballs.

The Italians also had the audacity to criticise Ken Aston for failing to control the match and his biased officiating.

When David Coleman introduced the BBC's highlights show on 5 June 1962, he famously remarked, 'The game you are about to see is the most stupid, appalling, disgusting and disgraceful exhibition of football in the history of the game. This is the first time these countries have met; we hope it will be the last. The national motto of Chile reads, "By Reason or By Force." Today, the Chileans weren't prepared to be reasonable, the Italians used force, and the result was a disaster for the World Cup.'

LAST MAN STANDING
1937

Not long after kick off in Chelsea's Division One game at home to Charlton Athletic on 25 December 1937, a thick fog descended over the stadium. Sam Bartram was keeping goal for Charlton at the far end of the pitch and watched the fog steadily creeping past the opposition goalie Vic Woodley and then engulfing the outfield players as it rolled towards him. His team-mates were attacking the Chelsea goal and within a short time, Bartram had lost sight of all the players on the field.

The next person he saw was a policeman appearing out of the fog. 'What on earth are you doing here?' he asked. 'The game was stopped a quarter of an hour ago. The field's completely empty.'

Bartram's reaction had been a mixture of laughter and embarrassment. The poor man had been heroically guarding his goal against nobody for 15 minutes!

All the other players from both teams were already back in the dressing rooms, languishing in the bath and downing cups of tea. Bartram hadn't heard the referee's whistle to end the match due to the cheering and shouting of the fans behind him in the stands, and had just assumed that his continued solitude meant his team-mates were still somewhere up the other end of the field doing their damnedest to get a goal. Little did he know that he was completely alone on the pitch and standing guard over a goal that no longer needed guarding.

What a way to spend your Christmas Day.

FLYING OBJECTS ABOVE THE STADIUM
1930 | 1954
AIRSHIPS

The 1930 FA Cup Final between Arsenal and Huddersfield is remembered for the sudden appearance of the world's largest airship, the *Graf Zeppelin*, drifting low over the stadium at the start of the second half. The 775ft-long, cigar-shaped craft passed slowly over the 92,000-strong crowd with the noise of its five 12-cylinder engines drowning out their cheers. Photos taken at the time seem to suggest that it almost skimmed the top of the stands.

The *Zeppelin* dipped its nose to salute George V, who was present at Wembley, and then continued south on its journey back across the English Channel.

The sight of a German airship hovering low above the stadium was both exciting and a little menacing. It was a symbol of Germany's rising power and for many it brought back memories of wartime when airships were used to bomb London and the Home Counties in 1915 and 1916. But while the crowd were stunned into silence by its presence, the players didn't even blink an eye. Play continued as if the appearance of a bloody great airship above their heads was commonplace at any FA Cup Final.

SPACESHIPS

The Italians went one better because they had UFOs appearing above one of their stadiums!

The referee stopped play just after half-time in the reserve match between Fiorentina and Pistoiese on 27 October 1954 when the crowd began pointing at the sky instead of pointing at the game. The fans and the players were left open-mouthed as they watched the cigar-shaped flying objects hovering above them for several minutes and dropping a 'silvery glittery' substance all over the Stadio Artemio Franchi in Florence.

The weird goings-on were reported throughout Tuscany and reports followed in the newspapers, with *La Nazione*'s headline reading 'Glass fibres fall on Tuscan cities after globes and flying saucers pass by'. There were no reports of anyone fleeing the scene screaming about alien invasions and the players just restarted the game once the novelty of seeing UFOs hovering above their heads had worn off.

ROCK, PAPER, SCISSORS
2018

Referee David McNamara had forgotten the coin he needed to decide which team should kick off the Women's Super League match between Manchester City and Reading on 26 October 2018. But rather than delay the start by running back to the dressing room to fetch it, he decided to play a little game of Rock, Paper, Scissors with the two team captains, City's Steph Houghton and Reading's Kirsty Pearce, instead.

However, the FA were not amused. They accused him of not overseeing an official coin toss, as required under football's laws, charged him with 'not acting in the best interests of the game' and then suspended him for three weeks!

TAKING THINGS A BIT TOO FAR
2002

AS Adema's 149-0 THB Champions League play-off win over their Madagascan rivals SO l'Emyrne holds the record for the highest scoreline in any football match anywhere in the world.

However, things weren't quite as straightforward as they seemed.

Adema and SOE were bitter rivals and this end-of-season match, which was part of a four-team round-robin play-off tournament, was supposed to be the title decider. But in their penultimate game, SOE had been held to a shock 3-3 draw by DSA Antananarivo due entirely to what they believed were some pretty contentious refereeing decisions, ending any hopes of them retaining the title and handing it instead to Adema. So, in a glorious display of pettiness, SOE sabotaged this dead rubber by putting the ball into their own net 149 times as a protest against the perceived poor refereeing in that match with DSA Antananarivo. For the whole game, they just kicked off, ran down the field and booted the ball past their own goalkeeper, while the Adema players stood idly by watching the mayhem unfold around them.

THE DECAPITATED REFEREE
2013

On 30 June 2013, Brazilian referee Otávio Jordão da Silva Cantanhede was officiating an amateur match in the remote northern town of Pio XII, Maranhão. After being dismissed, Josemir dos Santos Abreu refused to leave the field, resulting in a scuffle between the two men. Abreu threw a punch, which prompted Da Silva to pull a knife – and repeatedly stab him!

Abreu died on his way to hospital and when his family and friends, who had been watching the game, learned of the news, they invaded the pitch, stoned Da Silva to death, dismembered his body and stuck his head on a spike.

A graphic video of the incident later appeared online showing medical personnel collecting up the body parts and reassembling him!

THE CROSSBAR INCIDENT
1887

In 1863, the FA ruled that the goalposts should be eight yards apart and it's been that way ever since, becoming the international standard after FIFA joined the International Football Association Board in 1913. However, no mention was ever made about the height of a goal in the original Laws of the Game and while some clubs began stringing a piece of tape between the two posts set at whatever height they thought was appropriate, others did not, and this led to balls being hit 30ft into the air and a goal being awarded, leading to disputes between the teams and a lot of wasted game time. Three years later, in an effort to reduce the on-field arguments, the FA further ruled, 'The goals shall be upright posts, eight yards apart with a tape across them, eight feet from the ground.'

Experiments using permanent wooden crossbars began a few years later with Sheffield FC and Queen's Park both claiming to be the first clubs in Britain to use them. However, it wasn't until 1882 that they were made compulsory by the FA.

But even the new crossbars didn't stop disputes from arising.

After a 2-2 draw in the FA Cup fourth-round game between Swifts and Crewe on 10 December 1887, the two teams met again in a replay a week later at the Queen's Ground in London. Swifts won 3-2 but after the final whistle the Crewe players protested about the crossbars being set at different heights, with the *Crewe and Nantwich Chronicle* reporting, 'The height of the goal-posts formed the basis of an appeal against the result. A measurement revealed that they were within a few inches of the specified height.'

'Their appeal was upheld and the FA ruled that the game needed to be played again. Crewe eventually won 2-1 when the match was replayed at the Derby Cricket Ground on 31 December 1887.

After this debacle the FA ruled that any protests or complaints about the ground, the pitch, the goal, the markings or anything else should be made before the game and not after it had ended!

* * *

John Alexander Brodie was a civil engineer best known for designing the Mersey Tunnel in Liverpool but he also came up with the idea of fitting nets between the goalposts as a means of helping officials understand if a goal had been scored. It also prevented spectators from standing along the goal line and interfering with play. He first proposed the idea in 1889 but it wasn't until 1891 that they were finally used. Everton striker Fred Geary was the first player to act out that old football cliche of hitting the back of the net. He was playing in the North v South trial match at Nottingham Forest's Town Ground on 17 January 1891 and scored the first goal in a 3-0 win for North.

THE OUTFIELD GOALKEEPER
2005

Manchester City and Middlesbrough met on the last day of the 2004/05 Premier League season to fight for a seventh-place finish and the last UEFA Cup spot. The visitors may have taken an early first-half lead but City equalised in the 46th minute and were much the better side for the remainder of the game as they continued pushing forward in search of that elusive winning goal.

Two minutes from time, City manager Stuart Pearce took off his midfielder Claudio Reyna, sent on his reserve keeper Nicky Weaver and ordered his first-choice goalkeeper David James to change his shirt and ditch his gloves because he wanted him to unsettle the Middlesbrough back-line by playing as a centre-forward for the rest of the game.

Amazingly, the most desperate and bizarre set of substitutions ever seen in a Premier League match almost paid off. With James unwittingly fooling the Middlesbrough defence by running around like a headless chicken, Franck Queudrue handled the ball in the area and gave away a penalty two minutes into stoppage time – only for Robbie Fowler to see his spot kick saved by goalkeeper Mark Schwarzer.

The match ended in a 1-1 draw a few minutes later with Middlesbrough claiming the prize of European football.

Maybe James should have been allowed to take that penalty; there's a fair chance he might have scored the winning goal and it would have been the perfect finale to his weird cameo performance as a striker.

THE SQUARE GOALPOSTS OF HAMPDEN PARK
1976

The 1976 European Cup Final ended with a 1-0 victory for West German champions Bayern Munich over Saint-Étienne after a 57th-minute goal from Franz Roth.

But to this day the Saint-Étienne fans still believe they were robbed of a win by Hampden Park's infamous square goalposts.

In the 39th minute, Jacques Santini got on the end of a cross and headed the ball towards the Bayern goal; the ball struck the sharp-edged square crossbar, bounced down and back into play with the Bayern players then able to clear the danger. Every French fan was convinced that if the goalposts had been rounded, the ball would have gone in and their team would have won the trophy.

However, that might have been stretching credibility. Bayern were attempting to win a third consecutive European Cup, and their team included legends of the game such as Franz Beckenbauer, Gerd Müller and Sepp Maier, so it might have taken more than just a set of rounded goalposts to wrestle the trophy away from them. Nevertheless, the French remained convinced that the dreaded *les poteaux carrés* (the square posts) had cost them the game despite the rest of the world believing it was just because they were the second-best team.

In 1987, FIFA standardised the shape, thickness and material of goalposts used around the world and the square posts which had been used at Hampden Park since 1903 were finally removed and put into storage. The last game in which the famous old goalposts were used was the Rous Cup match between Scotland and Brazil on 26 May 1987.

In an extraordinary act of Gallic masochism, Saint-Étienne then decided to bid for *les poteaux carrés* when they were put up for auction by the SFA in 2013. They won the bidding war by paying around €20,000 (£17,000) and the square posts are now on display in their club museum.

THE LIVERPOOL COIN TOSS
1965

After knockout competition matches ended in a draw, there was a time long before the away goals rule and/or penalty shoot-outs when they just kept playing replays until one team emerged triumphant. Or they just tossed a coin to decide a winner.

After the two-legged European Cup quarter-final between Liverpool and Cologne on 10 February and 17 March 1965 ended in stalemate with two 0-0 draws, a play-off was quickly arranged in Rotterdam on 24 March – and this time there were goals. Liverpool took the lead with first-half goals from Ian St John and Roger Hunt but then Cologne hit back with two of their own and the match ended 2-2 after extra time.

After three games and 300 minutes of football in three different countries the tie was still deadlocked.

Referee Robert Schaut then called captains Ron Yeats and Wolfgang Overath into the centre circle for a coin toss to determine the winner. Yeats called tails, Schaut flipped the coin and everyone watched it fly up into the air, fall back down again – and then get stuck in a divot. It had landed at such a strange angle that it was impossible to tell if it was heads or tails. After a few words of encouragement from Yeats, Schaut decided to pick up the coin and try again. Overath wasn't too happy about it because the coin was definitely beginning to tilt and probably would have fallen on to heads if they'd all been prepared to wait around long enough to find out.

The referee tossed the coin into the air again and this time it fell flat on its face – tails.

Liverpool had won the tie and the German champions had been knocked out of the competition in the most bizarre fashion and without losing a game. *Liverpool Daily Post* journalist Horace Yates described it as 'the most amazing finish I have ever seen or am ever likely to see in football'.

WHEN NEEDS MUST
2012

The Greek financial crisis began in 2009 when a new government reported a much higher fiscal deficit than had previously been disclosed, resulting in a debt crisis which had a profound impact on the economy, leading to a decline in the country's GDP, a rise in unemployment, and significant social and political upheaval. As a way of navigating the financial storm and staving off bankruptcy, two amateur football clubs enlisted the help of two very unconventional backers to ensure their survival.

Voukefalas FC, from the central Greek city of Larissa, turned to former prostitute and brothel owner Soula Alevridou ('Madame Soula'), who provided them with dazzling bubblegum pink-coloured shirts emblazoned with the logo of her Villa Erotica brothel, while Palaiopyrgos FC, in the nearby city of Trikala, signed a deal with a local funeral parlour which meant playing in black shirts adorned with a large purple cross.

THE FALSE TEETH FIASCO
1957

This popular story revolves around Henning Erikstrup, the referee for the Danish League match between Nørager and Ebeltoft. With Nørager leading 4-3 and just a few seconds of the game remaining, their opponents pushed forward searching for an equaliser. Meanwhile, Mr Erikstrup consulted his watch and decided to end the match – except, as he went to blow the whistle, his loosely fitting false teeth flew out of his mouth! By the time he'd retrieved them and refitted them, and then finally blown his whistle, the score was 4-4. In the meantime, Ebeltoft had got that equalising goal and were busy celebrating their good fortune.

But they weren't celebrating for very long because Mr Erikstrup promptly disallowed the goal. He'd meant to blow his whistle and in his mind that was as good as actually doing it.

A REAL ASSET TO THE TEAM
2015

Richard Dunne made 431 appearances in the Premier League over 19 seasons between 1996 and 2015 – and holds the record as the player with the most career own goals. His first came playing for Manchester City against West Bromwich Albion on 28 December 2004 and his tenth and last came playing for Queens Park Rangers against Liverpool on 19 October 2014.

Dunne was such a classy player that he also holds the Premier League record for the most red cards too. He shares that unwanted honour with fellow bad boys Duncan Ferguson and Patrick Vieira having been sent off EIGHT times.

Goodness knows what his own goal tally might have been like without all those early baths!

FROM ZERO TO HERO
1998 | 2000

ZERO

A relatively dull and unremarkable first half between Sheffield Wednesday and Arsenal at Hillsborough on 26 September 1998 suddenly ended with one of the most famous incidents in Premier League history.

After the volatile Arsenal midfielder Patrick Vieira was bundled over by Wim Jonk, the Frenchman got up and pushed his assailant to the ground. Paolo Di Canio didn't take kindly to one of his own being pushed around, so he started running towards Vieira to do a bit of pushing and shoving of his own, only to be blocked by the Arsenal hardman Martin Keown. In holding Di Canio back, however, Keown accidentally caught him in the face with his elbow, leading the temperamental Italian to start kicking and lashing out at him instead. Then everyone started pushing and shoving everyone else.

Eventually, order was restored and unsurprisingly referee Paul Alcock then waved a red card at Di Canio and pointed towards the tunnel. The poor man hadn't even finished pointing when Di Canio yelled a few well-chosen words of abuse at him before dismissively pushing him away. Both hands landed hard on his chest and Alcock stumbled backwards and kept on stumbling until he eventually fell on his arse. It was comical to watch, as if someone had pulled out a chair from underneath him just as he was about to sit down. He took so long to hit the ground that Di Canio didn't even see this slapstick finale to their confrontation because he'd already turned his back on him and was marching off the pitch.

Di Canio later received a £10,000 fine and an 11-match ban for his violent conduct; he never played for Wednesday again and signed for West Ham the following January.

HERO

Two years later, in a Premier League game against West Ham at Goodison Park, on 16 December 2000,h Everton keeper Paul Gerrard had been left stranded outside the penalty area with an injury as Trevor Sinclair whipped the ball into the box for Di Canio to smash into the empty net. However, instead of hooking it into the goal as everyone had expected him to do, he caught it to stop play so his injured opponent could receive treatment.

The game had been level at 1-1 with just five minutes left so any goal would probably have been the winner. The Everton players thanked Di Canio for his good deed; the home fans applauded him from the terraces, and a year later FIFA presented him with a Fair Play Award for his 'special act of good sportsmanship'.

The only person who didn't appear to appreciate Di Canio's sportsmanship was his manager Harry Redknapp. He'd just cost them three points.

THAT ECUADORIAN REFEREE
2002

Ecuadorian Byron Moreno is often described as the worst referee of all time after he made a series of controversial decisions which appeared to favour co-hosts South Korea during their World Cup last-16 tie against Italy on 18 June 2002.

He constantly ignored a series of rough tackles from the Korean players, he disallowed two goals for Italy for being offside and awarded a penalty to the hosts but denied Italy a penalty, and red-carded Italy's charismatic forward Francesco Totti for two bookable offences. To add insult to injury, Moreno has always maintained that it was one of the best performances of his career.

The controversy began just three minutes in with a dubious penalty to South Korea after a bemused Christian Panucci was adjudged to have brought down Seol Ki-hyeon. But no harm done because the Italian goalkeeper Gianluigi Buffon managed to palm the ball clear and the score remained at 0-0. Totti was booked after 21 minutes for elbowing Kim Nam-il in the face while jostling for a high ball, notwithstanding the fact that his team-mate Christian Vieri had escaped a yellow card for a similar offence on Kim Tae-young just minutes earlier. Then, a few minutes into the second half, Kim Tae-young again was involved in a bit of shirt-pulling and elbow-swinging with Alessandro Del Piero inside the Korean penalty area. But instead of awarding a spot kick, the referee just had a little chat with both players and told them to calm down. Perhaps he hadn't been alerted to the severity of the tackle because Del Piero had foolishly stayed on his feet instead of diving to the ground, rolling around and clutching his face like he'd just been shot by a sniper in the crowd, as most other players would have done. Approaching the 90-minute mark, Italian defender Paolo Maldini cleared the ball while lying flat on his back on the ground after a goalmouth scramble but earned himself a big kick in the head from Lee Chun-soo for his trouble. Not only did the referee keep his cards in his pocket, he just waved play on.

Despite Moreno's best efforts, Italy had been leading 1-0 through an early strike from Vieri but then in the 88th minute Sol Ki-hyeon equalised and forced the game into extra time.

The defining moment came 12 minutes into the first period of extra time when Totti received a second yellow card and was then sent off. He should have had a penalty after being brought down by Song Chong-gug but Moreno booked him for diving instead. TV pictures have since shown that he couldn't have been more wrong.

Damiano Tommasi could have been the hero of the night when he put the ball in the back of the Korean net in the 20th minute of extra time, but he hadn't figured on Moreno being Moreno. By now every decision he was making was wrong, so it was no surprise to anyone when he ruled the goal out for a non-existent offside.

Instead, it was Ahn Jung-hwan who scored a 117th-minute 'golden goal' to send South Korea through to the next round where they met Spain – and benefited from further favourable officiating to win that game too!

The Italians were understandably furious, claiming that the match had been manipulated to ensure the co-hosts advanced to the later stages of the tournament. Allegations of incompetency and corruption were bandied about by their fans; *La Gazzetta dello Sport* called Moreno the 'worst referee ever', and Panucci stated, 'Moreno was put in place to eliminate Italy. He was a bandit. The game ended for us after an hour. We felt we might as well have gone home there and then. He was only interested in seeing Korea go through. FIFA had put him there for that reason. Moreno was certainly an incompetent, but the greater responsibility should be taken by those who made him referee the game.'

Doubts about Byron Moreno's integrity resurfaced again just a few months after that fiasco in South Korea. In a domestic match between LDU Quito and Barcelona de Guayaquil, he signalled an additional six minutes of extra time – only to play a total of 13 minutes, which allowed LDU to score twice and win the game 4-3. He also awarded two contentious penalties and handed out a couple of red cards just to make sure that he was the star of the show. Most interestingly, he was also running for election to the local council in Quito at the time, so appearing favourable towards their football team would have done him no harm at the ballot box! The Ecuadorian Football Federation were less than impressed by his performance and the surrounding controversy generated by his political ambitions, and suspended him for 20 matches.

Realising that his reputation had suffered and he'd never be allowed to officiate at the highest level again, he announced his retirement from the game and then spent the next couple of years exploiting his fame in Ecuador and his infamy in Italy by accepting whatever TV work came his way, appearing as a pundit in his own country and a figure of fun on Italian comedy shows. He soon became accustomed to the finer things in life; he began living well beyond his means and running up debts, and then, in 2010, he was caught at JFK airport in New York smuggling 6kg of heroin into the USA hidden in his pants!

'Six kilos of drugs?' exclaimed the *Azzurri* goalkeeper Gianluigi Buffon when hearing of his arrest. 'I believe

Moreno already had them in 2002, but not in his underwear – in his system.'

Byron Moreno was last heard of hosting a show analysing referee errors on Ecuadorian TV. You couldn't make it up.

PRIDE BEFORE THE FALL
1888

Preston North End were the overwhelming pre-match favourites to win the 1888 FA Cup Final against West Bromwich Albion and they were so confident of overcoming their opponents that they asked to be photographed with the trophy before the game. The FA president Francis Marindin turned down their request and was reported to have remarked, 'Hadn't you better win it first?' It seems that the West Brom players were just as unconvinced about their chances of success as everyone else that day as they'd refused to accept any bets offered to them by their opponents on the outcome of the game.

Marindin also happened to be the referee that day and was later accused of showing bias towards West Brom. At one point during the game he stopped play to award them a free kick just as Preston were about to score, despite no WBA player making an appeal for a foul, which was required by the Laws of the Game at that time. The Preston players, however, blamed their own pre-match routine for the defeat. They'd all gone off to watch the University Boat Race in the morning (which was a bigger sporting spectacle than the FA Cup Final) and then turned up at the Kennington Oval in the afternoon just a little bit worse for wear.

THE GHOSTLIEST OF ALL GHOST GOALS
2013

In the 70th minute of the Bundesliga match between Hoffenheim and Bayer Leverkusen on 18 October 2013, the visitors' Gonzalo Castro took an in-swinging corner, sending the ball into the Hoffenheim box, where his team-mate Stefan Kiessling appeared to head it down into the bottom-left corner of the goal to give Leverkusen a 2-0 lead.

From the normal TV angle it looked like a good goal but when a replay was shown from behind the goal, the commentator and everyone else realised that it wasn't. The ball had hit the *outside* of the net, passed through a small hole, and then ended up inside the goal. Kiessling had initially held his head in disbelief at the miss but then referee Felix Brych awarded the goal.

As Kiessling and his team-mates celebrated the phantom goal, the Hoffenheim players surrounded Brych in protest. They even persuaded him to inspect the goal net to see the hole. He did as he was told but then claimed that his decision couldn't be reversed, he'd awarded the goal and it was too late for him to change his mind.

The Leverkusen sporting director and former German international Rudi Völler later said how embarrassed everyone had been after being awarded such a bizarre goal but didn't seem quite so sympathetic when Hoffenheim demanded a replay. He immediately dismissed the idea and added, 'Hoffenheim have spent such a lot of money on a nice stadium, maybe next time they should buy some proper nets.' The Deutscher Fußball-Bund were equally as dismissive about the game being replayed and the result stood.

* * *

Perhaps the most famous ghost goal of all time was scored by England's Geoff Hurst against West Germany during the World Cup Final on 30 July 1966 at Wembley. The game kicked off in front of 96,924 spectators and a UK TV audience of 32.3 million people, making it the most watched event ever on British television. After only 12 minutes West Germany went 1-0 ahead with a fine shot from Helmut

Haller. However, six minutes later Hurst equalised with a header to make it 1-1. The teams were still level at half-time and then England took the lead after 77 minutes with a goal from Martin Peters. West Germany pressed for an equaliser and after 89 minutes Wolfgang Weber levelled at 2-2 which sent the final into extra time.

In the first period, England pressed forward and created several chances; Bobby Charlton struck the post and sent another shot just wide. Then, after 11 minutes, Alan Ball crossed the ball to Hurst who shot at the German goal from close range. The ball hit the underside of the crossbar and then bounced down on to the goal line before being headed out of play by Weber. The Soviet referee was uncertain if the ball had crossed the line but after consulting with his linesman he awarded the goal. The 1966 World Cup Final is always remembered for this controversial fifth goal and debate has long raged over whether the ball actually crossed the line or not. The Laws of the Game define a goal as when 'the whole of the ball passes over the goal line' but modern technology and the use of computer simulation has since proven that only 97 per cent of that particular ball had crossed that particular line.

The Germans have been banging on about that goal for years – turns out they were right.

In the dying seconds, England captain Bobby Moore picked out Hurst with a long ball, which he carried forward and then drove into the top corner of the German goal for England's fourth of the day. While all of this was going on, a celebratory pitch invasion had begun with the TV commentator Kenneth Wolstenholme famously describing the closing moments, 'Some people are on the pitch. They think it's all over … It is now!' Later, Hurst admitted that he was actually trying to hit the ball as high into the Wembley stands as possible to waste time.

The game finished moments later in a 4-2 win for England.

THE MASTER OF THE DARK ARTS
2010 | 2014 | 2021

The temperamental Uruguayan striker Luis Suárez is well known for his work rate, clever movement and clinical finishing. He is generally regarded as one of the best players of his generation and one of the greatest goalscorers of all time. At the same time, however, he's also been criticised for diving, biting, cheating, stamping, time wasting and using any other form of shithousery he can think of to win a game.

CHEATING

The 2010 World Cup quarter-final between Uruguay and Ghana was the first time the two teams had ever played one another. Ghana took the lead just before half-time with a Sulley Muntari goal and then Diego Forlán equalised shortly after the break. While both teams had their chances to win it, the score remained deadlocked at 1-1 after the 90 minutes, then through to the final moments of extra time.

With 120 minutes almost up, Suárez deliberately blocked a header from Dominic Adiyiah with his hands to stop what would have almost certainly been the match-winning goal. The referee stopped play, red-carded Suárez and awarded the Black Stars a penalty.

Asamoah Gyan stepped up to the spot. It was a great chance to be a hero by sending an African side into a World Cup semi-final for the first time, but instead of blasting his shot into the back of the net, he blasted it against the crossbar instead. The TV audience were then treated to pictures of Suárez standing around in the entrance to the tunnel shamelessly celebrating the miss.

In the subsequent penalty shoot-out, Gyan made amends by converting his shot, but his team-mates John Mensah and Dominic Adiyiah didn't and Ghana lost 4-2.

Suárez had the cheek to claim that he'd had no alternative and was acting on instinct when he stuck out his hand to stop the goal, and then inflamed the situation still further by commenting, 'I made the save of the tournament.' Referring to the infamous Diego Maradona handball incident against England in the 1986 World Cup, he added, 'The Hand of God now belongs to me.'

It was said that he'd enraged the whole of Africa by his shithousery that night with Ghana's coach Milovan Rajevac labelling him a 'villain' and a 'cheat', but in Uruguay he was hailed as a hero after sacrificing himself for the good of the team.

BITING

Four years later, at the World Cup Finals in Brazil, the group-stage match between Italy and Uruguay n 24 June 2014 was a rather slow and dull affair with both teams struggling in the Brazilian heat. Italy were reduced to ten men early in the second half after Claudio Marchisio was sent off for a studs-up challenge on Egidio Arévalo, and then Diego Godín scored the only goal of the game after 81 minutes, sending Uruguay through to the last 16 as the runners-up in Group D.

The only exciting thing to happen occurred in the 79th minute when Luis Suárez decided to take a bite out of Giorgio Chiellini. They'd both jostled for a loose ball and had fallen to the ground, Suárez clutching his teeth and Chiellini holding his left shoulder. The incident went unnoticed by the Mexican referee but an angry Chiellini chased after him, pulling up his shirt sleeve so he could see the bite mark, before Uruguay's Gastón Ramírez attempted to pull his sleeve down again, as if covering up the wound would somehow make it go away.

The TV images of the incident confirmed what everyone already suspected: Suárez had been up to his old tricks again.

In 2010 he'd bitten Otman Bakkal while playing for Ajax, and in 2013, as a Liverpool player, he'd gnawed away at Chelsea's Branislav Ivanović; now he'd completed his hat-trick by taking a bite out of Chiellini.

Of course, Suárez had his own version of events – he'd lost his balance and hit his face against Chiellini's shoulder, leaving him with a small bruise on his cheek and a bit of a toothache.

Rather predictably, his captain Diego Lugano and manager Óscar Tabárez backed his story. What else could they do? FIFA were less convinced, however, and began an inquiry, resulting in Suárez receiving an immediate nine-match ban and a fine of 100,000 Swiss francs. He was also forbidden from entering football stadiums and taking part in any football-related activities for four months. The Uruguayan FA launched an appeal but it was immediately rejected. Their country's president José Mujica then joined in the debate, claiming the punishment was grossly unfair and calling the FIFA officials 'fascists' and 'a bunch of old sons of bitches'.

Nothing like a bit of good old-fashioned name-calling when you've lost the argument.

By 2025, the great man was playing for Inter Miami in the USA – and biting his own team-mates!

On 12 April 2025, Inter Miami met their MLS rivals LAFC in the second leg of the CONCACAF Champions Cup quarter-final at the Chase Stadium in Fort Lauderdale, Florida. The visitors opened the scoring after nine minutes, giving them a 2-0 aggregate lead, but Inter Miami drew level after 35 minutes and then scored two second-half goals to win the tie. But it was Suárez biting people again that grabbed all the headlines.

A harsh tackle by LAFC's Marlon on their Argentinian superstar Lionel Messi late in the second half prompted a bit of a scuffle between the two sets of players. And, as always, Suárez was in the thick of it. At one point he felt a hand grabbing his shirt and believed it was the hand of an opposition player, so he instinctively bent his head, bared his fangs and took a bite.

Except it wasn't an opposition hand – it was the hand of his team-mate Jordi Alba.

TIME WASTING

The funniest exhibition of the dark arts ever seen on a football pitch occurred on 21 June 2021.

Eduardo Vargas gave Chile the lead after 26 minutes of a Copa América group-stage match, and Uruguay equalised through an Arturo Vidal own goal early in the second half. Then, with five minutes left to play, Suárez decided to entertain the crowd with a truly magical exhibition of his shithousery skills.

The ball had gone out of play for a goal kick, so Suárez took the opportunity to hinder the Chilean keeper Claudio Bravo from taking it quickly by standing just in front of the very spot where he would place the ball. He tried to disguise his trickery by pretending to readjust his footwear. It was the left boot giving him all the trouble apparently, so he slipped it off and fiddled about with it a bit before trying to wriggle his foot back inside it again.

Suárez might have had his back to Bravo the whole time but he knew perfectly well what was happening behind him. He presumably thought he'd done enough to prevent him from taking the kick but Bravo just moved a few steps to his right after spotting the body and the teeth of the Uruguayan striker blocking his way. However, Suárez had been watching his every move out of the corner of his eye – so he too took a few steps to his right.

It was glorious to watch. The way he did it without appearing to do it was pure genius. The move was executed with such nonchalance that it seemed totally natural. He'd never turned around and he'd continued adjusting his boot the whole time just to add that little extra touch of authenticity to the manoeuvre.

Check it out on YouTube.

WHEN ASTON VILLA LOST THE CUP 1982

Compared to some of England's other big clubs, like Arsenal, Liverpool and Manchester United, Aston Villa haven't won that many trophies. Probably just as well because they're not very good at looking after them. Not only did they manage to lose the FA Cup in 1895, they also lost the European Cup for a few hours in 1982 too.

Villa had beaten Bayern Munich 1-0 in the final in Rotterdam on 26 May 1982, and 24 hours later they'd somehow managed to lose the trophy in a Birmingham pub.

Two of the Villa players, Colin Gibson and Gordon Cowans, had taken the giant silver cup into the Fox Inn near Tamworth in Staffordshire, which was a popular pub with the squad at the time, so the fans could see it, touch it and have their photos taken with it. The players downed a few pints and sometime later they got involved in a game of darts, seemingly taking their eyes off European football's most treasured prize long enough for it to be stolen.

Nobody had the slightest idea what had happened to it, least of all the two red-faced players, and eventually the police were informed of the theft.

It wasn't until 3am the following day that there was a break in the case.

Some 100 miles away, a man had walked into a Sheffield city-centre police station, identified himself as Mr Sykes and then informed the officer on duty at the front desk that he had the European Cup stashed in the boot of his car. He'd then gone outside again and returned a few minutes later with the cup, still with the claret and blue ribbons attached. He'd admitted taking it from the pub but had then had a change of heart and was now returning it and handing himself in.

The South Yorkshire officers informed their colleagues in the West Midlands, who then informed the players and the pub staff still anxiously pacing around the Fox Inn. The cup was eventually returned, Aston Villa were saved from the cost and embarrassment of having to pay for another one and the mysterious Mr Sykes was apparently released without charge.

It was later revealed that Mr Sykes was actually a 28-year-old Fox Inn regular called Adrian Reed, who'd swiped the cup and taken it home to show his flatmates. They eventually persuaded him to hand it in to the police, and then, for some strange reason, he decided to drive all the way to Sheffield and return it to a police station there.

The officers on duty at the Sheffield station that night acted no differently from anyone else who might have suddenly found themselves in possession of the European Cup. They wanted their photograph taken with it but in 1982 mobile phones hadn't yet been invented, so they had to call in their scenes of crime officer who was the only person they knew with easy access to a camera!

WEDDING CELEBRATIONS
1909

Leicester Fosse had already been relegated from Division One by the time the final day of the 1908/09 season came around; they were away to Nottingham Forest, who were one of several clubs trying to avoid being the other team to join them. Forest were hoping for a win and maybe a few goals to improve their goal difference, which could prove vital in their battle to avoid the drop. Luckily for them, the game was as one-sided as the 12-0 scoreline suggests. So one-sided, in fact, that some of the other clubs protested to the Football League, who were obliged to hold an inquiry into why Leicester Fosse had been so bad.

It was soon discovered that two days before the showdown, the Leicester players had attended a team-mate's wedding and the celebrations had continued well into the early hours of the morning – on the day of the match. All the players were still hungover!

RELEGATED TWICE IN ONE SEASON
2015

Earlier in his career, Manchester United and England centre-half Harry Maguire was so good at being relegated that he managed it twice in one season. He turned out in the first half of 2014/15 for Hull City but was then sent out on loan to Wigan Athletic for the second half of the season. Both clubs were subsequently relegated: Hull to the Championship and Wigan to League 1.

For good measure, Maguire's debut season at Sheffield United saw the Blades relegated from the Championship in 2010/11; he even got relegated playing for England in the UEFA Nations League in 2022. There'd never been an international tournament where a team could get relegated before, but as soon as they introduced one, it seemed like he couldn't wait to get relegated from it! Fantastic achievement.

LAUGHING AT YOURSELF
1996

Aston Villa defender Gareth Southgate stepped up to take England's sixth spot kick of the sudden-death penalty shoot-out in the Euro 96 semi-final against Germany but fired a weak shot straight at Andreas Köpke who made an easy save. Andreas Möller then converted his kick to dump England out of their home tournament.

A few months after that fateful night, Southgate teamed up with fellow England players Stuart Pearce and Chris Waddle, who had both missed penalties against West Germany in the 1990 World Cup semi-final, to appear in a TV advert for Pizza Hut.

The 30-second ad shows the three lads dining out at a Pizza Hut restaurant. Southgate has a paper bag over his head, with the joke being that he was still too embarrassed to show his face in public after that horrific penalty miss. As 'Psycho' and 'The Waddler' take the piss out of him, the waitress arrives with their meal; Pearce remarks that it only took him six years to get over his miss, and then encourages Gareth Southgate to have a slice of the delicious deep-pan pizza which will make him feel a whole lot better.

The pizza seems to have the desired effect. Having devoured a slice, Southgate removes the bag and says, 'Thanks a lot, boys. I feel much better now,' before getting up and walking away – straight into a pillar.

The other two wince, with Pearce quipping, 'This time he's hit the post,' before they both start laughing.

WASTE OF MONEY
2021

Romelu Lukaku ranks as the most expensive flop in Premier League history.

The Belgian striker had just helped Inter Milan win the 2021 Serie A title after years of Juventus dominating the league.

Chelsea desperately needed a new centre-forward and sold nine of their players, including rising young stars Marc Guéhi, Tammy Abraham and Fikayo Tomori, to finance the move for Lukaku. They earned £98m from those sales and then promptly spent £97.5m of it bringing the superstar to Stamford Bridge.

He'd already played for Chelsea at the beginning of his career after being signed from Anderlecht for £18m in 2011. However, he only made ten appearances for them, without scoring a goal, before being loaned out to West Bromwich Albion and Everton. Having eventually been sold to Everton in 2014, he then moved to Manchester United three years later and finally Inter Milan in 2019.

Despite his disastrous first spell at Chelsea, the club didn't seem too bothered about paying a near-record British transfer fee for him. He returned to London on 12 August 2021 and started off well, scoring on his debut, but then things quickly went downhill after that. He got injured, contracted COVID-19 and then got injured again. Then he took part in an unsanctioned interview with Sky Italia in which he foolishly criticised his manager's tactics and professed his undying love for Inter Milan. As a consequence, he was immediately dropped from the squad and forced to issue an apology to the fans. Although he was later restored to the first-team, it was more often than not as a substitute, and he finished the season having scored only eight goals in 26 Premier League appearances.

It was obvious that Chelsea weren't particularly keen on keeping him on the payroll for another season. He was one of the Premier League's highest earners, he'd forgotten how to score goals, he didn't get along with manager Thomas Tuchel and Lukaku himself was clearly unhappy at the club.

Unsurprisingly, nobody else wanted him except Inter Milan – but only on loan, and Lukaku signed for Inter again on 29 June 2022 for a reported loan fee of around 6.9m.

Inter had only lost their star player for a year and had then made a healthy £90m profit on the deal.

THE BETTING SCANDAL
1915

Before the final Division One game of the season between Manchester United and Liverpool at Old Trafford on 2 April 1915, the visitors were sitting comfortably in mid-table but United had to win to avoid relegation. Their victory was never really in any doubt, however, as a few players from both sides had already hatched a plan to rig the match so United wouldn't drop down into Division Two.

They might have got away with it too if they'd been a little more discreet. But they'd all been seen together numerous times in various Manchester pubs beforehand; they'd all placed large bets on a 2-0 United win at odds of 8/1, which had alerted the local bookmakers, and they were all such bad actors on the day that nobody believed they weren't trying to manipulate the result.

It had already been agreed that one goal should be scored in each half and everything was going to plan when the two teams left the field at half-time. But in the Liverpool dressing room, the players not involved in the scam knew perfectly well that their team-mates were throwing the game and threatened not to return for the second half.

But they did go back out and both teams fielded the same players for the second half. United were awarded a penalty shortly after the restart with their captain Patrick O'Connell stepping up and hitting the ball so far wide of the goal that it nearly hit the corner flag. Although he was never actually implicated in the scam, there were reports of him laughing to himself as he walked back up the pitch, as if he already knew that his penalty miss wasn't all that important as they could get another goal whenever they wanted. Which is exactly what happened: United scored their second and final goal of the match and the teams then settled back to wait out the final whistle.

But that's not to say the rest of the game wasn't without incident.

United's top striker Enoch 'Knocker' West fell back into defence as the game progressed, citing an ankle injury as the reason for his move. According to the *Manchester Daily Dispatch*, he then spent the rest of the game kicking the ball as far out of play as he could, presumably in a poorly disguised attempt to waste time because back then they only played with one ball and had to wait for it to be returned by the crowd before play could be resumed. Then, in the dying seconds, Liverpool striker Fred Pagnam, who was not part of the conspiracy, hit a shot against the crossbar and some of his team-mates were seen yelling and screaming at him; he had almost ruined everything. Another player who'd been screaming at his team-mates all afternoon was United's star winger Billy Meredith. The 'Prince of Dribblers' wasn't involved in the scam and so nobody had passed him the ball for the whole of the match just in case he hit it into the back of the Liverpool net.

The match ended in a 2-0 win for United exactly as planned. George Anderson scored both goals and United picked up two points which were enough to earn them 18th place and avoid relegation. No doubt the players enjoyed a few pints to celebrate their good fortune and then made a visit to the bookies to pick up their winnings.

However, the 18,000 crowd had voiced their discontent throughout the match about the obvious poor play from both sides; the referee's report had highlighted all the weird behaviour he'd witnessed during the game and the newspapers had started asking some very awkward questions. The FA didn't need any further convincing and opened an investigation.

Then, on 20 April, league football was suspended indefinitely with the players being called up to fight in the war.

The FA finally reported their findings on 27 December 1915, concluding that no club officials had been involved in the conspiracy and therefore neither team would be fined nor have points deducted. However, seven players were found guilty of match tampering and handed lifetime bans with the FA commenting that 'they have sought to undermine the whole fabric of the game and discredit its honesty and fairness'.

Of the six players who later admitted their guilt, five of them earned a reprieve when returning from the trenches as heroes and promptly resumed their careers after the war. The odd one out was poor Sandy Turnbull who was killed at the Battle of Arras in 1917. Enoch 'Knocker' West, on the other hand, was never pardoned because he refused to admit his involvement in the scandal and remained suspended from playing professional football for the next 30 years. It was the longest ban in the league's history. Although it was eventually lifted in 1945, West was 59 years old by then and, needless to say, he never kicked another football again.

Ironically, the number of clubs allowed to compete in the top division was increased from 20 to 22 after the Football League resumed for the 1919/20 season. So even if Manchester United had lost that game to Liverpool, they wouldn't have been relegated anyway.

SIXTH TIME LUCKY
2004

With the score level at 1-1 seven minutes from the end of the second half of Serbia & Montenegro's 2004 Olympic Games group match against Tunisia on 17 August, the Africans were awarded a penalty.

Their experienced striker Mohamed Jedidi stepped up to the spot and took the kick – again, and again, and again. In fact, he took the penalty six times in total because players from both sides kept encroaching into the box. He scored with the first three kicks, missed the next two, and then put his team 2-1 up with his sixth and final effort.

It's probably fair to assume that the Tahitian referee Charles Ariiotima was a bit of a stickler for the rules.

THE CHEATING FRENCH
1993

Marseille might have been the inaugural winners of the new UEFA Champions League in 1993 but they were also the first club ever to be banned from the competition too.

The French club's president Bernard Tapie and the general manager Jean-Pierre Bernès were concerned about the fitness levels of their players and any possible injuries they might pick up in their league game against Valenciennes, which was due to be played on 20 May 1993, just six days before the Champions League Final, so they asked team captain Jean-Jacques Eydelie to contact a few of the opposition players and ask them to play nicely. Marseille won 1-0 with a goal by Alen Bokšić and in doing so also secured the Ligue 1 title. However, the Valenciennes defender Jacques Glassmann had refused to play nicely and duly informed his manager and the match referee about the attempted bribe prior to the game.

The scandal soon became public knowledge, arrests were made and a trial followed.

Tapie was exposed as the instigator of the fraud and later given a two-year jail sentence; Eydelie was also jailed, and some other players and officials received suspended prison sentences. Bernès actually admitted that it was common practice for Marseille to bribe other clubs around five or six times every season to underperform in matches!

Marseille were eventually stripped of their league championship by the Fédération Française de Football and banned by UEFA from taking part in the following season's Champions League, European Super Cup and Intercontinental Cup.

Meanwhile, Jacques Glassmann was rewarded for his honesty with a FIFA Fair Play Award.

THE BALL-BOY ASSIST
2019

Tottenham Hotspur had enjoyed a woeful start to their Champions League group game at home to Olympiacos on 26 November 2019, going 2-0 down after only 19 minutes.

It certainly wasn't the start that new manager José Mourinho was hoping for in his first European game in charge at the north London club. But then Dele Alli pulled a goal back for them just before half-time and Harry Kane scored the equaliser after 50 minutes.

It was the 15-year-old Tottenham ball boy Callum Hynes who provided the unlikely 'assist' for that second goal.

Without his quick thinking the goal would never have happened. After the ball went out of play in the Olympiacos half, he instantly threw another one towards Spurs defender Serge Aurier who quickly took the throw-in. The ball fell to his team-mate Lucas Moura who ran to the goal line and crossed the ball into the box where Kane was waiting to fire home the equaliser. It all played out in a matter of just a few seconds.

Young Callum didn't even see the goal because he was still too busy retrieving the original ball and had his back to the pitch; he only knew about it when he suddenly heard the cheers. Mourinho then sought him out at the pitchside during the goal celebrations to shake his hand and thank him for the 'assist'.

Aurier later scored a goal of his own after 73 minutes and Kane made it 4-2 four minutes later. The win for Tottenham that night ensured their qualification for the knockout stages.

Mourinho later remarked to BT Sport in the post-match interview, 'I love intelligent ball boys ... and this kid today was brilliant. He read the game, understands the game and made an important assist, an important moment for him and he will never forget it.'

Callum was later invited to a pre-match lunch with the players at the Tottenham Hotspur Stadium ahead of their Premier League game against Bournemouth the following weekend as a thank you for his part in their victory.

MOST VALUABLE PLAYER
1985

Morton ended the 1984/85 season bottom of the SFL Premier Division with just 12 points having won only five of their 36 games. Despite such a poor record, one of their players, Jim Duffy, went on to win the Scottish PFA Players' Player of the Year award that very same year. Goodness knows what Morton would have been like without him!

THE FIRST FOOTBALL HOOLIGANS
1880s

Having invented the game, it follows that hooliganism should also have been invented in England.

The first reports of hooliganism occurred as early as the late 19th century with organised gangs of supporters terrorising neighbourhoods, invading pitches, attacking referees, fighting with other fans and pelting the players with stones inside the grounds.

Most of the stories from that time seem to involve the Preston North End fans. They knocked a railwayman unconscious at Wigan station in 1881, they attacked the Bolton players and their fans at the end of a match in 1884, and then, in 1885, they were the protagonists of perhaps the most famous of all the early incidents, during a game against Aston Villa, when the officials and players from both sides were struck with stones, attacked with sticks, spat at and punched and kicked as they came off the field. One of their own players was beaten so severely that he lost consciousness. Preston actually won that game 5-0. It doesn't bear thinking about what might have happened if they'd lost.

The following year, those 'howling roughs' of Preston were at it again after getting involved in the first recorded instance of hooliganism and violence away from a ground when they had a bit of a set-to with some Queen's Park supporters at a railway station.

LEAVING THINGS TO THE LAST MINUTE
1999

Manchester United were the first team to win the Champions League without having qualified as champions of their own domestic league.

They had already become the first English team to secure three league and cup doubles after capturing their fifth league championship in seven seasons by winning the 1998/99 Premier League title and then beating Newcastle in the FA Cup Final on 22 May 1999. Four days later they took to the field again in Barcelona, this time against Bayern Munich in the Champions League Final with the aim of getting another win to complete a historic treble-winning season.

The two sides had already played each other in the group-stage with the games ending in 2-2 and 1-1 draws. Bayern had eventually finished top of the group, ensuring a fairly easy passage to the final with wins over Kaiserslautern and Dynamo Kyiv. United had a much tougher route, playing against Inter Milan and Juventus.

With only six minutes gone in the final, Ronny Johnsen fouled Bayern striker Carsten Jancker just outside the United area and Mario Basler placed a low free kick around the wall and past their flat-footed keeper Peter Schmeichel to score the first goal of the game. The rest of the first half was fairly predictable with United dominating the play looking for an equaliser and Bayern anxiously defending their lead and only occasionally threatening on the break.

The Germans started the second half in a more positive mood. Both teams missed chances but it was probably Bayern who were playing the better football at this stage. Realising that the game was slipping away from them, United manager Alex Ferguson introduced two substitutes, Teddy Sheringham after 67 minutes and Ole Gunnar Solskjær after 81. Both players forced Oliver Kahn into important saves, but it was probably Bayern who had the best chance of securing the win when Jancker hit the crossbar with an overhead kick late in the game.

Just as the fourth official signalled the three minutes of additional time, United won a corner. David Beckham floated the ball over the crowded penalty area, it fell to Dwight Yorke but was half-cleared, then played back in by Ryan Giggs towards Sheringham, who swiped at the shot and hit the ball into the bottom corner of the net. The goal was timed at 90:00.36 and it looked like the match was heading into extra time. But less than 30 seconds after the restart, United forced another corner. Again Beckham swung the ball into a crowded penalty area, this time finding the head of Sheringham who nodded it down across the face of goal. Solskjær reacted quickest, sticking out his foot and poking the ball into the roof of the Bayern net for United to take a 2-1 lead. Their second goal was timed at 90:02.17. Solskjær slid across the turf on his knees, mimicking the earlier goal celebration of Mario Basler, and was mobbed by the United players and coaching staff.

The game restarted with only a few seconds left with many of the Bayern players just too stunned to play on – and then referee Pierluigi Collina blew his whistle for full time.

Only three minutes earlier, the game had been nearing its conclusion, Bayern were leading 1-0 and about to be crowned champions of Europe, and their fans were already cheering their team's victory and letting off flares. But then, in a remarkable turn of events, United had drawn level and gone on to win the trophy and complete an unprecedented treble.

The ending was so unexpected that the UEFA president Lennart Johansson, who'd already left the stands before the stoppage time and was making his way down to the pitch to present the trophy, emerged from the tunnel and thought how strange it was that the winners were crying and the losers were dancing.

NO MEDALS FOR THE CHAMPIONS
1891

The Argentine Association Football League was the first official league championship outside of the British Isles, with the inaugural eight-game season, which began on 12 April 1891 and ended on 13 September 1891, being contested by just five teams.

The two works teams formed by Scottish immigrants, Old Caledonians and St Andrew's, both finished on 13 points and were declared champions. But then someone must have realised that they only had one set of medals, so they had to quickly arrange a play-off game to see who got to keep them.

Both teams were winners but in the end only the St Andrew's lot got a medal to prove it.

A REALLY SHITTY PERFORMANCE
1990

Striker Gary Lineker had been feeling ill before England's opening 1990 World Cup group-stage match against the Republic of Ireland, passing most of the previous night running to the toilet, but had decided not to inform his manager Bobby Robson about his dodgy tummy for fear of being dropped from the team.

He put England in front after only nine minutes and made it to half-time without incident – but he wasn't quite so lucky after the break.

Around 15 minutes in, his team-mate Chris Waddle hoofed the ball upfield, Lineker and the Irish defender Kevin Moran challenged for it, and then Gary's bottom exploded. He went down like a sack of potatoes and the referee gave a free kick to England believing that he must have been fouled. But he hadn't; he'd crapped his pants instead.

Linker just sat there nonchalantly shimmying back and forward across the grass trying to rid himself of the messy brown stuff which had suddenly appeared in his shorts. He even appeared to scoop some of it out with his hands, before wiping them on the grass and getting up, and then carrying on with the game as if nothing had happened. When recounting the story many years later, he explained how relieved he'd been that England were playing in dark blue shorts that day. Lineker was subbed off shortly afterwards and then sat on the bench stinking the place out until the end of the match.

Gary Lineker had quite literally shit himself on his big day, but he got away with it at the time. Nobody sitting in the stadium or watching the game at home on TV was any the wiser. It had been raining the night before and the ground was still wet, so anyone noticing the suspect brown stains on his shorts would have probably just assumed they were patches of mud.

Allaster McKallaster (the outrageous online persona of the US comedian/filmmaker Pete Reid) summed it all up in his hilarious YouTube piss-take of the incident, 'Gary Lineker: once a prolific shot hitter and now a horrific shorts shitter! An unfortunate incident that will undoubtedly leave an indelible stain on his career ... and his underpants!'

THE MOST BORING TITLE WINNERS
1998

Swedish club AIK were the first in the world to win a league title as the lowest-scoring team.

They scored only 25 goals in 26 games (0.96 per match) in their 1998 title-winning season. All of the 13 other teams in the top-flight Allsvenskan league scored more, including the two who were relegated!

AIK were a big club but they hadn't won much in recent times. Their last title win had been in 1992 (the first in over 50 years) and they'd had to console themselves with just a few Svenska Cupen wins in the meantime; they'd ended the 1997 league season in eighth place, and they'd lost most of their best players after a good run in the 1996/97 Cup Winners' Cup. But they did have a new manager, Englishman Stuart Baxter, who had been brought in from Japan to try and steer them towards winning the title again. He'd played and managed in Sweden before so he knew how things were done; he championed strong, disciplined and defensive play, and wasn't adverse to doing what it takes to win. Even if that meant winning every game 1-0.

After a shaky start, AIK went on a long unbeaten run – which included a lot of wins by just a single goal and a lot of draws – that left them occupying the top spot for most of the season.

But then, on the penultimate matchday of the season, 31 October 1998, they lost that top spot after drawing 0-0 with Trelleborg which allowed Helsingborg to sneak ahead of them after their easy 2-0 victory over Elfsborg.

The fight for the championship would now come down to the last day of the season.

Both clubs had to play duff teams on 8 November, AIK at home to 12th-placed Örgryte and Helsingborg away to 13th-placed Häcken, who had already been relegated. AIK were one point behind their rivals, so they had to win and also hope that Helsingborg dropped points too.

AIK did their part, winning 1-0 again, and unbelievably so did Häcken, who'd somehow managed to beat the top-of-the-table team 2-1 to hand the title to AIK. However, it was really only one Häcken player who'd won them the title. Their striker Mathias Larsson scored both goals and he was then invited to the AIK party to celebrate their title win. He turned up too! It was a surreal moment when he suddenly appeared on stage with all the AIK players for the toasts and the speeches, but he was the hero of the hour, and was probably worshipped more by the AIK fans than any of their own players at that moment, so why shouldn't he have enjoyed his 15 minutes of fame and joined in with all the revelry?

As the legendary Aberdeen and Manchester United manager Alex Ferguson once said, 'Attack wins you games, defence wins you titles.' And that was certainly the case with AIK with a record of 11 wins, 13 draws and two losses and a goal difference of +10, with 15 goals conceded against their 25 scored.

* * *

The lowest-scoring team won the title again in the 2009/10 season. But this time it was in Ghana when Aduana Stars won the country's Premier League after scoring only 19 goals in 30 games (0.63 per match). They ended the season on 53 points along with the second-placed team Ashanti Gold, but won the title on goal difference. They might not have scored many goals but they didn't let in many either. Aduana Stars were also the first newly promoted team in Ghana to win the championship.

THE FIVE-PENALTY MATCH
1989

This chaotic and often fiery Division Two meeting between Crystal Palace and Brighton on 27 March 1989 set a new world record for the most penalties awarded in a single game.

It also set two new British records – the most penalties awarded to one team in one game and the most penalties missed by one team in one game. Referee Kelvin Morton gave five spot kicks in less than half an hour (four of them to Palace) and wrote himself into the record books at the same time. The fact that the hosts then contrived to miss three of them only added to the surreal nature of a game involving two of British football's less obvious rivals.

Picking up points in this match was important for both sides with Palace looking to secure promotion back to the top flight after seven years playing Division Two football and Brighton hoping to avoid the drop back to Division Three.

Ian Wright opened the scoring for Palace after 23 minutes with a vicious half-volley from the edge of the box; five minutes later Mike Trusson of Brighton was red-carded for an equally vicious studs-up tackle on Eddie McGoldrick, and then, ten minutes after that, Mr Morton stepped into the spotlight for the first time that afternoon and awarded his first penalty. Mark Bright had been fouled in the area and then duly converted the spot kick to give Palace a 2-0 lead.

It wasn't long before Mr Morton was pointing to the penalty spot again, this time after a blatant foul on McGoldrick by Dean Wilkins, who'd already been booked and was lucky to stay on the pitch. However, Bright's shot was saved by Brighton keeper John Keeley who pushed it wide around the post to concede a corner. But when the ball was swung back into the area and made its way to Bright, he was hacked to the ground, and Mr Morton pointed to the spot again – less than 120 seconds after the last time and for the third time in only five minutes! As always, Mr Morton then sprinted to the edge of the box to stand defiant and wave away the protests from the Brighton players; by now it was a well-worked routine. Wright took over from Bright as the taker but blasted his shot against the post; the ball then fell to Bright, leaving him one-on-one with Keeley, but he couldn't put it in the back of the net either.

Despite being two goals and a man down at half-time, the Brighton fans were still strangely upbeat about their chances. After those two missed penalties, it somehow felt that their team was on top.

Their mood was buoyed even further ten minutes after the restart when Mr Morton finally awarded them a penalty. Palace's Jeff Hopkins held off Kevin Bremner, allowing a long ball to harmlessly pass over their heads and into the arms of his keeper. The Brighton striker turned around and instinctively appealed for a foul. It was a pretty half-hearted call but Mr Morton in his wisdom seemed convinced of a wrongdoing and awarded another penalty. It was probably the softest penalty of the match, a dubious decision that would never have passed a modern VAR check, but nonetheless Mr Morton stuck out his arm and pointed to the spot with his usual conviction. There was a sense among the fans at the time that he was just evening things up a bit after appearing to so obviously favour Palace during the first half.

Alan Curbishley showed everyone how it should be done by blasting the ball into the goal to make it 2-1 and all of a sudden Brighton were right back in the game.

But not for very long. Ten minutes later, Mr Morton blew his whistle again for the fifth penalty of the match after Brighton centre-back Ian Chapman was adjudged to have handled the ball in the area. This time it was Palace right-back John Pemberton who stepped up to the spot – and then probably wished he hadn't because it was the worst penalty of the day with the ball flying high over the goal and even higher over the terraces full of jeering away fans. If Selhurst Park's present two-tier stand had been in place back then, the ball would have most likely cleared that too! He'd never taken a penalty before and was probably never asked to take another one ever again!

Ten-man Brighton couldn't believe their luck. They pushed forward looking for an equaliser in the later stages but their best effort, a point-blank shot from Curbishley, was brilliantly saved by Perry Suckling and the game eventually finished with a 2-1 win for the home team.

Palace had got away with it. They'd missed three penalties but had still managed to walk away with the three points.

UNGENTLEMANLY CONDUCT
1891

With only a few seconds remaining in Aston Villa's home game against Stoke on 21 November 1891, the referee awarded the visitors a penalty. Villa keeper Bill Dunning wasn't impressed, so he picked up the ball and booted it out of the ground. By the time it had been retrieved, the referee had blown for full time. It has been suggested that the FA changed the Laws of the Game after this incident allowing for additional stoppage time to be played.

THE DEMISE OF GOAL AVERAGE
1966

Goal average was the forerunner to goal difference and was once used as a way of ranking league teams tied on the same number of points. It was calculated by dividing the number of goals scored by the number of goals conceded.

The system wasn't perfect. It seemed to penalise more deserving teams and encourage defensive play but nonetheless it was still used in the British leagues and even by FIFA in World Cups for a very long time as a way of deciding a team's final league position – right up until the 1966 World Cup, when England scored four goals and conceded none in their Group 1 games and someone at FIFA suddenly realised that dividing something by nothing just wasn't going to work!

A VERY CONVENIENT RESULT
1978

The 1978 World Cup in Argentina was marred by controversies and allegations of interference and match-fixing by the host nation's military junta who were accused of using the tournament for propaganda purposes.

Argentina and Brazil had both made it through the first group stage and were then drawn together along with Poland and Peru in Group B for the second round. Both teams easily won their first games with Argentina defeating Poland 2-0 and Brazil cruising to a 3-0 victory against Peru. Then they played each other in a tense 0-0 draw four days later, meaning that they went into their final games level on three points.

Whereas the last Group A fixtures were played at the same time, so no team had an advantage over another, this was not the case in Group B where Argentina had very conveniently managed to schedule their match to kick off later in the day. On 21 June, Brazil met Poland in the late afternoon and beat them 3-1 meaning Argentina knew they had to beat Peru in the evening by at least four clear goals to reach the final.

Argentina were only winning 2-0 at the break but then Peru suddenly crumpled and folded in the second half with the hosts notching up another four goals. And they did so with a suspicious degree of ease. It was rumoured at the time that the Peruvian government had either been bribed or threatened by Argentina's rulers to throw the game but nothing could ever be proved and it was a lot more convenient just to cast aspersions on the integrity of Peru's Argentinian-born goalkeeper Ramón Quiroga for their mysterious collapse.

Only many years later did it emerge that the Argentinian president Jorge Rafael Videla had visited the Peru dressing room to talk to their players before the game; 35,000 tonnes of wheat were suddenly gifted to Peru, Argentinian banks unexpectedly unfroze $50m of Peruvian government assets, and Argentina allegedly agreed to accept and imprison 13 political opponents of the Peruvian leader under the Operation Condor dissident-swap scheme.

WORD OF MOUTH
1970–2025

Perhaps they really said what they said, perhaps it's just anecdotal, or perhaps it's some kind of weird Mandela Effect-style collective memory fail that makes us all think it's what they said. Whatever the reason, these foot-in-the-mouth moments have all been fairly or unfairly attributed to certain players or managers when they've been in front of a microphone:

- 'Ally McCoist will always get you a goal, whether he's playing or on the bench.' – Rangers team-mate Mark Hateley

- 'Germany are a very difficult team to play … they had 11 internationals out there today.' – Northern Ireland's Steve Lomas

- 'Glenn Hoddle hasn't been the Hoddle we know. Neither has Bryan Robson.' – England manager Ron Greenwood

- 'I wouldn't say he [David Ginola] is the best left-winger in the Premiership, but there are none better.' – Ron Atkinson

- 'They [Argentina] are the second-best team in the world, and there's no higher praise than that.' – Kevin Keegan

- 'Today's top players only want to play in London or for Manchester United. That's what happened when I tried to sign Alan Shearer and he went to Blackburn.' – Graeme Souness

- 'We didn't underestimate them [Cameroon]. They were a lot better than we thought.' – England manager Bobby Robson after the 1990 World Cup quarter-final against the Africans

- 'What he's got is legs, which the other midfielders don't have.' – Lennie Lawrence on a player whose identity has never been confirmed

- 'I never comment on referees, and I'm not going to break the habit of a lifetime for that prat.' – Ron Atkinson, after West Bromwich Albion's controversial UEFA Cup defeat to Red Star Belgrade in 1979

- 'It's hit the facial part of his head, there.' – Michael Owen, on TV commentary duties in 2015

    Pretty sure that part of the body is just called the face!

RIPPING UP THE SEATS
1981

Coventry City's Highfield Road ground was the first all-seater stadium in England. When asked why he'd had the changes made, Coventry's chairman Jimmy Hill replied, 'You can't be a hooligan sitting down!'

It was like a red rag to a bull and the Leeds United fans seemed determined to prove him wrong when they visited on 12 September 1981. Only a few short months after his fancy new seats were installed, they took great delight in angrily ripping out several hundred of them to use as weapons against the home supporters.

THE HUMOURLESS CAPTAIN
2025

At the end of Eintracht Frankfurt's 4-1 Bundesliga home win over Werder Bremen on 23 August 2025, Bremen captain Marco Friedl swapped shirts with Frankfurt goalkeeper – and his former team-mate – Michael Zetterer and then wandered across to the pitchside interview station where the Sky Sports Germany presenter Katharina Kleinfeldt was waiting for him.

'We want to talk a bit about Eintracht, of course. Let's first focus on the game. You won 4-1 today – is that the opening victory you were expecting?' To which he very matter-of-factly replied, 'I'm a Bremen player, in case you didn't know.'

In fact, she did know. But she'd forgotten or she was just a bit confused because he was wearing a bright-orange Eintracht Frankfurt goalkeeper's shirt.

Whatever. No big deal, right?

She apologised for her mistake but instead of just laughing it off, the humourless Austrian footballer looked quite upset about it all. Friedl later told the German magazine *Bild*, 'I've never experienced that before. I talked to her before the game. Ninety minutes later, she doesn't recognise me any more. That's strange and also a bit ridiculous.'

Get over yourself, mate!

MORE IMPORTANT MATTERS TO ATTEND TO
2009

In the 63rd minute of the Spanish Segunda División B match between Jumilla CF and FC Puente Tocinos in September 2009, an urgent announcement was made over the PA system by the local police asking for the owner of an Audi A4 parked near the ground to contact them.

The owner recognised the licence plate number that was announced and went to find out what the problem was. It was just a pity that the owner also happened to be the referee! He stopped the game and sprinted off the field only to be told that his car had been vandalised.

The match was then held up for five minutes while he sorted out matters with the police.

THE STUFF OF LEGENDS
1927–1947

Giuseppe Meazza – the Italian superstar striker with a love for scoring goals, dancing the tango, swilling champagne and hanging out in brothels.

Meazza was possibly Italy's greatest-ever player and widely regarded as one of the best footballers of all time. The manager of Italy's 1934 and 1938 World Cup-winning teams, Vittorio Pozzo, once said of him, 'Having him on the team was like starting the game 1-0 up.'

He was the first world-famous player and the first to agree a personal sponsorship deal; a versatile player known for his technical ability and dribbling skills who spent most of his career at Inter Milan. In his favoured inside-forward role, he would pick the ball up on the halfway line, dribble past three or four defenders, dummy the keeper and shoot into the net. It was such a trademark move that it became known as a *Gol alla Meazza*, a term still used today to describe any goal involving a series of dribbles.

It was easier for the opposition defenders just to hack him down rather than try to win the ball off him. But that's not to say Meazza didn't give as good as he got – like the time he punched the Czech player Rudolf Krčil in the gut during the final of the 1934 World Cup. But Giuseppe was more of a lover than a fighter, probably because he was only 5ft 6in tall.

His passion for football was only matched by his passion for women; he even went out on the pull the night before a game. Once he woke up with a couple of women lying beside him and had to get a taxi to the ground still dressed in his PJs. Luckily, he didn't live too far away and was able to get there just in time for the kick off. He might have got a few strange looks from his team-mates but he quickly got changed and joined them on the field. Apparently, he'd overheard the Inter bosses saying they'd deal with him after the game but since he scored a hat-trick, not a word was said. He was just allowed to get away with it because his wild lifestyle off the pitch never seemed to affect his performances on it.

Another story has him going AWOL before a big game against Juventus. With only an hour before kick off, club officials were sent out to look for him, only to find their star striker still lying in his bed sleeping off the excesses of the night before. They bundled him into a car and then had to listen to him banging on about his night of lovemaking as he lay slouched on the back seat. But he was still the best player on the pitch that day, scoring both goals in Inter's 2-1 win.

Whereas most players were teetotal and liked an early night before a game, it seemed that Giuseppe thrived on partying, drinking and shagging until the early hours. He was also the only player in the Italian team allowed to smoke.

Meazza played in the victorious 1934 World Cup team and then captained Italy to the trophy again four years later. In the semi-final against Brazil on 16 June 1938, when Italy were awarded a penalty after Silvio Piola was fouled by Domingos da Guia, he stepped up to the spot with a chance to double his team's lead – but as he was about to take the kick, his shorts fell down. The elastic in the waistband had snapped. Brazilian keeper Walter couldn't stop laughing at him but, undeterred, he just pulled up his shorts and held on to them as he took the kick, striking the ball into the corner of the net to put Italy 2-0 up. And all of a sudden, Walter wasn't laughing any more.

That was the last of his goals for Italy as he retired from international football a year later after 54 appearances.

In 1980, the San Siro, home of AC Milan and Inter Milan, was renamed the Stadio Giuseppe Meazza in his honour. So he must have been good. You don't just get a stadium named after you for nothing.

THE SAUSAGE MAN
2006

This is without doubt the most insulting transfer fee of all time.

Romanian defender Marius Cioară moved from UT Arad to Regal Hornia for a fee of 15kg of pork sausages. He felt angry and embarrassed, and was so widely mocked about the deal that he quit football altogether the very next day and moved to Spain to work on a farm.

And then Regal Hornia asked for their sausages back!

THE WANNABE PROPERTY TYCOON
1996

When German striker Giuseppe Reina signed for Arminia Bielefeld from SG Wattenscheid 09 in 1996, he had a clause inserted into his contract stating that his new club had to build him a house for every year of the deal. Surprisingly, Arminia Bielefeld agreed to his ridiculous demand.

But as the contract didn't stipulate the size and type of property they had to build, they just constructed him a house made out of Lego every year.

A few other strange contract clauses worth a mention:

- Rolf-Christel Guié-Mien – the Congolese midfielder insisted on Eintracht Frankfurt arranging free cookery classes for his wife when he signed for them in 1999.

- Dennis Bergkamp – the Dutch striker had a fear of flying so he had a clause excluding him from travelling anywhere by aeroplane inserted into his contract when he signed for Arsenal in 1995. For European games, he was expected to travel by train or – just not bother at all.

- Ronaldinho – the Brazilian superstar managed to negotiate a contract with Flamengo in 2011 which included a clause allowing him to go out partying twice a week.

Of course, sometimes it's the clubs who insist on a particular condition of employment. It'll come as no great surprise to learn that Luis Suárez had a 'no biting' clause in his contract when he signed for Barcelona in 2014, and the Italian bad boy striker Mario Balotelli had a 'good conduct' clause in his when he joined Liverpool the same year.

THE TOP-SCORING GOALKEEPER
1977

Argentine goalkeeper Carlos Fenoy arrived at Celta Vigo, then playing in the Spanish Segunda División, from Club Atlético Vélez Sarsfield during the 1975/76 season and helped them to a second-place finish, earning them promotion to the Primera División (La Liga).

But it was during the following season that he made his name at the club.

In the third match, against Real Sociedad on 9 September 1976, he saved a penalty and then scored one in his team's 1-0 win. During the rest of the campaign he took another five spot kicks and scored with four of them – against Real Madrid, Las Palmas (twice) and Elche – taking his goal tally for the season to five.

As it turned out, Celta Vigo finished second from bottom and were relegated after just one season playing top-flight football. After 34 games they had the lowest goal tally in the league having scored just 22 times. Their strikers were so hopelessly bad that Fenoy actually ended up as the team's top scorer with his five goals.

FINAL WHISTLE

BIBLIOGRAPHY

11v11.com
allfootballapp.com
apnews.com
arbroathfc.co.uk
arsenal.com
bbc.com
bbc.co.uk
besoccer.com
bordercountiesadvertiser.co.uk
bournemouthecho.co.uk
byfarthegreatestteam.com
ccfpa.co.uk
cnn.com
corinthian-casuals.com
cpfc.co.uk
cultkits.com
dailymail.com
dailyrecord.co.uk
englandfootballonline.com
englandstats.com
en.wikipedia
espn.com
express.co.uk

facebook.com

fifa.com

fifamuseum.com

firstsportz.com

followfollow.com

footballhistory.org

football-italia.net

footballsite.co.uk

footballwhispers.com

footy-boots.com

footyfair.com

forzaitalianfootball.com

fourfourtwo.com

friendsofliverpool.com

gentlemanultra.com

givemesport.com

glasgowtimes.co.uk

goal.com

goalkeepersaredifferent.com

independent.co.uk

interclub.org.uk

it.wikipedia

ketteringtownfc.com

koha.net

liverpoolecho.co.uk

liverpoolfc.com

londonhearts.com

lookandlearn.com

lutontoday.co.uk

macanilari.com

mancity.com

mirror.co.uk

mtmg.wordpress.com

neverfeltbetter.wordpress.com

news.bbc.co.uk

nowiknow.com

onefootball.com

pastemagazine.com

planetfootball.com

planetworldcup.com

raithrovers.net

rangers.co.uk

readtheleague.com

scottishfootballmuseum.org.uk

scottishfootballstories.co.uk

soccerhistory.co.uk

spartacus-educational.com

sportbible.com

sportsgazette.co.uk

sportstoriez.com

squawka.com

stalbancityfc.com

standard.co.uk

talksport.com

teakdoor.com

telegrafi.com

theanalyst.com

thecelticstar.com

thecelticwiki.com

thefa.com

thefactsource.com

thefootballfreak.com

thefootballhistoryboys.com

theguardian.com

thescottishsun.co.uk

thesefootballtimes.co

thesetpieces.com

thestreaker.org.uk

thesun.co.uk

thisisanfield.com

time.com

transfermarkt.com

vice.com

wbur.org

wearebrighton.com

westaucklandtownafc.co.uk

westernfrontassociation.com

whufc.com

wsc.co.uk

wwfc.com

x.com

youtube.com